Richard Wiseman holds Britain's only professorship
in the Public Understanding of Psychology, at the
University of Hertfordshire. His research into a
range of topics – including luck, self-help, deception
and persuasion – has been published in the world's
leading academic journals, while his psychology-based
YouTube videos have been viewed over 150 million times.
He is the author of several books that have been
translated into over thirty languages, including
The Luck Factor, *Quirkology*, *Rip It Up* and
the international bestseller *59 Seconds*.

Richard Wiseman

Rip It Up

**Forget positive thinking
It's time for positive action**

PAN BOOKS

First published 2012 by Macmillan

First published in paperback 2013 by Pan Books

This edition published 2015 by Pan Books
an imprint of Pan Macmillan, a division of Macmillan Publishers Limited
Pan Macmillan, 20 New Wharf Road, London N1 9RR
Basingstoke and Oxford
Associated companies throughout the world
www.panmacmillan.com

ISBN 978-1-4472-7336-3

1 3 5 7 9 8 6 4 2

A CIP catalogue record for this book is available from the British Library.

Printed and bound by CPI Group (UK) Ltd, Croydon, CR0 4YY

The information provided in this book is for general informational purposes only.
None of the information constitutes a professional diagnosis or a treatment plan.
The information should not be relied on to suggest a course of treatment, nor be seen
as a substitute for personal diagnosis or hands-on treatment. You should never disregard
professional advice or delay in seeking it because of something you have read in this book.
If you have any health-care-related concerns, please call or see your physician or other
qualified health-care provider. Never discontinue treatment or medication
without first consulting your physician, clinician or therapist.

Visit www.panmacmillan.com to read more about all our books
and to buy them. You will also find features, author interviews and
news of any author events, and you can sign up for e-newsletters
so that you're always first to hear about our new releases.

To Ronald and Brenda

'If you want a quality, act as if you already have it'

Philosopher, William James, 1884

Contents

A Brief Introduction

It's time to Rip It Up

Self-help gurus and business coaches preach the same simple mantra: If you want to improve your life then you need to change how you think. Force yourself to have positive thoughts and you will become happier. Visualize your dream self and you will enjoy increased success. Think like a millionaire and you will magically grow rich. In principle, this idea sounds perfectly reasonable. However, in practice the approach often proves surprisingly ineffective, with research showing that people struggle to continually think happy thoughts, that employees remain unmoved by imagining their perfect selves, and that those dreaming of endless wealth fail to make their millions.

Over a century ago the brilliant Victorian philosopher William James proposed a radically different approach to change. Since then researchers from across the world have carried out hundreds of experiments into James's theory and discovered that it applies to almost every aspect of people's lives. Perhaps most importantly of all, the work has given rise to a series of easy and effective exercises that can help people feel happier, avoid anxiety and worry, fall in love and live happily ever after, stay slim, increase their willpower and confidence, and even slow the effects of ageing. This research has been presented at countless scientific conferences and published in academic journals, but has rarely made its way into the public domain.

In my previous book, *59 Seconds*, I described a handful of these exercises. *Rip It Up* builds on this work by presenting the first accessible and comprehensive guide to James's radical theory. It reveals how everything you currently believe about your mind is wrong, shows that change does not have to be challenging, and describes a series of easy-to-implement techniques that are designed to improve several different areas of your everyday life.

Throughout the book you are going to be asked to change your behaviour. To emphasize this key message I am going to invite you to do something that I suspect you have never done before. I would like you to destroy parts of this book as you work your way through it. I suspect that there are two possible thoughts running through your mind at the moment.

First, you might be thinking something along the lines of 'Noooooooooooooo, I hate the idea of ripping up my book!' That, of course, is the point of the exercise. Ask someone to alter their behaviour and they will quickly produce a long list of reasons why they should continue to act in the same old way. This attitude is perhaps understandable (after all, behaviours quickly become ingrained in our minds and soon start to feel like old friends), but it presents perhaps the biggest barrier to change. The most effective way of overcoming this problem is simply to do something that you have never done before. Something that makes you feel rather uncomfortable but is harmless. Like destroying a book.

Second, if you are looking at this on an ebook reader then you will realize that you obviously can't carry out the exercise. That's fine. Simply find a self-help book that encourages you to change the way you think and destroy that instead. Just kidding. Actually, please visit www.RipItUp.biz, download a copy of the 'Rip It Up workbook', and print it out. This workbook contains everything you will need to join in with the interactive exercises.

To help get the ball rolling, let's start with a small act of radical change. The following page contains a picture of 'The Rule Book'. Please rip out the page right now, tear The Rule Book into four pieces, and screw each of the pieces into a paper ball. Hopefully that wasn't too painful, and you felt your mind undergo a small but real change. I hope that you enjoyed the exercise because throughout the book I am going to ask you to alter many other aspects of your behaviour and, each time, experience much more significant and important shifts in your thoughts and feelings.

It's time to embrace a new approach to change. An approach that is grounded in science, overturns conventional thinking, and provides a basis for the easiest, quickest and most effective ways of changing your life.

So sit up straight, take a deep breath and prepare to Rip It Up.

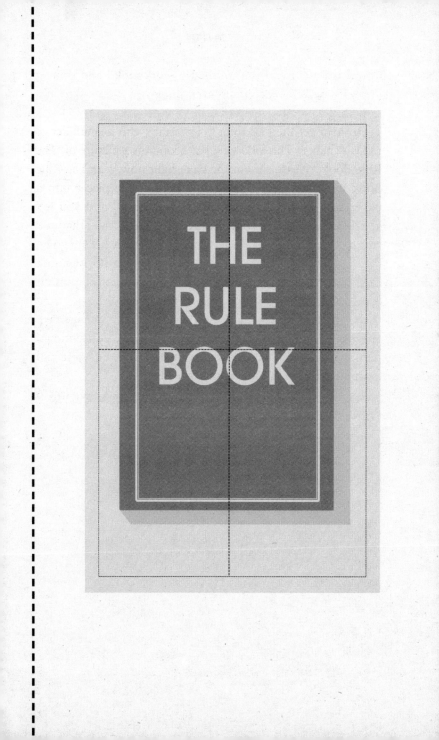

1. HOW TO BE HAPPY

Where we meet that adorable genius William James,
turn the world upside down, learn how to create good cheer
at will, and visit the fun factory.

'In the Beginning Was the Deed.'

Faust, Johann Wolfgang von Goethe

1. THE SIMPLE IDEA THAT CHANGES EVERYTHING

The world's first laboratory-based psychology experiment was carried out by the German psychologist Professor Wilhelm Wundt in 1879. This historic study was conducted in a small room at the University of Leipzig, and reveals all you need to know about how Victorian scientists approached the human mind.

Wundt could have celebrated the birth of experimental psychology by investigating any fascinating topic of his choosing. Perhaps why people fall in love, believe in God, or sometimes feel the need to kill one another. Instead, the 'humourless and indefatigable'[1] Wundt chose to conduct a strange and bizarre experiment involving a small brass ball.

Wundt and two of his students gathered around a small table and connected together a timer, a switch, and a carefully designed metal stand. A brass ball was then balanced on the stand and one of Wundt's students placed his hand a few millimetres above the switch. Seconds later the ball was automatically released from the stand and the timer sprang into action. The student slammed his hand down on the switch the moment that he heard the brass ball hit the table, which immediately halted the timer. By carefully recording the reading shown on the timer in his notebook, Wundt created psychology's first data point.

It would be nice to think that after a day or so of ball-dropping Wundt would have closed his notebook, reported his findings and moved on to something more interesting. Nice, but wrong. In fact, he spent the next few years of his life observing hundreds of people responding to the test. In the same way that physicists were trying to identify the fundamental nature of matter, so Wundt and his team were attempting to discover the fundamental building blocks of consciousness. Some of the participants were asked to press the switch the moment they first heard the ball hit the table, whilst others were told to react when they became fully aware of the sound. In the first scenario the observer was asked to concentrate their attention on the ball, whilst in the second instance they were required to focus more on their own thoughts. When the tasks were performed properly, Wundt believed that the first reaction would represent a simple reflex whereas the second involved more of a conscious decision. Perhaps not surprisingly, many participants initially struggled to recognize the alleged subtle difference between the two conditions, and so were required to complete more than ten thousand trials before moving on to the experiment proper.

After carefully wading through the resulting mass of ball-dropping data, Wundt concluded that the reflexive response took an average of one tenth of a second and left the participants with a very weak mental record of the sound of the ball. In contrast, consciously hearing the sound produced an average reaction time of two tenths of a second and resulted in a far clearer experience of the ball's impact.

Having solved the mystery of the reflexive response, Wundt devoted the rest of his career to carrying out hundreds of similar studies. His approach proved surprisingly influential, and almost every other nineteenth-century academic dabbling in matters of the mind followed in Wundt's footsteps. In psychology laboratories across Europe, researchers could hardly hear themselves think for the sound of brass balls dropping onto tables.

Over in America, a young philosopher and psychologist named William James was having none of it.

William James was a most remarkable man. Born in 1842 in New York City, James's father was an independently wealthy, well-connected, eccentric, one-legged religious philosopher who devoted himself to educating his five children.[2] As a result, much of James's childhood was spent receiving private tuition, visiting Europe's leading museums and art galleries, and rubbing shoulders with the likes of Henry Thoreau, Alfred Tennyson, and Horace Greeley. James's older brother, Henry, would go on to find fame as a novelist, and his sister, Alice, as a diarist.

Initially trained in painting, James abandoned the arts in his twenties and instead enrolled to study chemistry and anatomy at Harvard Medical School. In 1872, family friend and Harvard president Charles Eliot recruited James to teach courses in vertebrate physiology. James soon found himself drawn to the mysteries of the human psyche and in 1875 put together America's very first psychology course, later remarking that 'The first lecture in psychology that I ever heard was the first one I gave.'

Appalled by what he saw as the triviality of Wundt's work, James firmly believed that psychological research should be relevant to people's lives. Turning his back on brass balls and reaction times, James instead focused his attention on a series of far more interesting and pragmatic issues, including whether it was right to believe in God, what made life worth living, and if free will actually exists.

Wundt and James didn't just differ in terms of their approach to the human mind. Wundt was formal and stuffy, his lectures were serious and solemn, and his writing dull and turgid. James was informal and unpretentious, often walking around campus sporting '. . . a silk hat, cane, frock coat and red-checked trousers'. He would frequently pepper his talks with jokes and light-hearted asides to the extent that his students often felt the need to ask him to be more serious, and he produced accessible and often amusing prose ('As long as one poor cockroach feels the pangs of unrequited love, this world is not a moral world').

James and Wundt also developed completely different ways of working. Wundt recruited a large team of students to conduct his carefully controlled studies. On their first day in Wundt's laboratory each new intake of students would be lined up, and Wundt would move down the line handing each of them a description of the research that they were required to conduct. Once the work was completed, he would act as judge and jury, with any student reporting results that failed to support their master's theories running the risk of being failed.[3] In contrast, James loved to encourage free thought, loathed the idea of imprinting his ideas on students, and once complained that he had just seen a fellow academic 'applying the last coat of varnish to his pupil'.

The two great thinkers did little to hide their animosity for one another. James developed a poetic turn of phrase, causing some commentators to note that he wrote psychology papers like a novelist, whilst his brother Henry penned novels like a psychologist. Wundt, however, remained unimpressed and when asked to comment on James's writings, once replied 'It is beautiful, but it is not psychology.' In reply James complained about Wundt altering his theories from one book to the next, noting 'Unfortunately he will never have a Waterloo . . . cut him up like a worm and each fragment crawls . . . you can't kill him.'

Despite being vastly outnumbered by Wundt's army of supporters, James stood his ground. Whilst almost every psychologist in Europe was obsessively carrying out increasingly esoteric variations of Wundt's classic ball-dropping experiment, James continued to stroll around Harvard in his red-checked trousers encouraging his students to think about the meaning of life.

James's persistence paid off. Open any modern-day psychology textbook and you will struggle to find even a passing reference to Wundt or his brass balls. In contrast, James's ideas are still widely cited and he is seen as the founding father of modern-day psychology. First published in 1890, James's two-volume magnum opus *Principles of Psychology* was recently described by one leading historian as 'the most literate, most provocative, and at the same time the most intelligent book on psychology that has ever appeared',[4] and both volumes are still considered required reading for modern-day students of behavioural science. Harvard's psychology department have named their building after James, and each year the Association for Psychological Science give their William James Fellow Award to the academic judged to have made the most significant intellectual contribution to psychology.

James was perhaps at his best when he found mystery and substance in phenomena that most people tended to take for granted. In 1892 he reflected on the importance of this approach to understanding the human mind, and provided a few examples of the type of phenomena that had recently caught his attention:

> Why do we smile, when pleased, and not scowl? Why are we unable to talk to a crowd as we talk to a single friend? Why does a particular maiden turn our wits so upside-down? The common man can only say, 'Of course we smile, of course our heart palpitates at the sight of the crowd, of course we love the maiden, that beautiful soul clad in that perfect form, so palpably and flagrantly made for all eternity to be loved!'[5]

It was exactly this kind of thinking that led James to create his most controversial theory and turn our understanding of the human mind on its head.

On emotion

Towards the end of the 1880s James turned his attention to the relationship between emotion and behaviour. To the uninitiated, this may seem a strange choice of topic for a world-renowned philosopher and psychologist.

Common sense suggests that certain events and thoughts cause you to feel emotional, and that this, in turn, affects your behaviour. So, for example, you might find yourself walking along an unexpectedly dark street late at night, or being called into your boss's office and awarded a pay rise, or suddenly remembering a time you were five years old and fell down the stairs. These stimuli then cause you to experience certain emotions. Perhaps the dark street makes you feel anxious, the pay rise makes you feel happy and the memory of falling down the stairs makes you feel upset. Finally, these emotions then affect your behaviour. Feeling afraid may make you sweat, feeling happy may make you smile and feeling upset may make you cry. Seen from this perspective, the link between how you feel and the way you act is as straightforward as it is unsurprising. Mystery solved, case closed.

Behaviour and emotion

Common sense suggests that emotions cause behaviour:

Feel anxious $\longrightarrow$ Sweat

Feel happy $\longrightarrow$ Smile

Feel sad $\longrightarrow$ Cry

However, James's previous experience with seemingly straight-forward psychological phenomena made him well aware that conventional wisdom can often be deeply misleading. Take, for example, James's work on memory. For years armchair philosophers had suggested that memory operated much like a muscle, believing the more you used it, the stronger it became. James wondered whether this was really accurate.[6] To find out, he spent eight days timing himself as he memorized 158 lines of the Victor Hugo poem 'Satyr', and discovered that the task took him an average of fifty seconds per line. Then, to further exercise his memory muscle, he devoted twenty minutes each day for the following thirty days memorizing the entire first book of Milton's *Paradise Lost*. If the 'more you use it, the stronger it gets' theory was correct, James hypothesized that he should be able to return to 'Satyr' and learn the next 158 lines in less time than before. In fact, when he tried to learn another section of the poem he discovered that it took him longer than before. The 'memory as muscle' hypothesis was wrong.

James wanted to explore whether there was an alternative to the common sense theory of emotion, and began his intellectual quest by thinking about how we go about deciding how other people feel.

Look at the photograph below and try to imagine how the two people in the photograph are feeling.

Now do the same with the people in the following photo-graph.

Most people find this exercise easy. Almost everyone assumes that the couple in the first photograph are probably having a good time, and are likely to be experiencing happiness with just a hint of attraction. The second photograph elicits a quite different reaction, with most people concluding that the group are probably concerned and anxious, and that at least one of them appears to be in need of a comfort break.

This simple exercise is based on an experiment that was first conducted by the legendary naturalist Charles Darwin in the mid-1800s. Darwin published twenty-two books in his lifetime, including the groundbreaking *On the Origin of Species by Means of Natural Selection, or the Preservation of Favoured Races in the Struggle for Life*, and his lesser-known tome *The Formation of Vegetable Mould Through the Action of Worms, with Observations on Their Habits*. In 1872 Darwin published a seminal text on emotion entitled *The Expression of the Emotions in Man and Animals*, and described carrying out the first psychological study of emotions.[7]

A French physician named Guillaume-Benjamin-Amand Duchenne had previously applied painful electrical shocks to the muscles in a volunteer's face in order to study facial anatomy. When Darwin saw photographs of Duchenne's work he was struck by how easily he associated emotions with the volunteer's expressions. Intrigued, Darwin showed some of the photographs to his friends and asked them to say which emotion the volunteer appeared to be feeling. Darwin's friends also reliably and effortlessly associated certain expressions with particular emotions, proving that the ability to know how others are feeling on the understanding of their facial expressions is somehow built into our brains.

James read about Darwin's experiment and used it as a basis for his new theory about emotion. Darwin had shown that people are extremely skilled at knowing how another person feels from facial expression. James wondered whether exactly the same mechanism might also account for how they themselves experience emotions. He suggested that in the same way that you look at other people's facial expressions and work out how they feel, so you might monitor your own expressions and then decide what emotion you should experience.

James originally proposed that any emotion is entirely the result of people observing their own behaviour. Seen from this perspective, people never smile because they are happy, but rather always feel happy because they are smiling (or, to use James's more poetic way of explaining his radical hypothesis: '*You do not run from a bear because you are afraid of it, but rather become afraid of the bear because you run from it*'). James makes a clear distinction between our body's instinctive physical behaviour in the face of stimulus – whether it be pulling our hands away from a flame, smiling at a joke, or instantly starting to turn on our heels at the sight of an angry bear – and how our brain observes that movement and, a split second later, produces an emotion. You see the bear, your body behaves by starting to run, and your brain decides 'I'm afraid'. More modern-day versions of James's theory view the relationship between emotion and behaviour as a two-way street, suggesting, for example, that people both smile because they are happy but also become happier when they smile.

James never formally tested his theory because he found experimentation both boring and intellectually unrewarding ('The thought of brass-instrument and algebraic-formula psychology fills me with horror'). He was, however, a passionate pragmatist and lost no time exploring the potential practical implications of his idea.

The notion of behaviour causing emotion suggests that people should be able to create any feeling they desire simply by acting as if they are experiencing that emotion. Or as James famously put it, 'If you want a quality, act *as if* you already have it.' I refer to this simple but powerful proposition as the *As If* principle (see diagram, opposite).

Behaviour and emotion

Common sense suggests that the chain of causation is:

You feel happy   ⟶   You smile

You feel afraid   ⟶   You run away

The *As If* theory suggests that the opposite is also true:

You smile   ⟶   You feel happy

You run away   ⟶   You feel afraid

This aspect of James's theory clearly energized him more than any other. In one public talk he described the potential power of the idea as 'bottled lightning', and enthusiastically noted: '. . . the sovereign voluntary path to cheerfulness . . . is to sit up cheerfully, to look round cheerfully, and to act and speak as if cheerfulness were already there . . . To wrestle with a bad feeling only pins our attention on it, and keeps it still fastened in the mind . . .'[8]

James's theory met with a critical reaction from some of his peers. Wilhelm Wundt roundly condemned the idea, labelling it a 'psychologischen Scheinerklärungen' and presented his own account of emotion, which suggested that feelings were a 'Gefühl' – defined as 'an unanalyzable and simple process corresponding in the sphere of Gemuth to sensation in the sphere of intellection' (good to get that sorted out).

James defended his position, but the theory proved too radical for his many of his more conventional colleagues, and was quickly relegated to the filing drawer marked 'Years ahead of its time'.

And there it lay for more than sixty years.

2. TESTING A THEORY

In the late 1960s a young academic named James Laird was studying for his doctorate in clinical psychology at the University of Rochester.[9] During a training session there, Laird was asked to interview a patient whilst his supervisor watched through a one-way mirror. At one point in the interview a rather unusual smile spread across the patient's face. Laird was intrigued by the smile and wondered how the patient had felt when he had produced the rather odd facial expression.

As Laird drove home from the interview he replayed the session in his mind and became fixated on the smile. Eventually he forced his own face into the same expression to discover how it felt. He was amazed to discover that the smile instantly made him feel happier. Intrigued, he tried frowning and suddenly felt sad. Those few rather strange moments during his drive home changed the entire course of his career. When he reached his house that night Laird went straight to his bookshelf, where he searched for information about the psychology of emotion. By chance, the first book he picked up was William James's *Principles of Psychology*.

Laird read about James's long-lost theory and realized that it might explain why smiling in his car had made him feel happier. He was also amazed to discover that the theory had been confined to the history books and had never been properly tested. In order to do so, Laird invited volunteers into his laboratory, asked them to smile or frown, and then report how they felt. According to James, those who had been smiling should feel significantly happier than those who had forced a frown on their faces.

However, worried that volunteers might be tempted to tell him what he wanted to hear, Laird wanted to find a way of making people smile or frown whilst concealing the true nature of the experiment. Eventually, he hit upon a clever cover story.

He told the volunteers that they would be participating in a study examining the electrical activity in their facial muscles, and placed electrodes between the participant's eyebrows, at the corners of their mouth, and at the corners of their jaw. He then explained that changes in their emotion could affect the experiment, and so, to rule out this possible source of error, they would be asked to report their emotions as the experiment proceeded.

The electrodes were fake, but the clever cover story allowed Laird secretly to manipulate his volunteers' faces into a smile or frown. To create an angry expression the participants were asked to draw down and pull together the two electrodes between the eyebrows, and contract the ones on the jaw by clenching their teeth. For the happy expression they were asked to draw back the electrodes at the corners of the mouth towards the back of the face.

After they had contorted their face into the required position, participants were presented with a checklist containing a list of emotions (such as aggression, anxiety, joy and remorse) and asked to rate the degree to which they were experiencing each. The results were remarkable. Exactly as predicted by James at the turn of the last century, the participants felt significantly happier when they forced their face into smiles, and significantly angrier when they were frowning.

After the study Laird interviewed his participants and asked them if they knew why they had experienced various emotions during the study. Only a handful put their new-found emotional state down to their manipulated expressions, with the rest at a loss to explain the shift. In one of the interviews a participant who had had their face contorted into a frown explained: 'I'm not in any angry mood but I found my thoughts wandering to things that made me angry, which is sort of silly, I guess. I knew I was in an experiment and I knew I had no reason to feel that way, but I just lost control.'

Rip it up

How to be happy in an instant

Around the turn of the last century the Russian theatre director Constantin Stanislavski revolutionized drama by creating method acting. A key part of his approach involves encouraging actors to experience genuine emotion on stage by controlling their behaviour. This technique, often referred to as the 'magic if' ('If I was really experiencing this feeling, how would I behave?'), has been adopted by several famous performers including Marlon Brando, Warren Beatty, and Robert De Niro.

The same technique has been used in laboratory experiments exploring the *As If* principle. Let's imagine that you are taking part in a study to test the *As If* principle. At the start of the study you would be asked to rate how cheerful you feel on a scale between 'one' (how you would feel if you had just fallen down an open man-hole) and 'ten' (how you would feel if you had just seen your worst enemy do exactly the same thing).

Next, you would be asked to smile. However, there is more to acting happy than simply forcing your face into a brief, unfelt smile that finishes in the blink of an eye. Instead, you would be asked to follow these instructions.

1) Sit in front of a mirror.

2) Relax the muscles in your forehead and cheeks, and let your mouth drop slightly open. In scientific circles, the expression

that you have on your face right now is referred to as 'neutral', and acts as a blank canvas.

3) Contract the muscles near the corners of your mouth by drawing them back towards your ears. Make the resulting smile as wide as possible, and try to ensure that the movement of the cheeks produces wrinkling around the base of your eyes. Finally, extend your eyebrow muscles slightly upward, and hold the resulting expression for about twenty seconds.

4) Let the expression drop from your face and think about how you feel.

Do you feel more cheerful than before you started? What number would you give to this new feeling on the 'one to ten' manhole scale?

Most people report that the exercise has made them feel happier. As predicted by William James more than a century ago, just a few seconds changing your facial expression has a big impact on how you feel.

To boost your level of good cheer, incorporate this type of smiling into your daily routine. Create a fun way of reminding yourself to do this by drawing two self-portraits of yourself wearing a huge smile. One of the portraits should be drawn on a sheet of A4 paper and the other on a small piece of paper that is about two inches square. Make the portraits as humorous and happy-looking as possible. Finally, place the large portrait somewhere prominent in your home and the smaller one in your wallet or purse, and use them as a cue to help you to remember to smile.

To make sure that the remarkable effect was genuine, other scientists set about attempting to replicate Laird's ground-breaking result. Rather than repeatedly placing fake electrodes on people's faces, each laboratory produced its own cover story.

Inspired by photographers who make people smile by getting them to say the word 'cheese', researchers at the University of Michigan had participants repeatedly make an 'ee' sound (as in '*ea*sy') to force their face into a smile, or an 'eu' sound (as in 'yule') to produce an expression nearer to disgust.[10]

Psychologists at Washington University attached a golf tee to the inner ends of their participant's eyebrows and then asked them to carry out one of two facial contortions.[11] Participants in one group were asked to make the golf tees touch by drawing their eyebrows down and together, thus producing an unhappy facial expression. Those in the other group were asked to ensure that the ends of the golf tees didn't touch, thus creating a more neutral expression.

In perhaps the best known of the studies, researchers in Germany told participants that they were investigating a new way of teaching people who were paralysed below the neck to write.[12] Half of the participants were asked to support a pencil horizontally between their teeth (forcing their faces into a smile) whilst the other half were asked to hold the pencil between their lips (pulling their face into a frown).

Participants repeatedly chanting 'ee', keeping their golf tees apart, or supporting a pencil between their teeth suddenly felt significantly happier. Time and again, the research showed that Laird's results were genuine and that James's theory was correct. Your behaviour does influence how you feel and so, as a result, it is possible to manufacture emotions at will, as the *As If* principle (pages 17–20) predicts.

Excited by the results, researchers set out to discover the impact that the principle has on your body and brain.

Body and brain

Paul Ekman from the University of California has devoted his career to studying facial expressions and emotion. During a long and distinguished career he has produced the definitive guide to facial expression (a 500-page treatise showing how the forty-three facial muscles combine to produce thousands of expressions), advised law enforcement agencies across the world on the best ways of identifying whether someone is telling the truth from their facial expressions, and helped to create the hit American television show *Lie to Me*.

Towards the start of his career Ekman was intrigued to hear about the notion that altering people's facial expressions could make them feel either relaxed or angry, and wanted to discover how the *As If* principle affects the body. His remarkable results pay tribute to the power of James's theory.

What Ekman did was to invite volunteers into his laboratory, where he attached them to a machine that continually monitored their heart rate and skin temperature.[13] He then asked each participant to carry out two tasks. The first was designed to make them feel genuine anger, and involved thinking about an event in their lives that had made them feel angry, and mentally re-living that event as vividly as possible. For the second, they only produced the facial expression of anger (eyebrows down and together, raised upper eyelid, lower lip up and lips pressed together). By choosing different events and facial expressions, this procedure was repeated for several emotions, including fear, sadness, happiness, surprise and disgust.

Not surprisingly, the genuine emotional memories triggered certain patterns in participants' physiology with, for example, fear producing a high heart rate and low skin temperature, and happiness resulting in a low heart rate and higher skin temperature. Remarkably, exactly the same physiological pattern emerged when people adopted a facial expression. When they adopted a fearful facial expression their heart rate rocketed and their skin temperature dropped. When they put a smile on their faces their heart rate fell and their skin temperature increased.

Curious to discover whether this mechanism was 'hard-wired' into the human psyche, Ekman and his team journeyed across the world and repeated his study with the inhabitants of a remote island in western Indonesia.[14] The results were identical to those found in the West, suggesting that the *As If* principle is not a product of Western culture, but rather the deep-seated product of our evolutionary past.

Ekman's findings showed that behaving as if you are experiencing an emotion does not just influence how you feel, but also has a direct and powerful effect on your body.

More recently, researchers have built on this work by using the latest technology to discover how the *As If* principle affects the brain.

If you were to cut off your head and examine the region of the brain closest to the top of your spine, you would see two almond-shaped pieces of tissue either side of the spinal chord. These are known as the 'amygdala' (named after the Latin for 'almond'). They form a very small, but very well connected, part of the brain that plays a key role in almost every aspect of your everyday life. The amygdala is central to emotional experiences, especially fear.

The key role that the almond of horror plays in fear was recently illustrated by scientists studying a remarkable patient referred to as 'SM'.[15] SM suffers from Urbach–Wiethe disease, a rare genetic disorder that causes the amygdala to degenerate. After interviewing SM, the scientists noticed that she described several incidents in her life when she should have experienced fear, but didn't. In perhaps the most dramatic of these SM was unfortunate to be attacked in a local park. Her attacker held a knife to her throat, and threatened to stab her. SM said she didn't feel afraid at the time, but instead noticed a nearby church and calmly stated, 'If you're going to kill me, you're gonna have to go through my God's angels first.' Confused, the attacker suddenly let her go.

Intrigued, the scientists set out to scare SM. They took her to an exotic pet store and asked her to handle snakes and spiders. SM showed no reaction, and had to be stopped from touching the more dangerous ones. Next, they took her to an allegedly haunted house, and then showed her lots of horror movie clips. Again, nothing. Proof that a fully functioning amygdala plays a key role in experiencing fear.

A few years ago, scientists decided to conduct the ultimate test of James's hypothesis by putting participants in a brain scanner and asking them to contort their faces into a fearful expression.[16] Unlike the psychological studies that had been conducted throughout the preceding few decades, the participants did not have to tell the experimenters how they were feeling. Instead, the researchers just looked directly inside participants' brains, saw a highly active amygdala and could conclude that the participants were indeed experiencing genuine fear. In doing so, the researchers obtained the ultimate proof that behaving *As If* directly influences your brain.

The *As If* principle has been used to manufacture happiness in laboratories across the world, and has the power to impact instantly upon people's bodies and brains. But does the effect work in the real world? Could it even be employed to cheer up an entire nation? It was time to find out.

The science of happiness project

I have conducted several mass participation experiments during my career. These studies have involved tens of thousands of people and examined a range of topics including the psychology of lying, how a jury is swayed by a defendant's appearance, and whether people can tell the difference between cheap and expensive wine (they couldn't).

A few years ago I also arranged for thousands of people across Britain to take part in a large-scale study into happiness. Psychologists have created all sorts of techniques for promoting happiness, and I wanted to discover which was the most effective. Also, because other research had shown that happiness can spread through groups of people like a kind of infectious disease, with people 'catching' emotions from one another,[17] I wondered whether thousands of happier people might act as a catalyst and cheer up the entire country!

Before the start of the study I commissioned a national survey to measure the mood of the country. Everyone was asked to rate how cheerful they felt on a seven-point scale, where a 'one' corresponded to 'not at all cheerful' and seven to 'very cheerful'. Forty-five per cent of the population awarded themselves a five, six or seven.

The study was then announced in the national media. Everyone who was interested in participating was asked to visit the project's website and rate how happy they felt. More than 26,000 people responded. All of the participants were randomly assigned to one of a handful of groups and asked to carry out various exercises designed to make them happier. A number of the groups used some of the most popular 'think yourself happy' exercises, involving, for example, creating a sense of gratitude or re-living happy memories, whilst participants in one of the other groups were asked to follow James's advice and smile for a few seconds each day.

A week later the participants came back to the website and again rated how happy they were. When it came to increasing happiness, those altering their facial expressions came top of the class. Powerful evidence that the *As If* principle can generate emotions outside the laboratory, and such feelings are long-lasting and powerful.

After the study we conducted another national happiness poll. People were again asked to rate how cheerful they felt on the seven-point scale, and this time 52 per cent put themselves in the top half. Assuming there are 60 million people in the country, this 7 per cent rise corresponds to just over 4 million people reporting that they felt happier after the study. Was the increase due to our project? It is impossible to know for sure, but there were no obvious changes in the other factors that might have affected the mood of the country, such as a sudden rise in the amount of sunshine, drop in rainfall, or particularly heartening news stories, so we like to think that William James helped cheer up an entire nation.

3. THE VALUE OF FUN

William James not only speculated that smiling makes you feel happier, but also that all aspects of behaviour, including the way people moved and spoke, would influence how they felt. To discover if he was correct, psychologists started to walk the walk and talk the talk.

Research shows that in the same way that there are only a very small number of core facial expressions, so there are only six basic walking styles. Striders, for example, take long steps, walk with a bounce and let their arms swing back and forth. In contrast, shufflers tend to take small steps and have drooping shoulders. The work had also shown that people associate each of the walking styles with different emotions; with 'striders' being perceived as happy and 'shufflers' as sad.

Psychologist Sara Snodgrass from Florida Atlantic University wanted to discover whether changing the way people walked would influence how they themselves felt.[18] Whilst pretending to be conducting a study on the effect of physical activity on heart rate, Snodgrass asked people to take a three-minute walk in one of two ways. Half of the participants were asked to take long strides, swing their arms, and hold their head up high. In contrast, the others were asked to take short strides, shuffle along, and watch their feet. After enacting this real life version of Monty Python's Ministry of Silly Walks, everyone rated how happy they felt. The results demonstrate the power of the *As If* principle, with those who had been asked to take long strides feeling significantly happier than those who had been asked to shuffle along.

The *As If* principle can also help bring people closer together moments after they meet. Sabine Koch from the University of Heidelberg is fascinated by the impact of movement on the mind, and her work into the psychology of dance has revealed that people feel happier when they move in a fluid way, and unhappier when they make sharp and straight movements.[19] Aware that it isn't easy to persuade people to get in touch with their inner gazelle in everyday life, Koch turned her attention to a more down-to-earth behaviour: handshaking.

Koch trained a group of experimenters to shake people's hands in one of two ways. Some of them learnt how to shake hands in a smooth flowing way, whilst others were shown how to produce more sharp up-and-down movements. This crack team of intrepid handshakers then shook the hands of almost fifty participants. After each shake, Koch asked the participants how they felt. The results were remarkable. Compared to those subjected to the spiky handshakes, those who had been subjected to the smooth flowing handshake were happier, felt psychologically closer to the experimenter, and rated the experimenter as more likeable and open. The smooth handshake had made participants behave in a way that is associated with happiness and this had, in turn, made them both feel better and think more of the person they had just met.

Rip it up

How to shake hands

Sabine Koch's work can be used to help create a positive impression. Koch trained researchers to perform three 'smooth' and three 'sharp' handshakes, and discovered that the handshakes had a very different effect on people. To replicate one of Koch's 'smooth' handshakes, hold someone's hand and move your hand up and down in a slow flowing motion. In contrast, a 'sharp' handshake would involve you suddenly moving your hand down, keeping it there for a beat, and then quickly moving it back up again. At first the movements will appear artificial and strange; however, with practice they will feel far more automatic and natural. Focus on trying to recreate the 'smooth' hand movement as accurately as possible. Once you are confident of your new Koch-shaking abilities, use them in real life to create smooth hand movements and so make a good impression.

Other work has examined whether the words that you say, and the way that you say them, also influence how you feel.

In the late 1960s American clinical psychologist Emmett Velten wanted to create a quick and easy way of generating good cheer in the laboratory.[20] What would happen, Velten wondered, if people spoke as if they were happy and confident? To find out, he assembled a group of volunteers, randomly split the participants into two groups, and handed each group a stack of cards.

For the first group, the top card in the stack explained that they were about to see a series of statements and were required to read each statement out loud. The next card contained the first of the statements: 'Today is neither better nor worse than any other day'. As instructed, the participants read the statement out loud and then turned over the card and moved on to the second statement: 'I do feel pretty good today, though'. Slowly but surely the participant moved through all sixty cards, with the statements becoming increasingly positive.

Those in the second group were asked to read a series of statements that were not designed to get them talking like a positive person, and so spent the sessions reading various facts out loud, including 'Saturn is sometimes in conjunction, beyond the sun from the earth, and isn't visible', 'The Orient Express travels between Paris and Istanbul' and 'The Hope diamond was shipped from South Africa to London through the regular mail service'.

At the end of the procedure Velten asked all of the participants to rate how happy they felt. The participants who had said positive statements about themselves were in a wonderful mood. In contrast, those that had been reflecting on Saturn, the Orient Express and the Hope Diamond flat-lined.

Encouraged by Velten's results, other psychologists quickly adopted the procedure and it is now used to cheer up experimental participants across the world.[21]

And it isn't just about reading single statements. In another study, Elaine Hatfield from the University of Hawaii and her colleagues had a group of participants read a short paragraph describing a fictitious scenario in which their friends had thrown them a wonderful surprise birthday party.[22] In contrast, another group read a paragraph describing how they had just heard that a member of their family had been diagnosed with an illness.

Saying the two different sets of words affected the participants' moods, with the people hearing about a good time feeling much better than those speaking about the family illness. Getting the participants to speak as if they were in a good or bad mood had the power to genuinely affect their emotions.

The *As If* principle is not just about forcing your face into a smile, but instead applies to almost every aspect of your everyday behaviour, including the way that you walk and the words that you say. Excited by these findings, academics quickly set about exploring other ways of using the *As If* principle to cheer people up in an instant.

Rip it up

Happy talk

Can you really talk to yourself and make yourself feel happier? Find out by carrying out the following two exercises.

First, read each of the following statements out loud to yourself. Try to sound as convincing as possible, as if you are spontaneously saying the statements to a friend. Don't rush the task, but rather speak slowly and leave a little time before moving on to the next sentence. Most people find the task odd at first but quickly get used to it.

1) I feel surprisingly good about myself today.

2) I think that I can make a success of things.

3) I am glad that most people are very friendly towards me.

4) I know that if I set my mind to something, it will usually turn out well.

5) I feel very enthusiastic right now.

6) It's as if I am full of energy at the moment and enjoying what I am doing.

7) I feel especially efficient today.

8) I'm very optimistic at the minute and expect to get along very well with most of the people I meet.

9) I'm feeling very good about myself and the world today.

10) Given the mood that I am in, I feel particularly inventive and resourceful.

11) I am pretty certain that most of my friends will stick with me in the future.

12) I feel my life is very much under my control.

13) I am in a great mood and want somebody to play some wonderful music.

14) I am enjoying this, and I really do feel good about myself.

15) This feels like one of those days when I'm raring to go!

How do you feel now? For most people the procedure results in a boost in happiness.

Now, try reading aloud the following paragraph. Again, try to make your words sound natural and enthusiastic. It might help to imagine that you are having a telephone conversation with a friend. Feel free to improvise and come up with your own positive version of events.

This has been a great day. It's my birthday and you will never guess what happened. I was invited around my friend's house earlier this evening and when I arrived I found out that he had arranged a surprise birthday party for me! It was amazing. Almost everyone I knew was there, and some people had made a real effort to be part of the event. They had baked me a cake, brought me presents and even sang 'Happy Birthday'. I will remember the day for the rest of my life and am so lucky to have friends like that.

Make 'em laugh

In 1995 Dr Madan Kataria was working as a family physician in Mumbai, India. Whilst researching a magazine article on the science of laughter Kataria learnt about the medical benefits of laughter, and decided to try and introduce more chuckles and guffaws into people's lives.

Kataria came up with a strange plan. At seven o'clock one morning he went to his local park and persuaded four people to tell each other jokes, and laugh. Everyone enjoyed the session and Kataria decided to repeat the exercise the following week. The group soon grew and more than fifty people were turning up for the sessions. Kataria had created the world's first laughter club.

In his original meetings everyone would stand in a circle and then take turns to tell a joke. Initially, all went well, but after a few weeks people ran out of clean jokes and started to use more questionable material. The laughter came to a sudden halt when two women threatened to leave because of sexist jokes, causing Kataria to explore other ways of putting a smile on people's faces.

Eventually he had a world-changing 'ha-ha' moment – he wondered whether people would get the same benefits from laughter if they chuckled away without hearing any jokes. The laughter club was initially sceptical but eventually agreed to put their mother-in-law jokes on the back burner and try Kataria's new approach. Within moments of acting as if they had heard a great joke, many members of the group found themselves feeling surprisingly euphoric. Contagion quickly kicked in and soon almost everyone was giggling. Word about Kataria's new and surprisingly effective way of inducing good cheer quickly spread, and laughter clubs sprang up across the world.

Intrigued, psychologist Charles Schaefer from Fairleigh Dickinson University in New Jersey decided to discover whether behaving like someone who has just heard a great gag really does make people feel good.[23] Schaefer set up his own experimental laughter club and compared the effects of laughing with smiling.

He split volunteers into three groups. One group was asked to spend a minute smiling, whilst another was required to spend the same amount of time laughing out loud. Concerned that any changes reported by those in the second group may have been due to the physical exertion caused by side-splitting laughter, Schaefer wanted the third group to carry out a task that was equally energetic but not associated with having a good time. After much head-scratching, Schaefer asked the students in the third group to howl like a wolf.

Although a clever control, the 'howl like a wolf' exercise was not without its problems. At first the students in this group were somewhat confused and uncertain about how best to contact their inner werewolf. To solve the problem, Schaefer stood in front of the group and personally demonstrated how to role-play a wolf howling at the moon. He later reported that seeing a senior professor behaving in this way quickly caused the students to become significantly less self-conscious.

After much smiling, laughter and howling, Schaefer asked everyone to assess their mood. The more the students behaved as if they were having a good time, the happier they became.

Those that smiled became happier, but those that laughed out loud became elated. Howling like a wolf had very little effect on happiness, showing that the effect of the laughter was not due to physical exertion. William James's theory had been proved accurate again. Unfortunately, Schaefer didn't examine whether the students in the third group felt strangely attracted to dog food or nervous about silver bullets.

Schaefer's study revealed why laughter clubs are so popular. In the same way that smiling makes you feel happy, so behaving as if you find something funny brings the same psychological and physical benefits associated with genuine laughter.

Rip it up

Laugh and the world laughs with you . . .

Laughter clubs vary, but here is a rough guide to some of the basic procedures and exercises.

First, the group starts by forming a circle, with each person standing a few feet away from one another. One member of the group then takes the role of the 'leader' and stands in the middle of the circle.

The entire session lasts around twenty minutes and is made up of various exercises, each of which lasts about forty seconds. Here are some of the more popular exercises.

The big 'Ho-Ho Ha-Ha': Everyone starts chanting 'Ho-Ho Ha-Ha', clapping their hands together on each 'Ho' and 'Ha'. The chants should come from the stomach rather than the mouth, and everyone should try to keep a smile on their face throughout the exercise. This is often used as a warm-up and between other exercises.

Shake it all about: Everyone in the circle joins hands. The leader then says 'Now' and the group starts to quietly giggle. Then the leader beckons everyone towards the centre of the circle. As they move forward the intensity of their laughter increases. When the group nears the centre of the circle the leader beckons them back, and they return to their original positions and back to their quiet giggling.

Taming the lion: Everyone adopts a 'lion posture' by sticking their tongue fully out, opening their mouth and eyes as wide as possible, and holding their hands up like the paws of a lion. On a command from the leader, everyone roars like a lion for twenty seconds.

The humming bird: Everyone pairs up, closes their lips and tries to laugh whilst making a humming sound. Throughout the exercise people try to maintain eye contact with their partner.

Mockery: The leader separates the circle into two groups. The groups look at one other and start laughing, often pointing at members of the other group. This exercise is not recommended if members of the group suffer from low self-esteem, paranoia, or both.

After conducting some surprisingly serious science into laughter, psychologists turned their attention to the effect of other equally enjoyable experiences, such as dancing the night away.

Happy people like to dance, but can dancing make you feel happy? To find out, Sungwoon Kim from the Kyungpook National University in Korea enlisted the help of approximately 300 students.[24] The researchers split the students into four groups. Group one was asked to take part in an hour-long aerobic exercise class, the second group were invited to a body conditioning session, group three had fun hip-hop dancing, and group four were taken ice skating. After taking part in the activities everyone completed a questionnaire about their mood. It is well known that exercise makes people happier because it releases feel-good hormones called endorphins, and so the researchers expected all of the participants to be happier after the exercise. However, would the hip-hop classes make the participants feel especially good because they were behaving as if they were a happy person? The results revealed that those who had been sent hip-hop dancing were top of the class in terms of happiness.

And it isn't just hip-hop dancing that makes you feel good. Dr Peter Lovatt is a colleague of mine at the University of Hertfordshire, and carries out research into dance. Labelled 'Dr Dance' by the British media, Peter has examined a wide range of dance-related issues, including whether people with symmetrical bodies are better dancers (they are) and why 'dad dancing' makes us cringe (they have an overinflated opinion of their abilities). A few years ago Peter ran a ten-week experiment to examine the effects of dance on mood.[25] Each week he gathered together a group of willing volunteers at the university, taught them a new type of dance, and then asked them to rate their mood. From the foxtrot to flamenco, and salsa to swing, everyone had a jolly time. Once again, the results revealed that behaving as if they were happy made the participants feel better, with dances that were non-competitive and with an easily learned repetitive structure – such as Scottish country dances and line dancing – proving especially effective.

Rip it up

Fun Inc.

First, take a few moments to list nine activities that make you feel good. Here are a few questions to help you put your list together.

- Do you enjoy spending time with other people? If so, which of your friends and colleagues are the most fun to be around? What types of social activities do you really enjoy? Would you, for example, rather have a coffee with close friends, visit your family, or go out dancing with a large group of work colleagues?

- Which hobbies, interests or sports do you really enjoy? Do you have a good time going for long walks in the countryside, painting, taking photographs, skydiving, or visiting a museum? If you had a free evening, would you rather go to a cinema, stay in with a book, see a circus or head for the theatre?

- What did you do to have fun when you were a child? Did you enjoy skipping, dancing, baking, making a den, reading comics, playing in the leaves, or creating a drawing?

- Do you enjoy helping other people? Perhaps working for a local charity, or helping out at a local hospital? How does it feel when you give some money to a homeless person on the street or carry out an act of kindness for a stranger or friend?

- Do you like seeing the funny side of whatever happens to you? Do you enjoy playing silly games or generally messing around? Are there particular people or situations that seem to encourage this behaviour?

Second, tear out the following page and write one of your chosen activities in each of the boxes.

Third, rip up the page into nine pieces by tearing along the dotted lines, and screw each of the pieces into a ball.

Finally, place the balls into a box or bag. At the start of each week, randomly select one of the pieces of paper and make sure that you carry out the activity within the next seven days.

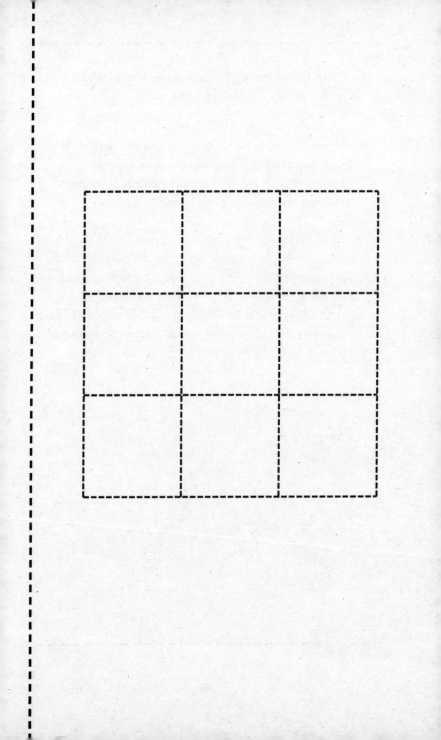

And if you have two left feet then worry not – you can always sing a happy song.

The seventeenth-century Spanish novelist and poet Miguel de Cervantes thought so, noting, 'He who sings frightens away his ills'. But was Cervantes correct?

Musicologist Grenville Hancox from Canterbury Christ Church University is a world-class clarinet player, conductor and researcher. Curious about the effect that music has on people, Hancox has carried out several large-scale investigations into whether singing makes people happy, including one study in which he interviewed more than 500 choral singers. The work has revealed one clear finding – singing makes people feel happy.[26]

Gunter Kreutz from the J. W. Goethe-Universität in Frankfurt had tackled the same issue under more rigorous circumstances.[27] Kreutz visited a choir during its rehearsal, asked the choristers to sing sections from Mozart's Requiem, and then rate how happy they were. As a control, a week later Kreutz again gate-crashed their rehearsal, asked them to listen to a recording of the same piece and again rate their happiness. Although listening to the music didn't make people feel any happier, singing made them feel far more cheerful.

The message from research into the *As If* principle and the fun factory is clear – rather than trying to cheer yourself up by thinking happy thoughts, it is far quicker and more effective to simply behave as if you are having a good time. Smile, put a spring in your step, hold your head up high, use happy talk, dance, laugh, sing, or do whatever else you enjoy doing.

Or, to put it another way, if you want to be happy and you know it, clap your hands.

2. ATTRACTION AND RELATIONSHIPS

Where we unpack the mysteries of the human heart, discover the power of footsie, invent a new type of speed dating, and learn how to live happily ever after.

'Whatever we learn to do, we learn by actually doing it; men come to be builders, for instance, by building, and harp players by playing the harp. In the same way, by doing just acts we come to be just; by doing self-controlled acts, we come to be self-controlled; and by doing brave acts, we become brave.'

Aristotle

1. WHAT IS LOVE?

In 1981 Prince Charles announced his engagement to Diana Spencer. In a now-infamous television interview about their forthcoming wedding, journalist Anthony Carthew asked the couple how they felt. Charles hesitantly explained that he was delighted and happy, prompting Carthew to add '. . . and I suppose . . . in love?' Diana quickly agreed, but Charles was far more circumspect, mumbling '. . . whatever "in love" means'.

Charles is not the first to be confused by the nature of love. Throughout history, poets, musicians and writers have struggled to define this most elusive of emotions. The Ancient Greek philosopher Aristotle thought that love was best viewed as '. . . a single soul inhabiting two bodies', whereas Elizabeth Barrett Browning attempted to capture the essence of passion when she wrote: 'What I do and what I dream include thee, as the wine must taste of its own grapes . . .' In contrast, the American actor John Barrymore took a somewhat more practical view, noting that: 'Love is the delightful interval between meeting a beautiful girl and discovering that she looks like a haddock.'

Although it is difficult to define love, there is little doubt that the emotion has always intrigued us. Archaeologists working in Iraq's Niffer Valley recently unearthed the world's oldest surviving love letter. Etched into a 4,000-year-old clay tablet, the love poem appears to have been written by a high priestess to her husband and describes her excitement about their forthcoming wedding night ('Goodly is your beauty, honeysweet. You have captivated me. Let me stand tremblingly before you. Can I borrow a tenner until the end of the week?'*).

Love also knows no cultural bounds. From the Amazon to Arizona, and the Sahara to Siberia, people in vastly different societies all appear to experience the joys and pains of passion. The few communities that have attempted to banish love have encountered nothing but failure. In the nineteenth century, for instance, both the Shakers and the Mormons believed that love was lust in disguise, and so attempted to prevent their followers from having romantic encounters. Love persisted in both groups, often taking the form of dangerous liaisons away from prying eyes.

Given the ubiquity of love, one might have expected psychologists to have had a long-standing interest in the emotion. However, research into the mysteries of the human heart is a surprisingly recent endeavour and was kick-started by the strangest of events.

'I'm just one of you in a bag'

In 1967 Professor Charles Goetzinger was lecturing on the science of persuasion at Oregon State University ('Speech 113: Basic Persuasion'). When Goetzinger's new cohort of students arrived for the first of their lectures they were greeted by a strange sight.[1] Sitting at one of the desks was a person

---

* I added the final line.

completely covered in a large black cloth bag, with their bare feet poking out through two slits in the base of the bag.

Goetzinger explained to his class that a male student had decided to attend the course enclosed within a black bag, and wished his identity to remain a complete secret. In the absence of a name for their anonymous classmate, the students agreed to refer to him as 'Black Bag' (presumably having just skipped 'Speech 112: Very Basic Creativity').

The class met three times a week and each time Black Bag sat silently at his desk. When the time came for the students to give a three-minute presentation on persuasion, Black Bag simply stood in front of the class in total silence. Initially Goetzinger's students were antagonistic towards Black Bag. One poked him with an umbrella, another placed a 'Kick Me' label on his back, and a third tried to punch him.

The story soon caught the attention of the local, and then national, media. News crews from across America descended on Goetzinger's classes, CBS legend Walter Cronkite tried to interview the mysterious man in the bag, and *Life* magazine devoted several pages to the story.

Then something unexpected began to happen. After a few weeks the students started to bond with Black Bag. Despite still not knowing who he was or what he looked like, the punching and poking was replaced with compassion and kindness. As alienation evolved into acceptance, the students grew increasingly fond of their anonymous classmate, involving him in their activities and protecting his identity. When Goetzinger asked the class to vote on whether Black Bag should be asked to reveal his identity, the majority of students were opposed to the idea.

At the end of Goetzinger's persuasion course several

camera crews were lined up outside the school building waiting for Black Bag to emerge from class. Without a word being said, the students formed a human wall around Black Bag and protected him as he moved through the media scrum. The episode humbled Black Bag, causing him to utter a rare but memorable comment: 'I'm just one of you in a bag.' To this day, the identity of Black Bag remains a mystery.

Both the media and public turned to psychologists in an attempt to understand why Goetzinger's students had slowly warmed to their anonymous classmate. There was, however, one small problem – psychologists at the time had almost no idea how to explain what had happened.

Prior to the 1960s most psychologists saw the experimental examination of friendship, attraction and love as taboo. Perhaps eager to distance themselves from Freud's unscientific and overly sexual view of the human psyche, universities discouraged their staff from investigating people's personal lives. Entering the forbidden zone could have very real consequences, with one professor severely reprimanded for carrying out a survey in which he asked people whether they had ever blown into someone's ear in an attempt to arouse passion.[2]

Even by the start of the 1960s researchers had only developed the most rudimentary of ideas about how people come to like and love one another. Somewhat embarrassed by the lack of insight that their work could shed on the mystery of Black Bag, a handful of researchers began to wander into the academic wilderness, and investigate the psychology of friendship, attraction and love.

In 1975, psychologist Elaine Hatfield from the University of Wisconsin received funding from the National Science

Foundation to carry out one of the first systematic programmes of research into love and attraction. Although many researchers saw this as a major breakthrough, not everyone was thrilled. American Senator William Proxmire launched a blistering attack on Hatfield's work, awarded her a 'Golden Fleece Award' (for allegedly 'fleecing' taxpayers), and publicly announced:

> I believe that 200 million other Americans want to leave some things in life a mystery, and right on top of the things we don't want to know is why a man falls in love with a woman and vice versa . . . So National Science Foundation – get out of the love racket. Leave that to Elizabeth Barrett Browning and Irving Berlin. Here if anywhere Alexander Pope was right when he observed, 'If ignorance is bliss, tis folly to be wise.'

Unperturbed, Hatfield ploughed on. In one of her initial studies[3] she teamed up with fellow romance researcher Russell Clark from the Florida State University and examined a very straightforward question – if a reasonably attractive member of the opposite sex asked a man or woman to sleep with them, would they get lucky?

Hatfield and Clark asked five women and four men to walk up to complete strangers at the university and say: 'I have been noticing you around campus. I find you very attractive. Would you go to bed with me tonight?' The experimenters carefully recorded the response in a notebook, and then explained that they were actually conducting a social psychology study and thus their offer had been made solely in the spirit of scientific enquiry (the experimenters did not record people's responses to this part of the procedure). Describing their findings in a paper entitled 'Gender Differences in Receptivity to Sexual Offers', Clark and Hatfield reported major differences between the sexes. None of the women who were approached accepted the offers of sex from the male experimenters. In contrast, a remarkable 75 per cent of men ticked the 'your place or mine?' box.

Perhaps, not surprisingly, Hatfield's study generated a storm of controversy, with some arguing that the findings provided a vivid demonstration of how those with societal power exploit the powerless, and others being equally adamant that they provided support for the 'man = shallow' hypothesis. The study has also had an unintended effect on popular culture. In 1998 the British jazz ensemble Touch and Go sampled a woman reciting Hatfield's experimental script and used it as the basis for their song 'Would You . . . ?' The song reached number three in the UK singles chart and has been viewed 2 million times on YouTube.

The success of this initial work prompted Hatfield and her colleagues to conduct other experiments into the psychology of attraction.

Some of the subsequent work revealed that both friendship and love tended to be greatly enhanced by prolonged contact. According to this theory, the more you hang around someone, the greater the likelihood of them liking and eventually loving you. This principle was used to explain why people often end up marrying people from their neighbourhoods, and why Goetzinger's students slowly came to bond with Black Bag. The theory also apparently motivated one man to write over 700 letters to his girlfriend, resulting in her marrying the postman (only joking).

The trickle of research into love soon became a tide, and from the mid-1970s onwards hundreds of researchers conducted thousands of experiments in an attempt to unravel the mysteries of the human heart.[4]

Love Factually

Research into Cupid's deepest secrets took many forms, including secretly observing people flirting in singles bars, staging scientific speed-dating sessions, posting fake personal ads, testing testosterone levels during kissing, and examining the lives of happily married couples.

It soon became apparent that love was going to be a tough nut to crack. In the early 1970s, for example, psychologist Donn Byrne declared that he had discovered the equation for love, proudly announcing that . . .

$$Y= m[\Sigma PR/(\Sigma PR+\Sigma NR)]+k$$

. . . where Y stands for attraction, PR for positive reinforcement, NR for negative reinforcement and k is a constant.[5] The response to Byrne's alleged discovery can be summed up by the mathematical formula . . .

$$X < 1$$

. . . where X stands for the number of people that were impressed.

Other academics took a slightly more constructive approach, arguing that you unconsciously carry around a list of desirable traits in your head, and when you meet someone who ticks all of the boxes your brain suddenly goes into overdrive and you fall in love.

Although the work struggled to discover exactly how Cupid's arrow found its target, it did reveal that there are two main varieties of love.[6]

The first is referred to as 'passionate love' and is associated with feelings of intense exhilaration, infatuation, and an emotional high. It is the type of love that makes two people stay up all night chatting and watch the sun rise in the morning. Some psychologists have taken a romantic view of this experience, focusing on the upside of a couple yearning to be together and thinking endlessly about one another. Others have taken off their rose-tinted glasses and adopted a more down-to-earth approach, pointing out that passionate love activates the parts of the brain commonly associated with drug abuse and alcohol addiction.

The second type of love, known as 'compassionate love', is far more about attachment than attraction. Rather than focusing on the thrill of the chase and intensity of that first kiss, this form of love is experienced by those in a secure and comforting long-term relationship.

Over the years researchers have devised questionnaires to measure these two very different varieties of love (see pages 63–4). A few years ago, Elaine Hatfield and her colleagues gave the questionnaires to three different types of couple – those who had just started dating, newlyweds, and long-term married.[7] The results allowed Hatfield to track how love evolves over the course of a relationship.

First, the good news. Those who have just started dating experience a very high level of passionate love, and a moderately high level of compassionate love. Next, the even better news. Newlyweds report even higher levels of both passionate and compassionate love. Now, the not so good news.

Within a year of being married the rot starts to set in, with both passionate and compassionate love declining to the levels first experienced during dating. Finally, the bad news. Over the next thirty years of marriage both passionate and compassionate love decline, with the demise of the former being far more rapid than the latter. Love may never die, but it certainly takes a dramatic nosedive as time passes. On the upside, as we will discover later in this chapter, once you understand the truth about love it is relatively easy to maintain a sense of passion in even the longest of relationships.

Couple Hatfield's somewhat depressing findings with the human need to be loved, and it's not surprising that throughout history those offering ways of manufacturing long-lasting love have never been short of clients.

Rip it up

Are you in love?

Please complete the following questionnaire by imagining your partner's name in each of the following statements, and then assigning a number between 1 (Definitely not true) to 5 (Definitely true).[8]

1) I would feel heart-broken if _____ left me.

2) _____ is always on my mind.

3) Of all of the people I know, I would rather be with _____.

4) If _____ were to fall love with someone else I would feel extremely jealous.

5) I tingle all over when _____ touches me.

6) I feel very sad when I see _____ going through a difficult time.

7) _____ and I make a great team.

8) Helping _____ provides me with a strong sense of meaning to my life.

9) I would rather help _____ than help myself.

10) I feel very comfortable when I am together with _____.

Scoring

First, add up your answers to questions 1 to 5. This is your 'Passionate Love' score. Use the following chart to discover how your score compares to others.

Less than 5: You didn't read the instructions properly.
5–7: Extremely cool, the thrill feels like it has gone.
8–10: Feels somewhat cool and tepid.
11–15: Average, with the occasional periods of passion.
16–20: Passionate but still room for improvement.
21–25: Congratulations, you are wildly and passionately in love.

Next, add up your answers to questions 6–10. This is your 'Compassionate Love' score. Use the following chart to find out how your score compares to others.

5–7: Slight evidence of friendship.
8–10: The two of you have bonded, but it isn't strong.
11–15: Average, with the occasional burst of strong compassion.
16–20: Highly compassionate.
21–25: Congratulations, you are in compassionate love.

In search of Cupid

For centuries, magicians and witches claimed to be able to create spells and potions that can make two people fall in love. The Byzantines believed that Cupid's arrow would strike the moment they consumed a special 'love cake' made from donkey's milk and honey. Throughout the Middle Ages the humble tomato was widely seen as the 'apple of love', causing Puritan leaders to try and prevent their followers from eating the vegetable by spreading the rumour that it was poisonous. When spells, donkey's milk and tomatoes failed to hit the mark, people turned to more down-to-earth ways of finding the love of their life, including the creation of personal ads.

Personal ads have a surprisingly long history, with the first one appearing in 1695 in a British publication entitled *The Collection for the Improvement of Husbandry and Trade*.[9] The item was sandwiched between an advert for an Arabian stallion and a second-hand bed, and was placed by a well-heeled gentleman who was searching for a 'Gentlewoman that has a fortune of £3,000 or thereabouts'. Unfortunately, history doesn't record whether the young man's quest was successful. Nevertheless, the idea quickly caught on, with people placing increasingly demanding and humorous ads. One eighteenth-century ad appealed for respondents with 'no bodily deformity', another wanted only those with a 'shapely ankle', and a third advertised for '. . . a wife with two or three hundred pounds; or the money will do without the wife'.

Skip forward a few hundred years and the search for love shows no signs of fading away. In the 1950s, two enterprising Harvard students created 'Operation Match', the first computer-based matchmaking system. To test the system, the students asked over 7,000 people to complete questionnaires designed to assess their personalities. This information was then transferred onto punch cards and run through a mainframe computer that was the size of a small room. Six weeks later each participant received a list containing the addresses and telephone numbers of compatible dates. Nowadays, online dating sites employ the same concept, and have developed increasingly sophisticated algorithms to match accurately millions of people using a variety of factors.

The matchmaking industry's latest innovation was created in the late 1990s, when Rabbi Yaacov Deyo wanted to help Jewish singles meet one another and so came up with the concept of speed dating. The idea quickly caught on, leading to millions of people around the world trying to find love on the basis of a three-minute chat.

The love industry does not just cater for those in search of Cupid's arrow, though. If couples experience difficulties in their relationship, counsellors, DVDs and self-help books offer a wide range of advice that claims to help people stay together.

But are these techniques effective? Research suggests that there is about a 4 per cent chance of having a relationship with someone you have met at a speed-dating event.[10] Online dating fares better, with one survey carried out by a major online dating agency showing that about 17 per cent of couples that tied the knot in the three years prior to the survey met via an online dating site.

The recent figures for those wanting to stay in love are somewhat more depressing, with around half of American's first marriages failing, along with two thirds of second marriages and three quarters of third marriages.

Encouraged by work showing how the *As If* principle (pages 17–20) can be used to manufacture happiness, researchers wondered whether it could also help people find the love of their life and encourage couples to stick together when the going gets tough.

Cue Dr Stanley Schachter and his hula-hoop of love.

2. THE MISATTRIBUTION OF
BODILY SENSATIONS

Think about the last time you experienced a really strong emotion. Perhaps you felt anxious before giving a talk, nervous during an important job interview, excited after a successful date, or angry when someone insulted you. In any case, unless you are a psychopath, you probably noticed a dramatic change in your bodily sensations. Your heart rate may have increased, your mouth might have become extremely dry, and perhaps your palms felt sweaty.

Much of the initial work into the psychology of emotion attempted to identify the exact patterning of bodily sensations that accompany various feelings. Researchers invited participants into the laboratory, wired up their bodies to various sensors, and then made the participants angry by insulting them, scared by bombarding them with loud noises, and happy by offering them cake. The research teams then pored over the reams of data, looking for the pattern of bodily sensations associated with each emotion. Was anger associated with a sudden increase in heart rate coupled with faster breathing? Was fear linked with a very dry mouth and sweating? Was joy accompanied by a decrease in heart rate and much shallower breathing?

After spending years trying to create a physiological dictionary of emotion it was obvious that something was very wrong. Although almost all of the participants experienced a vast array of emotions, the bodily sensations that accompanied these feelings were often surprisingly similar. Something just didn't add up.

Then, in the 1960s, psychologist Stanley Schachter finally solved the mystery.

Schachter worked at Columbia University and studied a wide variety of interesting topics, including obesity, nicotine addiction, cults, and miserliness. Early on in his career he conducted a now-classic experiment exploring what happens inside your body when you experience an emotion.[11] Let's imagine that you are taking part in his study.

You're walking along the street minding your own business when suddenly you see a poster asking for participants to take part in an experiment investigating the effects on vision of the vitamin compound suproxin. Eager to earn some money for a few hours' work, you call the number on the poster and are asked to come along to Schachter's laboratory the following day.

When you arrive at the laboratory a researcher gives you an injection of suproxin, explains that the shot takes time before it has any effect, and asks you go to a nearby waiting room. When you enter, you smile politely at a man already sitting there. The two of you start chatting and the man explains that he is also a participant in the experiment. Like you, he is waiting for the injection of suproxin to take effect.

After a few minutes your new-found friend becomes full of the joys of spring. He finds a hula-hoop in one corner of the waiting room and starts playing with it, cracks several jokes, climbs on the furniture, and throws balls of paper into the waste-paper bin. After spending about fifteen minutes with Mr Euphoric, the researcher enters the waiting room and asks you to complete a short questionnaire about your current mood. When you have completed the form the researcher explains that the experiment has finished. But as is often the case with psychology, nothing was quite as it seemed.

Schachter was convinced that the scientific search for the bodily sensations associated with emotions had failed because it was based on a fundamentally flawed assumption. To him it seemed obvious that each emotion couldn't possibly be associated with a particular pattern of heart rate, breathing, sweating and so on. There were simply too many emotions, and too few bodily sensations. Instead, Schachter thought that the situation was far simpler.

He hypothesized that all of your bodily sensations were caused by a physiological system that operated much like a tug of war match.

At one end of the rope is the red team. When this team bursts into action you feel more aroused and active. Adrenalin and sugar are quickly released into your bloodstream to help provide energy, your heartbeat and breathing rate increase to get more oxygen to your muscles, there is a reduction in blood flow to your skin to help reduce bleeding if injured, and the digestive juices in your stomach go into overdrive to help produce more energy. In short, your body undergoes the well-known 'fight or flight' response. If you decide not to engage in fisticuffs or run away, the unspent energy in your body can make you feel light-headed, weak at the knees, experience butterflies in your stomach, and tremble.

On the other end of the rope is the blue team. When they

pull on their end of the rope it calms down your body. Your heart rate slows and your digestive system returns to normal.

Similarly, when you lie down and take it easy, the blue team pulls on their end of the rope, causing your heart rate to decrease and your breathing to become slow and shallow. The moment you stand up and walk about the red team bursts into action and restores your heart rate and breathing to normal.

Most of the time, the red and blue teams work together to ensure that your bodily sensations are appropriate for your surroundings. If, for example, you were to spot a tiger in some bushes, the red team would jump into action and you would feel your heartbeat suddenly increase. However, the moment you remember that you are at a zoo and therefore perfectly safe, the blue team would pull on their end of the rope and your heartbeat would slow down.

According to Schachter, there is not a different bodily reaction associated with each emotion, but rather one system that simply varies in intensity.

Rip it up

Body talk

People vary in the degree to which their bodies produce the type of sensations that drive emotional feelings. Use this questionnaire to discover the degree to which your body is responsive.[12]

Imagine that you are in a fairly stressful situation. Please rate the degree to which each of the ten statements would apply to you using the following scale:

1: Never 2: Occasionally 3: Sometimes 4: Usually 5: Always

During stressful situations . . .

Your rating:

. . . my face either blushes or becomes especially pale. _____

. . . my legs feel weak and my hands start to shake. _____

. . . my breathing becomes rapid and shallow. _____

. . . my heartbeat increases. _____

. . . my palms start to sweat. _____

. . . my stomach starts to rumble. _____

. . . the hair on the back of my neck stands up. _____

. . . my mouth feels dry. _____

. . . my eyes start to feel wet. _____

. . . my face and ears feel hotter. _____

Scoring

Add up all of your scores. Use the following chart to find out how your score compares to others.

10–20:   Very low reactivity.
21–30:   Above low but below average reactivity.
31–40:   Average reactivity.
41–50:   Very high reactivity.

Being a high or low reactive is neither inherently good nor bad. Low reactives tend to keep calm in stressful situations, whereas high reactives are good at responding to early signs of threat.

Schachter's theory faces one major problem. If your bodily sensations only vary in intensity, how can you experience such a vast array of emotions? His solution involves moving away from your body and into your brain. According to his theory, when you experience a surge in bodily activity you look around, try to work out what is going on, and then label the emotion accordingly. So if, for example, someone shouts at you, you would feel your heart beat faster, hear some insults and conclude that you must be angry. Similarly, when you are with someone you find very attractive you might experience exactly the same increase in heart rate, but instead assume that it is due to desire.

Schachter's idea turned the common-sense view of emotion upside down. According to common sense, emotion seems to precede bodily sensations. You see a lion, become afraid and start to sweat. Or see a roller coaster, become excited and your heart beats faster. Schachter suggested the exact opposite. The lion makes you sweat, then you look at the dangerous situation you are in and start to feel afraid. Or the sight of the roller coaster makes your heart beat faster, then you see that you are in a theme park and so you feel excited. As such, Schachter's idea is an extension on William James's theory of emotion. James believed you monitor your facial expressions and behaviour and then figure out how you are feeling. Schachter extended this idea to your bodily sensations (see diagram, opposite).

Bodily sensations and emotion

Common sense suggests that the chain of causation is:
See an oncoming car ⟶ Feel afraid ⟶ Stomach lurches

Walk past your favourite celebrity in the street ⟶ Feel excited ⟶ Start to sweat

Schachter's theory suggests that the reality is:

See an oncoming car ⟶ Stomach lurches ⟶ Look at your situation ⟶ Feel afraid

Walk past your favourite celebrity in the street ⟶ Start to sweat ⟶ Look at your situation ⟶ Feel excited

This extension of the *As If* principle (pages 17–20), if correct, leads to an intriguing prediction. It should be possible to get you to experience vastly different emotions by increasing your heart rate in different contexts. And this was exactly what your time with Mr Euphoric was all about.

The vitamin compound 'suproxin' doesn't exist and the study was nothing to do with vision. Also, as you may have figured out by now, Mr Euphoric was actually a stooge working for the experimenters.

The injection that you received during the experiment contained a shot of adrenalin so would have activated your physiology. Moments after the chemical entered your body the red team would have burst into action, making your heart beat faster, your hands tremble and your mouth become dry. According to Schachter's version of the *As If* principle, spending time with Mr Euphoric would have encouraged you to label your strange bodily sensations as signs of good cheer, and so made you feel especially happy.

And this is what the results revealed. Time and again, when participants who had hung out with Mr Euphoric completed Schachter's mood questionnaire they ticked the 'I feel strangely delighted' box.

The *As If* principle suggests that if exactly the same bodily sensations were experienced in a different context they would give rise to a very different emotion. To find out if this was the case, Schachter carried out the second part of his study. He invited a group of participants into his laboratory and injected them with 'suproxin' (actually adrenalin). They were then given a questionnaire about their background and asked to complete it in the waiting room.

When each participant entered the room they didn't encounter Mr Euphoric and his hula-hoop of joy. Instead, the same man had been asked to play Mr Angry – a very unhappy individual who started to complain about the questionnaire. Faced with a series of increasingly personal questions ('With how many men (other than your father) has your mother had extramarital relationships? Options: 4 and under ____, Between 5 and 9 ____, 10 and over ____'), Mr Angry became progressively more agitated, and eventually screwed up the form and stormed out of the room.

Would Mr Angry's behaviour cause the participants to attribute their high heart rate to annoyance? Yes. In fact, when this second batch of participants described their mood they felt furious.

In both parts of the study people's bodily sensations were identical. However, in the first part Mr Euphoric encouraged people to view their high heart rate in a positive way and so ended up feeling happy. In the second part of the study Mr Angry put a dampener on the situation, causing people to view their heart rate in a more negative way and end up feeling annoyed.

To ensure that participants' emotions were not just the result of playing with hula-hoops or being asked about their mother's morality, Schachter added other parts to the experiment, including two more groups that were injected with an inert saline solution rather than adrenalin. These participants didn't feel their heart race, and so were not acting as if they were especially emotional. As a result they didn't feel especially happy or furious after spending time with Mr Euphoric or Mr Angry.

The *As If* principle also explains many curious aspects of emotion, such as people crying when they are either extremely sad or deliriously happy. Conventional theories of emotion struggle to explain why such different emotions should produce exactly the same behaviour. According to Schachter's approach, the bodily sensations associated with every emotion are the same, and so emotions of equal intensity will provoke the same bodily response.

Curiously, several studies have also suggested that when the temperature rises there is an increase in serious and deadly assaults.[13] Once again, the *As If* principle has no problem explaining this phenomenon. When people are in environments that they find unusually hot their heart beats faster and they start sweating. Some people will look around for an explanation for this change in their physiology, misinterpret these signals as signs of them being angry, and behave accordingly. It is an interesting explanation, but is it correct? To find out, one group of researchers heated up their laboratory to the mid-nineties Fahrenheit, and gave participants an opportunity to administer electric shocks to one another. The result was that the hotter the room, the higher the shocks. The researchers then cooled people down by asking them to drink a bottle of cold water, and then gave them another opportunity to shock others. Suddenly they became far less aggressive.[14]

However, by far the most significant impact of the *As If* principle was on those wishing to make love not war.

The chemistry of love

Schachter likened the relationship between bodily sensations and emotion to a jukebox. In the same way that a coin is necessary for the jukebox to operate, so an event makes the body jump into action. And just as the user selects which tune they would like to hear, so people unconsciously look at what is happening around them, decide how their bodily sensations should be interpreted, and experience an appropriate emotion. Following in the footsteps of James, Schachter had used his version of the *As If* principle to create happiness and anger. But could it really be used to produce passion?

To find out, Gregory White from the University of Maryland and his colleagues carried out two groundbreaking studies into heart rate and love.[15] In both studies White made men's hearts beat faster, showed them a videotape of an attractive woman talking about her hobbies, and then asked the men to rate how sexy she was and how much they would like to kiss her.

In his first experiment White had one group of men run on the spot for two minutes (high heart rate) whilst another group carried out the same exercise for just a few seconds (low heart rate). In the second study the groups of men listened to a tape of comedian Steve Martin's 'A Wild and Crazy Guy' routine or to a grisly account of a mob killing a foreign missionary (high heart rate), or a dull description of the frog's circulatory system (low heart rate).

As predicted, the men who had their heart rate increased by the two-minute run, Steve Martin, or the tale of the murdered missionary, found the woman in the video far more attractive than those who had only exercised for a few seconds or heard about frog physiology.

There have been other confirmations too.[16] In perhaps the best known of these, psychologists Donald Dutton and Arthur Aron famously arranged for a female 'market researcher' (actually a stooge) to approach men on one of two very different bridges across the Capilano River in British Columbia.[17] One bridge was swaying precariously in the wind whilst the other was far more solid. The precarious footbridge caused the men's heart rate to increase and they then misattributed this as a sign of passion, and found the woman particularly attractive. In another study, psychologists Cindy Meston and Penny Frohlich from the University of Texas visited theme parks and interviewed people a few moments before, or after, they had been on a scary roller coaster ride.[18] The researchers presented people with a photograph of a woman and asked them to rate how attractive they found her. Those rating the photographs after the ride misattributed their sweaty palms as a sign of love and found the woman especially attractive.

As I noted in my previous book, *59 Seconds*, this work has important implications for anyone who wants to find the love of their life – if you are going on a date, keep away from country walks and meditation classes, and instead head to theme parks, high bridges, comedy shows and cinemas showing scary films about mutilated missionaries.

This aspect of the *As If* principle also helps to explain several other curious aspects of love.

O Romeo, Romeo, wherefore art thou Romeo?

Unrequited love often increases a person's sense of longing for an unobtainable partner. Such effects can be dramatic, with one spurned lover eventually kidnapping his former sweetheart and later tearfully explaining, 'The fact that she rejected me only made me want to love her more.'

Most psychological theories would struggle to explain these events because humans tend to go out of their way to avoid people that make them feel bad. However, the *As If* principle presents a possible explanation for the phenomenon.

When someone is prevented from doing something that they want to do, that person tends to become frustrated and angry. If that person happens to be in love they may misinterpret the physiological signs of their frustration as evidence of passion. The more they are spurned, the more they are attracted to the unobtainable apple of their eye.

The theory also explains the rather strange effect that barriers to love can have on the human heart. The Greek writer Vassilis Vassilikos once created a story about two mythical creatures. One was a fish that was a bird from the waist up, whilst the second was a bird who was a fish from the waist up. The two creatures were passionately in love with one another, and one day the Fish-Bird expressed its annoyance that the two of them could never live together (sex wouldn't have been easy either). Looking on the bright side of a tricky situation, the Bird-Fish replied: 'No, what luck for both of us. This way we'll always be in love because we will always be separated.'

Vassilikos is not the first writer to suggest that separation fans the flames of love. In the Roman myth of Pyrasmus and Thisbe a couple fall in love but their parents disapprove of the relationship and so try to prevent the lovers from seeing one another. Confined to separate rooms in adjoining houses, they whisper to one another through a crack in the wall, with writer Edith Hamilton noting in her version of the story, 'Love, however, cannot be forbidden. The more the flame is covered up, the hotter it gets.' Similarly, in Shakespeare's famous tragedy *Romeo and Juliet*, the more the lovers' feuding families try to push Romeo and Juliet apart, the deeper their passion for one another.

To discover if this rather curious phenomenon exists in real life, psychologist Richard Driscoll from the University of Colorado tracked the lives of more than a hundred couples during the course of a year, measuring both their level of mutual love and any attempts by their parents to prevent the relationship.[19] The more the parents attempted to prevent a relationship, the greater the couple's love for one another developed. In honour of the great Bard, Driscoll labelled the phenomenon 'The Romeo and Juliet' effect.

Most conventional theories of love would adopt an 'out of sight, out of mind' approach to the issue, and predict that separating two lovers would cause them to slowly lose interest in each other. In contrast, the *As If* principle has no problem explaining the phenomenon. The more lovers are kept apart, the more angry they feel, and so the more likely they are to misinterpret these feelings of frustration as signs of passion.

The *As If* principle may also explain the infamous rebound effect. When a relationship ends people often feel especially anxious. If they meet a new potential partner soon after a previous relationship has finished, they may misinterpret their anxiety as a sign of passion. Evidence for this effect comes from a study in which researchers arranged for a group of men to take a personality test and receive either positive feedback (to make them feel good) or negative feedback (to make them feel anxious). The men were then asked to wait in a cafeteria and, whilst there, were approached by an attractive woman. The men who had just received the negative feedback found the woman especially attractive,[20] as Schachter had predicted.

One further effect, the Stockholm syndrome, also adheres to Schachter's version of the *As If* principle. When people are unfortunate enough to be taken hostage they often develop a strange sense of affection towards their captors. The effect is surprisingly common, with the FBI's Hostage Barricade Database System suggesting that just under a third of hostages show some evidence of the syndrome. Interestingly, the effect usually only emerges when the captors have shown some degree of kindness to the hostages, and so may well be the result of hostages misattributing the anxiety caused by being denied their freedom as a sign of liking. The same idea may also help to explain why some individuals are attracted to partners who treat them badly.

For years psychologists believed that people's emotions affected their physiology; that feeling angry made their heart beat faster, and that feeling anxious made them sweat. In the same way that research into James's theory proved that people's behaviour causes them to experience emotion, so Schachter showed that the way in which people interpret their bodily sensations determines which emotion they feel. Depending on the context, the same thumping heart can be seen as a sign of anger, happiness or love. Schachter's theory was used to create love by showing people funny films, having them walk across precarious bridges and ride on scary roller coasters. The theory also explains many curious aspects of love, including why rejection leads to increased attraction, why trying to keep lovers apart only fuels the flames of passion, and why some people find it difficult to walk away from partners who are treating them badly.

Encouraged by this work, researchers began to explore other ways in which the *As If* principle influences Cupid's arrow.

3. LOVE IN THE LABORATORY

Around the turn of the last century the maverick Victorian scientist Sir Francis Galton devoted much of his life to the study of strange psychological phenomena.[21] Adhering to his mantra 'Whenever you can, count', he determined whether his colleagues' lectures were boring by measuring the level of fidgeting in their audiences, tested the power of prayer by calculating the average lifespan of priests, and spent months trying to brew the perfect cup of tea.

In an essay entitled 'Measurement of Character' Galton suggested that it might be possible to calculate the degree to which two people are in love by recording the 'inclination' that they have for one another.[22] He had noted that when two lovers sit at a dinner table they visibly slope towards one another, and in so doing place greater weight on the front legs of their chairs. The great scientist suggested that it might be possible to secretly incorporate 'a pressure gauge with an index and dial' into the legs of everyday furniture, and thus objectively measure the extent of love. Galton ends his discussion of the matter by noting that 'I made some rude experiments, but being busy with other matters, have not carried them on as I had hoped.' Unfortunately, Victorian scientists were reluctant to modify their furniture along the lines suggested by Galton, and the idea of measuring how lovers behaved faded away.

In fact, the idea of trying to record the behaviour of those in love didn't re-emerge until the 1970s. Rather than adopt Galton's idea of concealed gauges and dials, the work took a more observational approach. For several years a small group of dedicated researchers boldly went where few psychologists had gone before, and visited bars and parties. Once there, the researchers secretly observed the behaviour of couples in love. The results confirmed what most people would have suspected: those struck by the love bug move physically close to one another, spend a long time looking into each other's eyes, play footsie under the table, mimic one another's body language, touch each other's hands and arms, and share secrets.[23]

Inspired by the way in which the *As If* principle had been used to manufacture happiness, researchers wondered whether people would fall for one another if they behaved as if they were in love.

One of the first studies was conducted by Kenneth Gergen from Swarthmore College in the United States.[24] Couples often spend quality time together in the dark, and so Gergen wondered what would happen if he encouraged complete strangers to do the same. He first covered the floor and walls of a ten-foot square room with padding, and asked groups of four men and four women to spend an hour in the room. After that, Gergen turned out the lights in the room and asked other similar groups of participants to spend sixty minutes in total darkness.

Gergen used normal and infrared cameras to record what happened in the room and also interviewed each participant after the experiment had finished. Describing his findings in an article entitled 'Deviance in the dark', he noted that when the lights were on none of the participants purposefully touched or hugged one another, and that 30 per cent of them felt sexually aroused. However, when the group was plunged into darkness the situation was very different. Now, almost 90 per cent of them touched one another on purpose, 50 per cent hugged, and 80 per cent were sexually aroused. In addition, the people who were in the dark room were far more likely to start talking about important events in their lives, and find each other attractive. Gergen's footage revealed that a few of the participants even started stroking each other's faces and kissing. Simply by finding themselves in the sort of situation enjoyed by lovers, people quickly started to behave as if they had been struck by Cupid's arrow, and so found one another more attractive.

When it came to making love in the laboratory, this was just the tip of the iceberg.

The power of footsie

Harvard psychologist Daniel Wegner wondered whether, in the same way that smiling makes people feel happy, having two strangers secretly play footsie might make them feel attracted towards one another.[25] Mindful of the way in which those investigating the 'smiling makes you happy' hypothesis had used various cover stories to prevent participants telling the experimenter what they wanted to hear, Wegner pretended he was conducting a study in which the psychology of poker was examined.

Volunteers were invited to Wegner's laboratory in groups of four. The experimenters scheduling the volunteers ensured that none of the group knew one another, and that each foursome consisted of two men and two women. The researchers then split the volunteers into two teams, with each consisting of one man and one woman. The teams were told that they were going to play poker against each other, and the experimenters took the teams to two separate rooms to explain the rules. In reality, one of the teams was taught how to cheat by secretly sending codes to each other during the game. And how were these codes relayed? The cheating couple were told to keep their feet constantly in contact throughout and tap out information to each other.

Without realizing it, they were made to play footsie. As soon as the game had finished all of the volunteers were asked to rate the attractiveness of the other players. The couple who had been behaving as if they were in love found each other more attractive.

Wegner was not the only one to try and conjure up love in the laboratory. In 2004, psychologists Arthur Aron and Barbara Fraley from the State University of New York at Stony Brook carried out a similarly strange, but equally insightful, study into the topic using several blindfolds and a packet of drinking straws.[26]

Young lovers often have fun together and so the researchers wondered whether encouraging people to behave as if they were having a good time in each other's company might pull them closer together. To find out, they invited participants to their laboratory, randomly paired them up, and then allocated them to one of two groups.

In one of the groups the couples had a great time. The researchers blindfolded one member of the couple and had the other hold a drinking straw between their teeth, after which the researchers arranged for the blindfolded person to try and learn dance steps by listening to instructions read by their straw-holding colleague. After that, the blindfold and drinking straw were removed, and one member of the couple was given a pad and pen. The other was then secretly given the name of a simple object, such as a tree or a house, and without naming it had to describe it whilst their partner attempted to draw the object. The couples in the other group weren't given the straws and blindfolds, and were asked to learn the same dance and draw the object under more straight-faced circumstances.

After the fun and games had stopped, all of the participants were asked to draw two overlapping circles to indicate the degree of closeness that they felt with their partner. The pairs who had been behaving as if they were a happy couple suddenly felt significantly closer to one another.

Over the years researchers have conducted many similar studies. In some experiments psychologists have pretended to test for extrasensory perception and had people stare into each other's eyes, whilst in others they have encouraged complete strangers to share their innermost secrets. Time and again the results have shown that it is possible to conjure up Cupid.[27]

Making love

Encouraged by these findings, American psychologist Robert Epstein decided to take things one stage further. Was it possible, he wondered, to use these techniques to produce passion outside of the laboratory?

Epstein has had a colourful career.[28] In his late teens he felt a calling to become a rabbi and so sold his possessions and headed for Israel. Six months later he decided that he had misunderstood the nature of his calling, and returned to America, determined to make a 'significant and lasting contribution to mankind'. He developed an interest in psychology and eventually enrolled as an undergraduate at Harvard. Publishing a remarkable twenty-one scientific papers in just four years, the head of Harvard's psychology department excused Epstein from having to write a dissertation, and instead advised him to 'staple some of your publications together and get out while you still can'. A few years later Epstein became the editor of a popular magazine called *Psychology Today* (back issues are affectionately referred to by psychologists as 'Psychology Yesterday'). In 2003 he left the magazine and has since been researching a range of topics, including creativity, stress, adolescence . . . and love.

Epstein is convinced that when it comes to love, the Western world is being sold a dangerous lie by fairy tales, romance writers and Hollywood blockbusters.[29] From a very young age children read stories in which damsels in distress are swept off their feet by knights in shining armour, and love is portrayed as a mystical emotion created by magical kisses, mysterious potions, or the will of gods. Later in life adults read books and watch films about people searching endlessly for the 'One' and, if successful, living happily ever after. According to Epstein, these inaccurate conceptions of love seep into our minds and wreak havoc in our lives.

He believes that love is not a magical process and that people are not destined to be with one specific person. Instead, Epstein is convinced that love develops according to established psychological principles, and that almost any two people could fall for one another by behaving as if they are in love.

The idea may sound outlandish, but there is some evidence that it might be true.

Many celebrity couples have fallen for one another after

acting out an onscreen romance. Richard Burton famously fell in love with Elizabeth Taylor when they were making the film *Cleopatra*. Brad Pitt and Angelina Jolie fell in love with one another whilst playing husband and wife in *Mr. & Mrs. Smith*. And in *Bugsy*, Warren Beatty plays the role of the gangster Benjamin 'Bugsy' Siegel, who instantly falls for a Hollywood starlet played by Annette Bening. Beatty and Bening married soon after filming. In each instance, the celebrities acted as if they were in love, and promptly fell for one another for real.

In June 2002 Epstein, then in his late forties and single, announced that he intended to carry out a 'bold, very personal' study to discover whether his theory about love was correct.[30] Writing in *Psychology Today*, he described how he would try to find a woman who was willing to join him in an experiment to discover if it were possible for two strangers to learn to love one another. Rather than go through the horrors of dating, Epstein and the selected woman would spend between six and twelve months following a simple set of rules designed to bring them together (such as them agreeing not to date others and to participate in exercises designed to promote love), and would then co-author a book about their experiences (working title: 'The Love You Make: How We Learned to Love Each Other, and How You Can Too'). Explaining that the idea was not just a publicity stunt, but rather a serious study into the nature of love, Epstein described how several large publishing houses had already shown an interest in the book.

The idea was quickly picked up by the media and more than 1,000 women volunteered for the experiment. Epstein met fifteen of the applicants, but rejected them all, later explaining that many of them appeared more interested in obtaining publicity than genuinely learning to love him.[31]

Then, on Christmas Day 2002, Epstein was on a flight and found himself seated next to a Venezuelan ex-ballerina named Gabriela Castillo. The two of them started to chat and Epstein eventually explained his experiment and asked Castillo whether she would like to be the One. At first she was reluctant to get involved, but eventually succumbed, and on Valentine's Day 2002 Castillo and Epstein signed the 'Love Contract'. Unfortunately, the couple struggled with the long-distance nature of their relationship (Castillo was based in Venezuela, Epstein in America) and, despite several visits to relationship counsellors, they eventually decided to abandon the experiment after a few months. In 2008 Epstein married a woman he met after giving a lecture on the Isle of Man.[32]

Unperturbed by the failure of his personal love project, Epstein has since created a series of exercises designed to promote love outside the laboratory, and road-tested them on students at the University of California, San Diego. These exercises encouraged pairs of strangers to carry out a variety of love-inducing tasks, including gently embracing one another, synchronizing their breathing, gazing longingly into each other's eyes, falling into each other's arms, and getting physically close to one another without touching (Epstein reports that this last exercise apparently often ends with kissing).

Epstein asked his romantic guinea pigs to rate the degree to which they felt emotionally close to one another before and after the exercises, with the results showing that afterwards the couples did find each other attractive and did move emotionally closer to one another.[33]

The results sounded encouraging. Could this approach to love help those genuinely searching for Cupid's arrow? It was time to find out.

Rip it up

Moving on

Struggling to get over a relationship? The *As If* principle can help.

Researcher Xiuping Li from the National University of Singapore Business School asked eighty people to write down a recent decision they regretted. Li then asked some of the participants to hand their descriptions to a researcher and others to seal them in an envelope. The participants who sealed their experience in an envelope felt significantly better about their past decision compared with those who handed it over. Sealing the description in an envelope meant that the participants were acting as if they had reached psychological closure and were moving on.

Next time you want some help getting over the end of a relationship, write a brief description of what happened on the next page, rip out the page, put it in an envelope, and kiss the past goodbye.

And if you really want to have fun, reach for the matches and convert your envelope into a pile of ashes.

Write about your past relationship opposite, rip out the page, put it in an envelope and kiss it goodbye.

Speed dating in the fast lane

Speed dating can often be a dull and repetitive process, with people talking about the same topics time and again throughout the evening. I wondered whether it might be possible to use the *As If* principle to create a new form of speed dating that was more interesting and effective.

First, hired a gorgeous Georgian ballroom in the centre of Edinburgh, and advertised for single people who wanted to take part in a study exploring the science of seduction. I then invited twenty single men and twenty single women to my love laboratory.

Before the start of the evening we placed candles on each of the tables, turned the lights down low and piped in romantic music. The scene was set. As each of our participants arrived they were seated at a long table, men on one side, and women on the other. Everyone was handed a 'book of love' containing the instructions for the evening (see pages 97–9).

Once everyone was sitting comfortably, we began. In the first exercise everyone was asked to chat with the person opposite them, and find out the person's name and background. Then we handed them all a blank cardboard badge and some marker pens, and asked everyone to make a badge for their partner. The badge had to incorporate their partner's name and something interesting about them. Finally, we asked everyone to give the badge that they had just made to their partner. Loving couples often make and give little gifts to one another, and this exercise was designed to get our participants to behave as if they found each other attractive.

At the end of this first exercise everyone was asked to tick one of two boxes to indicate whether or not they would like to see their partner after the speed-dating evening. All of the women then swapped seats, moved on to their next partner, and carried out the second exercise. This process carried on throughout the entire evening, with each exercise involving a different behaviour and a different partner. Some of the time the participants were asked to gaze into each other's eyes or hold hands, at others they swapped secrets or worked together to achieve a single goal.

Rip it up

The book of love

Here are some of the most successful love games used during the experimental speed-dating study. With a little ingenuity, they can be used to promote attraction in everyday life.

Reading minds (eye contact)

Secretly draw a simple picture in the space below.

Next, spend forty-five seconds staring into your partner's eyes trying to 'transmit' the drawing to them telepathically, and 'receiving' their picture in return. Draw the picture that you think your partner was trying to send you in the space below.

Finally, compare the two pictures. Spend a few minutes discussing whether the pictures match, why you drew your picture and why your partner drew theirs.

Secrets (sharing secrets)

Both you and your partner discuss the following five questions:

1. Name something that you have always wanted to do, and explain why you haven't done it yet.

2. Imagine that your house or flat caught fire. You can only save one object. What would it be?

3. What advice would you give your ten-year-old self?

4. What do you like best about your life?

5. When was the last time that you cried with laughter?

Knowing me, knowing you (exploration)

Take turns in answering the following five questions:

1. If you had a superpower, what would it be?
2. Which celebrity would you most like to go to dinner with?
3. If you travel back in time, what era would you visit?
4. If you could have any job in the world, what would it be?
5. If you won the lottery tomorrow, how would you spend the money?

Everyone had fun staring into each other's eyes and discussing their innermost secrets, but did the exercises help promote that loving feeling? I have run several other conventional speed-dating sessions over the years and around 20 per cent of the encounters result in both participants ticking the 'yes, I would like to see this person again' box. When the *As If* principle was at work, the success rate was a remarkable 45 per cent. Just spending a few moments behaving as if they found one another attractive was enough to help them get in touch with their inner Cupid.

At the start of the evening Lianne and Nick arrived as singletons. When they were paired up, they were asked to take part in the palmistry test (see opposite). This game is designed to get couples talking about their lives and touching one another in an acceptable way, and to have fun together. During the game Lianne and Nick made lots of eye contact and enjoyed the excuse to hold one another's hands. Their post-game chat revealed that the two of them had lots in common and made each other laugh.

Both of them indicated that they would like to see one another again, and so I arranged for an email introduction. Lianne and Nick arranged to meet up for a quick coffee the following week. Once again, everything went very well and the coffee turned into dinner and a couple of glasses of wine. After meeting again a few days later Lianne and Nick fell for one another, and are now in a loving relationship.

The *As If* principle can clearly help people get together, but can it make them live happily ever after?

Rip it up

The power of palmistry

Are you single and would you like to use the *As If* principle to improve your love life? Or perhaps you want to re-energize an existing relationship? Happy couples hold each other's hands, talk about their lives, and this fun exercise encourages two people to behave as if they find one another attractive.

Rip out the page with the palmistry diagram on page 103 and keep it in your wallet or bag. Then, if you are single and meet someone you like, ask them whether they would like a fun and completely inaccurate palm reading. If they say yes, take out the paper and ask them to hold out their hand, palm up. If you are already in a relationship then simply tell your partner that you have recently developed a strange sixth sense, and ask them to hold out their hand.

Either way, gently place your hand under their palm-up hand, with your other hand gently touch the lines on their palm, and use the diagram to tell them something about themselves. Try to make the reading as enjoyable as possible, so please avoid the temptation to look at their 'life-line', appear concerned and say 'I'm sorry'. Also, try to get the person to talk about themselves, and draw attention to ways in which the two of you seem similar. Finally, at some point it is important to stress that palmistry is total nonsense and that you are only doing this for fun.

To help kick-start each section of the reading, the diagram has ten prompts, each of which refers to the following statements:

1) This line suggests that you had a happy childhood and that you had one particular toy that you loved to play with . . .

2) (After looking at a line) You've experienced several ups and downs over the past few years, haven't you . . . have you been on lots of roller coasters?

3) You have a creative streak, as shown by this beautiful curvy line here, but you feel as if something in that area is holding you back . . .

4) Wow! A strong 'head-line'. You are an independent thinker, aren't you? Someone who doesn't just agree with statements, but rather likes to check out all of the facts . . . but also trusts their intuition.

5) Can you hold your hand a bit higher? Look at this line – it shows that you are not a fan of being told what to do and have a bit of an issue with authority.

6) Well, this line is curious and suggests that you get bored easily . . . which might account for the look on your face right now.

7) Hummm . . . this line suggests that you sometimes worry about situations that are outside of your control, and that you sometimes live under a cloud. Is that right?

8) Your 'imagination line' is very strong, suggesting you are something of a daydreamer and often drift away from dull conversations. You are doing well to stay focused here!

9) Oh, I *love* this – this line shows that you tend to be very honest and trust-worthy. Can I borrow a fiver until the end of the week?

10) Overall, the future looks very bright. I can see you settling down, and having a long happy life with the person of your dreams. Someone who is . . . (insert description of yourself here).

Palmistry: A quick guide

Creating a happy ending

When people first fall in love they tend to go out and about together, and try lots of new exciting experiences. However, as time goes on it is all too easy for couples to get stuck in a rut. Finding themselves having the same conversations and visiting the same places time and again, they can become bored with each other's company. Indeed, several research projects have discovered that boredom is one of the main sources of an unhappy marriage.[34] Psychologist Arthur Aron (he of the shaky bridge, blindfolds and straws fame) wondered whether getting long-term couples to behave as if life was fun again would make them feel more loving towards one another.

Aron recruited fifty married couples who had been together for an average of fourteen years, and persuaded them to take part in a ten-week experiment.[35] He presented everyone with a long list of activities, and asked them to rate how enjoyable and exciting they found each of the items. Next, he split the couples into two groups, and asked those in one group to spend one and a half hours each week carrying out an activity that they found enjoyable, and those couples in the other group to spend the same amount of time on an activity that they found exciting.

At the end of the study Aron asked everyone to rate how happy they were in their marriage. Those who had spent time engaging in exciting activities (such as skiing, hiking, dancing, or going to concerts) were significantly happier with their relationship than those who had been encouraged to carry out pleasant activities (such as going to see a film, eating out, or visiting friends).

His results show that the key to long-term love involves couples avoiding the lure of the familiar and instead inviting excitement into their lives. By acting as if they are out on an exhilarating date, they can turn back the hands of time and easily recreate that loving feeling.

Rip it up

The Dice Man

This exercise is designed to help existing couples bring back the magic of their first few years together. You and your partner should each complete part one of the exercise separately.

Part One: Take a look at each of the following activities and circle the ones you find exciting.

Go for a walk in the countryside

Go to see a live concert

Play sport

Plan a trip or holiday

Go on a shopping trip

Go to the beach

Create some kind of artwork

Rearrange/redecorate your home

Go to a sports event

Go to a new restaurant

Go to a lecture or talk

Go camping, hiking or boating

Invite friends around for a meal

Learn to windsurf

Go dancing

Visit a fair or zoo

Go for a trip in a speedboat

Eat snails

Fly a kite

Go on a long car journey

Bet on a horse race

Kiss on a fairground ride

Place a pin in a map and go there

Enter a pub quiz

Learn some circus skills

Go canoeing

Arm wrestle

Dive or jump off a high board

Sleep out under the stars

Fly in a seaplane

Go on a long train journey

Write a love letter

- -

Get a massage/go to a health club   Ride on a huge roller coaster

Go to the gym   Go paintballing

Plan a major purchase   Travel on a hot air balloon

Visit a museum or art exhibition   Swim with some dolphins

Go to see a film   Do a parachute jump

Now list two other activities that you find exciting:

Activity 1:
....

Activity 2:
....

Part Two: Sit down with your partner and look at your ratings and answers. Select six activities that you both find exciting and write them in the spaces below.

In the early 1970s author Luke Rhinehart published a novel entitled *The Dice Man*. The book tells the story of a psychiatrist who starts to make major decisions based on the roll of a die. It is time for you to play the role of the dice man. Find a die, roll it and read out the corresponding chosen activity. Ensure that you carry out this activity during the next two weeks, and repeat this process every fortnight.

The Dice Man

1
....

2
....

For centuries scientists have struggled to understand the mysteries of love. According to the small number of conventional theories that have been developed, it is love that makes your heart beat faster and motivates you to stare longingly into your partner's eyes. The *As If* principle shows that the exact opposite is true – behaving *as if* you are in love can ignite the flames of passion. Encourage complete strangers to hold hands and play footsie, and suddenly Cupid loads his bow ready for action. Have long-term couples behave as if they are re-living the excitement of their first date, and suddenly they find each other irresistible all over again. This simple but important principle can help people find love and live happily ever after.

It is not that love changes everything, but changing your behaviour can create the world's most desirable emotion.

3. MENTAL HEALTH

Where we meet the 'Napoleon of neuroses',
find out why watching sport is bad for your health,
and discover how best to deal with phobias,
anxiety and depression.

'Action is the antidote to despair.'

Joan Baez

1. PARALYSIS AND EMOTION

As you read this, millions of people across the world will be struggling with some form of psychological disorder. Some will be trying to live with an irrational phobia, others will be overly anxious, and many will be depressed. For more than a century scientists and psychologists have attempted to cure these problems. They have adopted many different perspectives, including giving people drugs, operating on their brains, and talking to them. Can the *As If* principle help them to move away from the dark side?

William James first outlined his radical theory in an essay entitled 'What Is An Emotion?' The essay ended with a brave and bold prediction. James reasoned that if behaviour created feelings, then people who were totally paralysed shouldn't be able to experience emotion. He also realized that it would be tricky to carry out this test, in part because of the difficulties in determining the emotional life of someone who was completely immobile ('It must be confessed that a crucial test of the truth of the hypothesis is quite as hard to obtain as its decisive refutation'). Eighty years after James wrote his now-classic essay, researchers devised a clever way of carrying out a version of his test and, in so doing, have laid the foundations for a new approach to pain management, phobias, anxiety and depression.

To appreciate their remarkable study it is important to understand what is happening inside your body. You are amazing. No, really, you are. At this very moment, millions of electrical impulses are zipping around a biological super-highway that covers you from head to toe.

One lane of this highway is carrying information from your sensory receptors to your brain. These receptors will be hard at work as you read these sentences. If you are sitting down, then the receptors in your legs and buttocks will be continuously sending 'I am being squashed by the weight of my upper body' signals to your brain. Each time you turn a page (or, if you are using one of those newfangled ebook readers, whenever you press the forward key) the receptors in your fingertips will send information about their movements up to your head. Your bladder and digestive system are also using the superhighway to tell your brain whether you need to go to the toilet or get something to eat. Similarly, the million or so fibres that continually carry information from the back of your eye to your brain will be buzzing with excitement, busily communicating the shape of each letter on the page and delighted to get a name check in such a prestigious book.

The other lane in the biological superhighway carries information in the opposite direction, transmitting signals from your brain to your body. If you are sitting down at the moment then these impulses will be continually sending small signals to your major muscles to ensure that you remain balanced on the chair. Each time you turn a page, or press the forward button, the signals control the delicate actions made by your hands and fingers. When your brain gets excited it uses the highway to send signals that speed up your heart and increase your rate of breathing. And as you read these words, other signals on the highway will be rapidly scanning each of the the lines on the page, slightly annoyed that they just missed the two 'the's in the middle of this sentence.

The superhighway starts at the base of your brain, runs down your spine, and is peppered with junctions that allow information to travel to and from various parts of your body. Junctions towards the base of your spine take information to and from your feet and legs, those towards the middle of the highway carry impulses to and from your hands and arms, and those towards the top of the highway communicate with your face and eyes. Similarly, information to and from your bladder joins the highway towards the bottom of your spine, your digestive organs join slightly further up, and your heart is controlled by signals coming from the junctions towards the top of the spine.

If this entire complex system of interconnected signals were to suddenly fail then you would experience multiple organ failure and die in an instant. However, the good news is that for most people the system works extremely well. Each moment of your life information zips around the highways and byways of your body and brain, allowing you to perceive your surroundings, move around and stay alive. Not only that, but the entire system has evolved to operate outside of conscious control, allowing you to focus on the finer things in life, such as appreciating great art, trying to understand scientific advances, and finding a plumber on a Sunday.

In the mid-1960s psychologist George Hohmann was working at the Veterans Administration Hospital in Arizona. Hohmann was a paraplegic and realized that his patients provided a unique opportunity to test James's 'immobility will prevent emotion' prediction.[1] Many of Hohmann's patients were paralysed because they had suffered an injury to their

114

spinal cord, and the level at which the injury had occurred was directly related to their degree of immobility. An injury towards the base of the spine, for example, would have severed the lower part of the superhighway and so resulted in a loss of movement and feeling in the legs. In contrast, an injury higher up the spine would have disrupted a much larger part of the highway and so resulted in a loss of feeling and movement in both the legs and arms. Hohmann reasoned that if James were correct, the higher the lesion on the spine (and therefore the less bodily movement) the greater the loss in emotional experience.

Hohmann tracked down patients who had received an injury to one of five sections of the spine, and interviewed them about their emotional experiences.

In one part of his study he asked his patients to compare how often they were afraid before and after their injury. Patients with injuries to the lower parts of their spine reported very little difference, whilst those with lesions towards the top of the spine reported becoming fearless. The patients' reports provide a remarkable insight into life without emotion, with one fearless patient noting: 'Sometimes I act angry when I see some injustice. I yell and cuss and raise hell, because if you don't do it sometimes, I've learned people will take advantage of you, but it just doesn't have the heat to it that it used to. It's a mental kind of anger.'

When Hohmann asked the patients about other emotions, such as grief, the same pattern emerged – the higher the spinal damage, the less able they were to move around and the less likely they were to experience emotion.

Hohmann's findings are a remarkable tribute to James's genius, and demonstrate the vital role that your body plays in determining how you feel. Exactly as predicted by James over eighty years before, the higher the damaged area on the spine, the more dramatic the drop in emotional experience.[2]

More recently, other researchers wanted to discover whether James's idea is also true for facial expressions. Would people who are unable to move their faces also show a drop in emotional experiences? The researchers could have spent years tracking down individuals with different levels of facial paralysis, and then assessing their emotional experiences. Instead, they adopted a lateral approach to the problem, and saved themselves a great deal of time and trouble by working with an easily available group of people who had voluntarily paralysed their own faces.

Botox (or, as it is known in scientific circles, 'botulinum toxin') is one of the most popular cosmetic treatments in the world. Originally developed to help those suffering from facial muscle spasms, Botox paralyses the nerves that cause the facial muscles to contract. In the early 1990s researchers discovered that injecting the chemical into the frown lines between the eyes caused partial paralysis of the forehead and so significantly reduced wrinkling. Although this can result in a more youthful appearance, it can also sometimes make people's faces appear a tad expressionless and robotic.

Joshua Ian Davis from Barnard College of Columbia University and his colleagues wondered whether such attempts to turn back time could form the basis of a remarkable test of James's theory.[3] Davis recruited two groups of women for the experiment. One group had just undergone treatment with Botox injections whilst the other group had opted for a different treatment that involved injecting a kind of 'filler' into the forehead. Both treatments aimed to create a more youthful appearance, but only the Botox paralysed the facial muscles. Davis asked the women to watch several video clips, including one scary clip of a man eating live worms, a hilarious clip from America's funniest videos and a serious documentary about Jackson Pollock. After seeing each of the clips the women were asked to rate how they felt. Compared with those who had had the filler treatment, the Botox women reported less of an emotional reaction. So evidence that James was right and that immobility (in this instance of facial expressions) causes a loss in emotional experience.

The message from the patients with spinal injuries and the women injecting Botox is clear – inhibiting people's behaviour and facial expressions prevents them from feeling certain emotions. On the downside such individuals are less likely to experience positive emotions, such as happiness and joy. However, on the upside they are also less likely to feel negative emotions, such as anger and anxiety. Researchers became curious and began to examine whether this latter result could be used to help avoid unwelcome feelings.

2. ELIMINATING PAIN, ANGER AND ANXIETY

In the 1970s British doctor Peter Brown visited a children's hospital in China to observe how medics there carried out tonsillectomies.[4] He was stunned by what he saw.

Patients undergoing tonsillectomies in the West often report experiencing a great deal of pain. In China the situation was quite different. Brown reported seeing a queue of smiling five-year-old children standing outside the doctor's surgery. Each child was given a quick anaesthetic throat spray by a nurse and then led into the room. Once inside, the still-smiling child climbed onto a table and opened his mouth. Within seconds the doctor had whipped out their tonsils and dropped them into a bucket of water. The child then walked to a recovery room showing few signs of discomfort.

The vast difference in discomfort by patients undergoing tonsillectomies in the West and China illustrates the subjective nature of pain. It isn't an isolated example. Often people experience exactly the same hospital operation, event, illness, or accident, but report very different levels of pain. Why should this be the case? According to the *As If* principle, a large part of the answer has to do with different ways in which they behave.

Some social psychology experiments involve telling participants that they are administering dangerous electric shocks to another person when, in reality, the 'shocks' are harmless and the other person is a stooge. However, before the creation of university ethics committees (an era that many psychologists nostalgically refer to as 'the good old days') some studies actually did involve administering genuine and painful shocks to volunteers.

One such study was conducted by John Lanzetta and his colleagues from Dartmouth College.[5] Lanzetta invited volunteers to his laboratory one at a time and connected them to two machines. First, the experimenters placed electrodes on the volunteer's legs and left hand, and plugged the wires into an electric shock generator. Second, they attached sweat sensors to the volunteer's right hand in order to be able to continuously measure their stress levels. After ensuring that the machines were ready to shock and sense, the experimenters retreated to an adjoining room.

A closed-circuit television system ensured that the experimenters could see, talk to, and hear the participant. They told the volunteer that they were about to receive a series of electric shocks of varying intensity, and that the participant was to rate the pain associated with each shock by calling out a number between one ('whatever') to a hundred ('just you wait until you come back in here'). The experimenters then administered twenty electric shocks and carefully noted down the numbers screamed out by each volunteer.

After a short break, Lanzetta explained that there was going to be a second series of shocks, but that this time the volunteers should do their best to hide how they felt. Each volunteer was asked to play tough, squash any emotional expressions, avoid screaming out, and adopt a relaxed posture. A second round of twenty shocks were then administered and each time the participants shouted out their ratings.

The results were quite remarkable. When the volunteers acted as if they were not in any discomfort they experienced much lower levels of pain. Not only that, but the data from the sweat sensors revealed that they were indeed far less stressed. The study has been repeated many times over the years and the same results have been obtained.

This rather counter-intuitive effect helps explain why the Chinese children appeared so unperturbed during the tonsillectomies. At the time of Peter Brown's visit, Chinese children were taught to view operations in a positive way, and so would often smile and behave in a relaxed manner when undergoing medical procedures.

The effect also helps explain several other curious pain-related phenomena. For example, people experience less pain during minor medical procedures if they look away from the incision or injection. In doing so, they are far less likely to adopt a pained facial expression or tense up, and so feel less discomfort. The same goes for other effective pain-reduction techniques that involve distraction, such as imagery, hypnosis and relaxation techniques. Each time, people are behaving as if they are not in any discomfort and this causes them to actually experience less pain.

Inspired by this effect, researchers then examined whether behaving as if you are a strong and powerful person would result in even lower levels of pain. Vanessa Bohns from the University of Toronto and colleagues told a group of volunteers that they were taking part in a study about the health benefits of exercise at work.[6] Some of the volunteers were asked to adopt a posture associated with dominance and power by puffing out their chests and moving their arms away from their body. In contrast, others were encouraged to curl up in a powerless-looking ball. Next, the experimenters placed a tourniquet around each volunteer's arm and slowly inflated it. The band gradually reduced blood flow and so became increasingly painful, and volunteers were asked to say when they could no longer tolerate the discomfort. Remarkably, those in the powerful posture were able to tolerate much tighter tourniquets than those curled up in a ball. Behaving as if they were powerful and strong helped push away an unwanted emotion, and showed that the age-old expression 'keep your chin up' may be literally true.

Results from the early work into the *As If* principle and pain motivated researchers to examine whether the same idea could be used to help minimize other unwanted emotions. Could it, for example, help pour cold water on those seeing red?

You wouldn't like me when I am angry

Anger is bad for you. It often makes you act foolishly, take irrational risks, blurt out comments that you later regret, and lash out (the vast majority of murders committed in the United States are due, at least in part, to the effects of anger[7]). It is also bad for those around you. Psychologist Martin Seligman tracked the lives of 400 children for five years, focusing on families in which the parents routinely fought with one another.[8] Seligman's findings show that the children from warring families were more likely to be diagnosed with depression and struggle later in life.

So what is the best way of keeping your inner Hulk under

control? To find out, we have to travel back to the turn of the last century and spend some quality time with one of the world's most famous psychologists.

Jean-Martin Charcot has been described as 'the Napoleon of the neuroses'. A charismatic lecturer with a flair for the dramatic, this nineteenth-century French clinician paved the way for modern-day neurology, has over fifteen diseases named in his honour, and carried out groundbreaking research into the causes of both multiple sclerosis and Parkinson's disease. Despite such impressive achievements, Charcot is actually best known for his remarkable journeys into the unconscious mind.

Charcot was fascinated by the secret life of the brain. To carry out his investigations, he would frequently team up with patients from Parisian asylums and embark on bizarre explorations into the unconscious. Much of the work was carried out live as Charcot lectured to fellow medics. In 1887 the French artist André Brouillet attended several of Charcot's lectures and painted the Napoleon of neuroses in action.[9] The image shows Charcot standing on the right-hand side of the painting wearing a smart black suit. On the left of the scene a group of around thirty men are carefully watching him and taking notes. An unconscious woman is draped across Charcot's outstretched left arm.

The woman in Brouillet's painting is one of Charcot's star performers, Blanche Wittmann. Described by historians at the time as having 'a large and strong body' with 'very large bosoms', Wittmann had been admitted to an asylum after having several attacks of hysteria, frequently urinating on herself, and admitting to sexual intercourse with her employer. During his lectures, Charcot would place Wittmann in a hypnotic trance and then ask her to exhibit a range of strange phenomena including falling into a catatonic state, maintaining an odd arched position by balancing on top of her head and the points of her feet, performing mirror writing, and making selected words appear scratched on her skin. Charcot argued that these phenomena were manifestations of Wittmann's unconscious mind and so could be used to explore the innermost workings of the brain. At the end of each session, Charcot would compress Wittmann's 'ovarian region' to awaken her from the trance, whereupon she would return to the land of the living with her pupils 'greatly dilated'.

Charcot's dramatic approach to the human psyche quickly became the talk of the town and academics from across Europe travelled to see his curious demonstrations. In 1885 a twenty-nine-year-old Austrian physician named Sigmund Freud attended one of Charcot's demonstrations. Before seeing Charcot in action, Freud had intended to pursue a career in medicine and had previously carried out a considerable amount of research in which he had dissected hundreds of eels in an unsuccessful search for their reproductive organs. Having seen Charcot dilate the pupils of several young female patients, Freud became convinced that the unconscious played a key role in a number of psychological disorders.

After taking vast amounts of cocaine, and with a cigar rarely out of his mouth (make of that what you will), Freud eventually came up with a dramatically new form of psychology known as psychoanalysis. According to him, people tend to push unwanted thoughts out of their conscious awareness and into the unconscious. Once there, the threatening thoughts bubble away and build up psychic energy. When they have gained sufficient psychological strength, these thoughts start to affect consciousness in a variety of unhealthy ways, creating, for example, feelings of unease, neurosis and anxiety.

Freud believed that it was psychologically healthy to get rid of these repressed thoughts before they became too powerful, and so attempted to develop therapeutic techniques that could act as a release valve for the unconscious mind. Initially following in the footsteps of Charcot, he started off by trying to hypnotize his patients. When this had little effect, Freud promptly abandoned the method and instead explored several other approaches, including dream analysis (where the therapist attempts to reveal the symbolic meaning of patients' dreams) and free association (where the patient is asked to say the first word that enters his head when the therapist says carefully chosen stimulus words, such as 'chair', 'table' and 'orgasm'). Applying these techniques to his own unconscious, Freud became convinced that he had developed sexual feelings towards his mother when he was around two years old.

Freud's ideas quickly caught on, and by the turn of the last century psychoanalysis was starting to spread across the world. In 1909 he was invited to Clark University in Massachusetts to give a series of prestigious lectures. It was the first and only time that Freud spoke in America, and he used the opportunity to deliver an overview of his beloved psychoanalysis.

At the time of Freud's visit William James was sixty-seven years old and suffering from a painful heart condition. Despite his poor health, he travelled to Clark University to hear Freud talk.[10] James was less than impressed, later describing Freud's idea of dream symbolism as 'a dangerous method', and believing that the great psychoanalyst himself was both deluded and 'obsessed by fixed ideas'.

James and Freud differed on many topics, including the causes and treatment of excessive anger. According to Freud, people become angry because they are repressing violent thoughts, and it would therefore be cathartic for them to release these feelings in a safe way by, for example, punching a pillow, shouting and screaming, or stamping their feet. In contrast, James's theory predicted that people become angry because they are behaving in an angry way, and that Freud's cathartic therapy will simply make them angrier. For years psychologists have carried out studies to discover which of these two great thinkers was right.

One of the first into the fray was sociologist Murray Straus from the University of New Hampshire.[11] In the early 1970s Straus became concerned with what he saw as the overly Freudian advice being given to couples struggling to maintain their relationship. Much of this advice came from the Therapeutic Aggression movement, who thought that couples shouldn't hold back when it came to telling one another what they thought. Manuals from the time encourage couples to 'Get rid of your pent-up hostilities', 'Let it be totally vicious', and encourage them to bite a plastic baby's bottle whilst imagining that it is their partner.

To find out if such radical behaviour helped or hindered a relationship, Straus carried out a simple study. He reasoned that if the cathartic theory were valid, couples who are verbally aggressive would be less likely to carry out acts of actual physical aggression towards one another. Straus also realized that couples might not be the best ones to report accurately on their aggressive behaviour, and so asked his students to secretly monitor their parents' level of verbal and physical aggression. More than 300 students carefully completed checklists about how their parents responded when faced with a problem. Did they tend to discuss the issue in a constructive way? Did they become verbally aggressive, perhaps yelling and storming out of the room? Did they become physically aggressive, perhaps throwing objects at one another or hitting their partner?

When Straus analysed the results, an obvious pattern emerged. The more the couples engaged in verbal aggression, the *more* likely they were to be physically aggressive. Just as James predicted, shouting and yelling wasn't cathartic, but rather encouraged them to behave in an angry way. Freud 0, James 1.

Next were studies carried out in the workplace. Ebbe Ebbesen from the University of California, San Diego and his colleagues discovered that a local engineering firm was going to lay off many of its employees.[12] The employees had every right to be angry because they had been promised a three-year contract but were being put out of work after just one year. Ebbesen interviewed some of the employees in one of two ways. One group were encouraged to talk about how angry they felt towards the firm ('So, how do you feel about the way in which you have been treated?'), whilst the other group were asked much more neutral questions ('So, can you describe the firm's technical library?'). After the interviews all of the employees rated their level of hostility and anger towards the company. Did those who had been encouraged to rant and rave show lower levels of hostility? No. Once again, the exact opposite pattern of results emerged. The employees who had vented their feelings of anger were much more hostile than those who had been asked about the company's technical library. Freud 0, James 2.

Finally, there is the work investigating the link between hostility and watching sport. When people attend football games they often cheer on their team and shout abuse at the opposition. Freudians had argued that such aggressive behaviour was cathartic, and so individuals would feel significantly less hostile after the game. In contrast, proponents of James's ideas thought that all of the shouting and jeering would make them feel far angrier. Jeffrey Goldstein from Temple University decided to discover which camp was correct.[13]

Goldstein arranged for a small army of researchers to attend a major American football game. Before the start of the match the researchers hung around the stadium turnstiles and interviewed a randomly selected group of spectators. The interviews were short, and included asking each spectator which team they supported and how aggressive they felt. Once the game had ended the researchers took to the turnstiles again and interviewed randomly selected spectators as they left the match.

The results revealed that regardless of whether the spectator's team won or lost, they were significantly more aggressive after the match. Worried that this increase in aggression might be due to spectators being in a crowd, or simply watching a competitive situation, Goldstein reassembled his crack research team and had them carry out the same interviews at a local gymnastics competition. Even though the spectators attending the event were crowded together in a competitive context, they didn't shout and jeer, and weren't significantly more aggressive after the event. Goldstein's data suggests that the football game encouraged the spectators to behave in an aggressive way, and that this behaviour made them feel more hostile. Freud 0, James 3.

Such induced hostility can have a very real impact on society. Glasgow in Scotland has two professional football clubs. Celtic is based in the east of Glasgow and has traditionally had support from the Catholic community, whilst Rangers has its base in the south-west of the city and has historically attracted a Protestant following. The clubs have a long-standing and fierce rivalry, with supporters from both sides often singing hostile and intimidating chants during matches. In 2011, researchers working for the Scottish Police compared the levels of reported crime after Rangers–Celtic matches with times when the teams were not playing.[14] The figures are remarkable. When Rangers played Celtic on Saturday lunch-times, violent crime in Glasgow almost trebled and incidents of domestic abuse more than doubled.

The power of calm

Psychologist Brad Bushman from Iowa State University has carried out several experiments showing how feelings of anger can quickly be quashed by acting like a calm person. In one study, for example, Bushman had college students spend twenty minutes playing either a relaxing or violent computer game.[15] Students in one of the relaxing games swam around a quiet underwater habitat looking for sunken treasure, whilst in the violent games they tried to dispatch as many zombies as gorily as possible. The students were then asked to play another game against an unseen player and, if they won, were given the opportunity to blast their opponent with a loud noise. In reality, there was no other unseen player and the students always won this second game. Those who had previously spent some time quietly swimming around the underwater habitat were significantly less aggressive, choosing a quieter and shorter noise blast for their imaginary opponent.

Bushman has also demonstrated the calming power of prayer.[16] He angered a group of Christian college students by again giving them extremely negative feedback about their work ('Christ, this is one of the worst essays I have read'), and then asked them to read a newspaper article about a woman suffering from a rare form of cancer. Next, some of the students were asked to spend five minutes putting their hands together and praying for the woman, whilst others were asked to think about her. Afterwards, the students who had prayed were significantly less angry than those who thought about the woman. Acting in a relaxed and calm way produced relaxed and calming thoughts.

Also, in my previous book, *59 Seconds*, I described how Bushman used the same essay-based anger-inducing procedure to enrage another group of students.[17] Some of those students were then given a pair of boxing gloves, shown a photograph of the person who had allegedly marked their essay, and told to think about that person whilst they hit a seventy-pound punch bag. Another group were asked to sit in a quiet room for two minutes. The findings came down firmly against Freud – punching the bag made people feel more angry whilst quietly sitting down made them feel much more calm.

Many anger management courses teach people to work hostility out of their system by behaving like an aggressive person. This is unhelpful and, if anything, will tend to make the problem worse. Other approaches involve trying to figure out the deep-seated psychological root of the anger in the hope that changing the way you think will change how you feel. In reality, there is a much quicker and more effective way of dealing with the problem. To calm down, act like a calm person (see opposite). In the same way that smiling will make you feel happy, and gazing into the eyes of another person will make you feel as if you are in love, so acting in a calm fashion will quickly make you feel calm.

Rip it up

Calming down*

Those needing to deal with anger in a quick and effective way often benefit from a deep-breathing exercise. To try the technique, put your tongue on the roof of your mouth just behind your front teeth. Now breathe in slowly through your nose for the count of five and hold your breath for the count of seven. Then exhale slowly through pursed lips for the count of eight. Repeat this exercise four times.

For a more long-lasting solution, learn how to carry out 'Progressive Muscle Relaxation'. This approach involves deliberately tensing various muscle groups and then releasing the tension.

To try this technique, remove your shoes, loosen any tight clothing and sit in a comfortable chair in a quiet room. Focus your attention on your right foot. Gently inhale and clench the muscles in your foot as hard as possible for about five seconds. Next, exhale and release all of the tension, allowing the muscles to become loose and limp. Work your way around your body performing the procedure in the following order:

---

* The exercises described here are designed to provide a general insight into the sort of techniques used by psychologists. If you believe that you have an anger management issue, consult a professional.

1) Right foot

2) Right lower leg

3) Entire right leg

4) Left foot

5) Left lower leg

6) Entire left leg

7) Right hand

8) Right forearm

9) Entire right arm

10) Left hand

11) Left forearm

12) Entire left arm

13) Abdomen

14) Chest

15) Neck and shoulders

16) Face

Little Hans and Albert B.

John B. Watson changed the entire course of psychology and shaped our current understanding of the human psyche.[18] Working at Johns Hopkins University just after the turn of the twentieth century, Watson was, by any measure, a strange and complex man. To outsiders he appeared flamboyant, outgoing and confident. In reality he was deeply insecure, petrified of the dark, and emotionally frigid. A tad socially awkward, Watson would shake hands with his children rather than kiss them goodnight, and would leave the room whenever anyone tried to discuss his emotions.

Watson firmly rejected both Wilhelm Wundt's introspection and Sigmund Freud's psychoanalysis. Arguing that as it was impossible to know for certain what was really going on in people's minds, he believed that psychologists should instead focus their attention on observing and measuring behaviour (thus giving rise to the joke wherein two behaviourists make love, and then one turns to the other and asks 'That was good for you, how was it for me?').

Watson loved to run rats through mazes. In his early years he constructed a miniature version of the medieval maze at London's Hampton Court Palace, placed hungry rodents in it one at a time, and carefully observed them running around trying to find a strategically placed pile of food. After testing hundreds of rats in this real-life version of 'Who moved my cheese?', Watson worked out the rodent rules of basic learning, including how the rats explored the maze, and how long they would continue to visit a location that used to contain food even after the food had been removed.

Watson became convinced that his results applied to human behaviour, and that the whole of life was like a huge maze. Even more controversially, he thought that it was possible to shape any human mind by simply applying the rodent rules of learning that he had uncovered during his maze experiments, causing him to famously remark:

> Give me a dozen healthy infants, well-formed, and
> my own specified world to bring them up in and
> I'll guarantee to take any one at random and train
> him to become any type of specialist I might select
> – doctor, lawyer, artist, merchant-chief and, yes,
> even beggar-man and thief, regardless of his talents,
> penchants, tendencies, abilities, vocations, and race of
> his ancestors.[19]

Watson's total focus on the measurement of behaviour quickly caught on, and soon researchers across the world started to run more and more rats through increasingly complex mazes, causing one commentator to remark: 'Psychology, having first lost its soul to Darwin, has now lost its mind to Watson.'

The behaviourists started to expand their empire away from the rules of learning and into other areas of psychology, with Watson taking a particular interest in the cause and treatment of phobias. Like many behaviourists, he was driven by a desire to provide an alternative to what he saw as the pseudoscientific ramblings of Sigmund Freud.

Freud encouraged an inner circle of supporters to help develop psychoanalytic theories by secretly observing the sexual life of their young children. In 1904 one of his closest associates reported that his five-year-old son, referred to as 'Little Hans', had developed an irrational fear of horses and suggested that this might make for an interesting case study. Freud agreed and began to explore what might be causing the young boy's fear. Hans's father initially attributed the phobia to his son being sexually overexcited when his mother cuddled him, coupled with Little Hans being shocked by the large penises of horses. Freud disagreed, and instead noted that the boy had described dreaming about a giraffe, and that the long neck of the giraffe was a symbol for the large adult penis. After much back and forth, Freud described his thoughts in a paper entitled 'Analysis of a Phobia in a Five-year-old Boy', and suggested that Little Hans's disorder was the result of several factors, including a repressed desire to make love to his mother and conflicting thoughts about masturbation.

Watson was appalled by Freud's speculations about Little Hans's alleged emotional inner turmoil, and became determined to come up with a far more down-to-earth explanation of phobias.

Watson's approach was heavily influenced by the work of the Russian researcher Ivan Pavlov. A few years before Watson had started running rats through mazes, Pavlov had been observing the impact of ringing bells on dogs. Pavlov had carried out a now-classic set of studies in which he had rung a bell and then presented a dog with a bowl of food. Not surprisingly, the dogs had salivated at the sight of the food. After just a handful of these 'bell-food' trials, Pavlov discovered that just ringing the bell was enough to cause the dogs to salivate, and so demonstrated that brains are extremely skilled at learning such associations (a procedure that is known in the trade as 'classical conditioning').

Pavlov's simple but important discovery has several practical applications. In one study, for example, animal researchers laced some sheep carcasses with a poison that made coyotes vomit, and put the carcasses out in a field. In the same way that pairing the bell with the presentation of food made Pavlov's dog salivate, so wolfing down the poisoned sheep made the coyotes feel ill whenever they saw a sheep. As a result, the number of coyote-sheep attacks dramatically declined.[20]

Watson wondered if the same mechanism might also account for phobias. Perhaps, he reasoned, phobic reactions were simply the result of an object or situation having being paired with a stimulus that made people behave as if they were afraid.

To find out, Watson followed in the footsteps of Freud and conducted a study on an unsuspecting infant. In 1919 he teamed up with a student named Rosalie Rayner, and together the two of them experimented with an eleven-month-old boy that they referred to as 'Albert B'. Watson speculated that if Albert could be made to behave as if he were afraid of something, he would quickly develop a Pavlovian response to that object and become phobic about it. Perhaps influenced by his laborious work with mazes, Watson decided to try to make Albert phobic about rats.

Before starting the study he needed to know that Albert didn't already have a phobia of rats, and so showed him a variety of rats and rat-like objects, including a rabbit, a monkey, and various hairy masks. The fearless Albert didn't flinch. Next, the intrepid researchers wanted to get him to associate the rat with something that made him behave as if he were afraid. Watson knew that infants jump out of their skin whenever they hear a very loud noise, and so went out and bought a large steel bar and a hammer.

Watson and Rayner then placed a white rat near to Albert and, whenever their young participant went to touch the rat, hit the steel bar with the hammer as hard as they could. Exactly as planned, the resulting bang made Albert start to cry. After several 'rat-bang' trials, Watson stopped banging the bar and showed Albert the rat. In the same way that Pavlov's dogs came to salivate when they simply heard the bell, so the mere sight of the rat caused Albert to become extremely distressed. Watson had indeed created a phobia.

Two months later Watson and Rayner visited Albert again, and discovered that he was still terrified by the sight of the rat. Not only that, his fear had generalized to other similarly furry objects, including a dog, a seal-skin coat, and Watson wearing a Santa Claus mask.

Could the same idea explain Little Hans's fear of horses? When discussing the onset of his phobia, his father described Hans having been terrified by the sight of a carthorse collapsing in a local park and being especially frightened by the sound of its hooves clattering against the cobbled road. Hans's phobia was nothing to do with repressed sexual thoughts about his mother or concerns about masturbation. Instead, it was simply a Pavlovian response to a situation that had made him afraid.

Little is known about what happened to Albert following the study, although Watson did joke that when he was older a Freudian analyst would probably manage to persuade him that his fear of fur was due to him being told off when he was trying to play with his mother's pubic hair aged three. In contrast, a great deal is known about the adult life of Freud's unsuspecting subject. 'Little Hans' was actually the pseudonym for Herbert Graf. Graf went on to enjoy a highly successful career as an opera producer, and is perhaps best remembered for his highly innovative adaptation of Wagner's *The Ring of the Nibelung*, in which Brünnhilde's horse was replaced by a giraffe with an especially long neck.*

The experiment with Albert had a huge impact on Watson's personal life. Whilst running the study, the then married Watson had an affair with his co-experimenter Rosalie Rayner. When Watson's wife found out about the relationship she sued for divorce, and when the President of John Hopkins University heard what was happening he demanded Watson's resignation. Watson left academia and went to work for a major advertising company, using his behavioural insights to help sell deodorants, baby powder and cigarettes. In one of his most successful campaigns, he introduced the

---

* I added the bit about the giraffe.

idea of a 'coffee break' to America as part of a campaign for Maxwell House.

Once psychologists understood how phobias developed, they were quickly able to understand more about the disorder and discovered that it was fairly easy to eradicate the problem.

Closer and closer

One of the most effective procedures was created by South African psychiatrist Joseph Wolpe and is known as 'systematic desensitization' (see pages 141–2). During this technique, people are first trained how to relax. Next, they are asked to establish a 'continuum of anxiety', that runs from a not very scary version of the phobia to a full-blown terrifying situation. So, for example, if a person was afraid of snakes, one end of the anxiety continuum might be opening a book and seeing a picture of a snake whilst the other end might involve meeting an estate agent. At the start of the first session the person is encouraged to relax and then experience a situation (or, in some cases, imagine it) from the lower end of the anxiety continuum. By acting as if they are not afraid, the situation quickly ceases to become associated with any sense of anxiety, and then the person moves on to the next situation on the continuum.

About 10 per cent of the population suffer from some kind of phobia, and for about 1 per cent this disorder has a dramatic and debilitating effect.[21] They could be afraid of open spaces, humiliation, the sight of blood and even the number thirteen. Often they end up talking about their fears with a psychotherapist who attempts to uncover the deep-seated nature of the problem. They are wasting their time. From snakes to spiders and flying to fear of public speaking, there is a much quicker and more effective way forward. By changing their behaviour one small step at a time they will slowly change their mind for ever.

Rip it up

Overcoming phobias*

The techniques designed to help people overcome phobias often involve the following three stages.

1) Learning how to relax – See the previous 'Calming down' box, pages 131–2.

2) Constructing an anxiety continuum – People are encouraged to write down ten events that make them feel anxious and are associated with their phobia. They then grade the anxiety associated with each event by assigning it a number between 0 (very low) and 100 (very high). For example, if you have a fear of flying, your anxiety continuum might be: Packing luggage, Making reservations, Driving to the airport, Checking in, Boarding the plane, Taxiing, Climbing to cruising altitude, Moving around the cabin, Turbulence, Landing, Crashing.

3) The Pairing Procedure – Finally, people are asked to go through their relaxation procedure and then experience the first item in the continuum for as long as they can (if it is not possible to actually experience the item, they are asked to imagine experiencing it).

* The exercises described here are designed to provide a general insight into the sort of techniques used by psychologists. If you believe that you have a serious and problematic phobia, consult a professional.

After they have stopped experiencing or imagining the situation they are asked to rate how anxious they feel using the 0–100 scale. They then repeat this procedure until their anxiety rating for that event is less than 10. When that happens, they move on to the next item in the continuum. Each session lasts around thirty minutes.

Hitting the 'panic' button

About 5 per cent of people have experienced a panic attack. The symptoms are obvious and unpleasant. Without warning, they start to experience chest pains, sweat, hyperventilate and feel faint. During the episode they might think that they are losing their mind or are about to die. The attacks usually last for about ten minutes, and then vanish over the course of an hour or so.

Many medics and psychoanalysts used to try to prevent these episodes by pumping people full of drugs or chatting to them about their childhood memories. In fact, there is a simple explanation for them and a quick and effective solution.

In the previous chapter I described the work of Stanley Schachter. Schachter showed that experiencing an emotion often involved a two-step process. First, an event or thought causes your body to jump into action. Perhaps you hear a gunshot and suddenly your palms become sweaty. Or maybe you catch the eye of an attractive stranger at a party and feel your heart miss a beat. Second, you then look around and try to work out what caused your body to act in this way. If you were in the street when you heard the gunshot then you might feel anxious, whereas if you were walking past a shooting gallery at a funfair then you might feel fine. Similarly, if you believe that the person at the party finds you attractive then you might experience a strong sense of joy, whereas if it turns out they were looking longingly at the person behind you then you might feel a tad embarrassed.

In the 1990s psychologist David Clark from the University of Oxford applied Schachter's thinking to panic disorders.[22] Clark thought that such attacks were due to people misinterpreting their bodily sensations in a catastrophic way. According to this idea, people who are prone to panic attacks have a tendency to feel their heart race and palms sweat, and assume the worst. Convinced they are about to have a heart attack or die, they then become even more stressed, which makes their heart beat even faster and their palms sweat even more. The process feeds on itself until they enter a state of extreme panic.

Clark believed that treating these attacks didn't need to involve taking drugs or discussing childhood memories. Instead it was a case of either preventing the sensations in the first place by teaching people how to relax or, even better, encouraging them to reinterpret their bodily sensations in a more productive way.

To discover if he was correct, Clark gathered together a group of patients who were prone to panic attacks and asked them to see themselves in a new way. The patients were told that they shouldn't panic when they felt their heart race or suddenly felt short of breath, but instead to see such sensations as evidence of their bodies simply feeling slightly anxious. Some patients were worried that they might pass out during their panic attack, even though this had never actually happened. Clark eased their fears by explaining that this feeling was due to the blood travelling away from the brain and to the major muscles, and that the resulting increase in blood pressure meant that they were actually less likely to faint.

Clark's procedure proved remarkably effective, with

research showing that getting people to reinterpret their bodily sensations was more effective than either relaxation therapy or drugs.[23]

The same approach has been used to treat many of those who are overly anxious about taking exams, going to a job interview, speaking in public or going into hospital. In each instance, people have benefited from learning why their bodies sometimes get overly excited, and how to reinterpret these feelings in a more positive way ('Exam nerves usually help focus attention', 'A little extra adrenalin makes for a better interview or talk', 'It is perfectly natural to be nervous before going into hospital').[24]

An understanding of the way in which the body creates emotion has led to the development of quick and effective treatments for anger management, phobias, panic attacks and some anxiety disorders. But can it also help with one of the most prevalent and problematic of psychological problems – depression?

Rip it up

The guilt trip

The following page contains a photograph of my grandfather, William Wiseman. I would like you to rip out the page and abuse the photograph. Do whatever you want to it. Add devil horns and a moustache. Write a horrible message about William right across the photograph. Tear off his head and poke out his eyes. Away you go . . .

All done? Let me tell you something about William Wiseman.

William lived in Luton and worked in the hat trade. He was a kind man who devoted much of his time to raising money for various charities, and was especially giving to the homeless and unemployed. Indeed, every Christmas William would visit local hospitals and orphanages and hand out presents to children in need. One of the children, George Cunningham, later became a well-known sculptor and produced a bust of my grandfather in tribute to his generosity. This bust currently stands on the site of my grandfather's house as a touching memorial to the positive effect that he had on the community.

Now take a look at what you did to my grandfather's photograph. Quite frankly, I hope you are ashamed of yourself. However, worry not, because the *As If* principle can help to ease your guilt.

Simone Schnall from the University of Plymouth knew that unethical behaviour often produces a look of disgust, but wondered whether forming a disgusted facial expression makes people think that an event is more unethical. To find out, Schnall and her colleagues armed themselves with several descriptions of dodgy scenarios and a can of fart spray.[25]

Schnall's experiment took place on a busy high street close to a rubbish bin. The researchers stopped passers-by, asked them to read short scenarios describing various types of questionable behaviour (including items about first cousins marrying, a man knocking over a dog in his car and then eating the dog's body, and a man being sexually aroused by his pet kitten), and then rate how moral they found each situation. Beforehand the researchers had either applied a liberal dose of fart spray to the rubbish bin or left it alone. The passers-by who were subjected to the fart spray made disgusted facial expressions and also judged the scenarios as significantly more immoral.

Encouraged by this work, other researchers had participants remember a time when they had acted in an immoral way, asked them to clean their hands with an antiseptic wipe, and then had them rate how guilty they felt and whether they would like to volunteer for charity work.[26] Washing their hands made them feel significantly less guilty.

So, to get over your little moral indiscretion with my grandfather's photograph, go and clean your hands and let the As If principle wash away your sins.[27] When you face even larger guilt trips, try taking a shower.

3. DEALING WITH DEPRESSION

According to the Bible, King Saul was not a happy man. Chosen to be King of Israel mainly because of his height ('he was higher than any of the people from his shoulders and upward'), Saul became embroiled in several wars, and was frequently very moody ('an evil spirit from the Lord troubled him'). Eventually, a young musician named David was summoned to the king's court, and his harp-playing proved surprisingly effective at alleviating Saul's bad moods. A man of many talents, David then went on to slay Goliath and defeat the Philistines. This, in turn, made Saul jealous of the harp-player's success and caused him to try and smite David with a javelin.

Liubov Ben-Noun from Ben-Gurion University of the Negev in Israel has carefully analysed the biblical description of Saul in an attempt to diagnose his psychological difficulties using modern-day psychiatric criteria.[28] After ruling out substance-induced mood disorders (the Bible makes no mention of Saul taking drugs) and schizophrenia (Saul is one of the few people in the Bible not to hear voices), Ben-Noun concludes that Saul may have been suffering from major depression. In a later paper, Martijn Huisman from the University Medical Center Groningen in the Netherlands suggests that this disorder was probably brought on by work-related stress due, in part, to Saul's army of just 3,000 men having to face Philistine forces consisting of 'thirty thousand chariots, and six thousand horsemen, and people as the sand which is on the seashore in multitude'.[29]

Modern-day epidemiology demonstrates that depression is not, unfortunately, confined to the pages of the good book. It is estimated that in most Western countries one in twenty people will be suffering from depression at any one time, with some research suggesting that women are nearly twice as likely as men to struggle with the problem.

The symptoms include feelings of hopelessness, finding it difficult to get out of bed, avoiding contact with other people, a dramatic loss or gain in appetite, an inability to concentrate, and sleep problems. When trying to explain what if feels like to be depressed, some clinicians ask people to imagine 'the anguish of grief with the sluggishness of jet lag'.[30] Although everyone feels sad from time to time, in depressed individuals these symptoms continue for long periods and so have a more damaging effect on lives. Sometimes depression appears to emerge as a response to a negative event, such as being made redundant or the death of a loved one, whilst at other times it just seems to emerge without any apparent cause. Although fierce arguments have been waged over the causes and treatment of depression, most medics, psychologists and psychotherapists originally believed that the solution to the problem involved changing what was happening inside people's heads.

During the 1940s American physician Walter Freeman believed that people became depressed because of a problem in the signals travelling between the front and centre of the brain. Based on this reasoning, he developed a strange medical procedure to cut the communication channels between these two parts of the brain. During this operation the patient would first be rendered unconscious by an electric shock. Next, Freeman would insert the end of an ice pick-like instrument called a leucotome through the patient's tear duct. After a few taps with a surgical hammer, the leucotome would move into the patient's frontal lobe, where Freeman would wiggle it about to destroy the offending parts of the brain. Freeman carried out over 3,000 of these operations during his career and, ever the showman, would sometimes set up a production line of patients, once lobotomizing twenty-five women in one day.

His operation became known as a 'frontal lobotomy' (a term derived from the Greek word *lobos*, meaning 'lobes of the brain', and *tomos*, meaning 'barbaric and ineffective hogwash'). Although some of Freeman's patients improved after their brief encounter with the leucotome, many suffered terrible side effects, including having to be re-taught basic functions such as eating and drinking. Perhaps Freeman's most high-profile failure was American President John F. Kennedy's sister, Rosemary. After experiencing dramatic mood swings and the occasional violent outburst, Rosemary was subjected to a frontal lobotomy when she was twenty-three years old. Unfortunately, she was incapacitated by the operation, and spent the remaining years of her life requiring full-time care because of severe learning difficulties and urinary incontinence.

After seeing the negative effects of destroying patients' frontal lobes, other medics started to examine less traumatic ways of changing people's brains. By far the most popular procedure to emerge has involved antidepressant drugs. Electrical impulses travel from one part of the brain to another via cells known as neurons. These neurons communicate with one another by releasing a chemical known as serotonin, and shortly after each communication the serotonin is reabsorbed back into the neuron. In the 1960s scientists discovered that high levels of serotonin in the brain were associated with good moods, and so developed drugs that blocked the neuronal re-absorption of the serotonin in the hope that this would help cure depression. Although there is considerable controversy about the effectiveness of these drugs and their potential side effects, many researchers claim that they help reduce depression and they are now one of the most popular forms of medication.

Reluctant to put pickaxes into people's brains or pump them full of drugs, psychologists have developed other ways of changing how people think.

The allure of attribution

Imagine that you take an exam and get a poor grade. How, in general, would you explain your failure? People come up with all sorts of replies to this question. Some say that perhaps they didn't revise hard enough, others may say they just had an off day or perhaps their questions didn't come up. Psychologists think that you can tell a great deal about a person from their answer, and tend to rate replies in three different ways.

Firstly, did you blame yourself? If you thought that you failed the imaginary exam because you are not especially bright or didn't revise properly then you are blaming yourself for your failure. If, on the other hand, you just thought that you had an off day or got unlucky with the questions, you are blaming something outside of yourself.

Secondly, there is the issue of permanence. Does your explanation suggest that you will do badly in future exams? Thinking that you are not very bright suggests that you will fail again in the future, whereas believing that you had an off day means that there is no reason to expect other tests to go badly.

Finally, what does your explanation say about what will happen in other areas of your life? If, for example, you think that you are not especially bright, or are especially lazy, then you might expect to do badly at work or in the local pub quiz. However, thinking that you failed the exam because you had an off day wouldn't have any implications for your career or other situations.

When bad things happen to depressed people they tend to come up with explanations in which they take the blame, causing them to expect to fail again in the future, and casting a dark cloud over every aspect of their lives. In contrast, those who are not depressed are far more likely to avoid personal shortcomings, expect the future to be bright, and prevent the failure from influencing other areas of their life.

When treating people with depression, psychotherapists often try to encourage their clients to recognize, and change, their explanations for the events that happen in their lives. This technique forms a central part of 'Cognitive Therapy' (or 'CT' for short). Other aspects involve getting clients to identify additional types of problematic thinking, including 'mind reading' (where they jump to conclusions about what other people are thinking), 'catastrophizing' (where they transform into drama queens and make mountains out of molehills) and 'fusion' (where they confuse their beliefs for facts).

Researchers have conducted several studies comparing CT with drug-based therapies, and have discovered that they are equally effective at tackling depression.[31] Because of this, governments and health systems across the world have adopted the approach, encouraging millions of people to reconsider their thinking. After years of experimenting with different cures, all looked well. In fact, this was far from the bigger picture.

Rip it up

From behaviour to memory

Let's conduct a small-scale experiment.

Stage One: Spend a few moments painting a happy expression on your face. Pull the sides of your mouth back towards your ears and hold them there. Sit or stand up straight, pull your shoulders back and push your chest forward. Now look at the three words below and, for each word, think of an event in your life that is associated with the word. Next, jot down a couple of words from each memory in order to remind you of the experience.

TREE   Words to remind you of your memory

HOUSE   Words to remind you of your memory

CAT   Words to remind you of your memory

Stage Two: Spend a few moments forcing your face into a frown. Pull the sides of your mouth down and hold them in that position. Next, if you are sitting down, slump forward. If you are standing up, let your shoulders drop down. Now look at the three words below and, for each word, think of an event from your life that is associated with the word.

BOAT   Words to remind you of your memory

CAR   Words to remind you of your memory

DOG   Words to remind you of your memory

Stage Three: Think about the six memories that you have just produced. Would you say that they were positive or negative?

This study was first conducted by researchers Simone Schnall and James Laird from Clark University.[32] They discovered that when people adopted a happy facial expression they tended to remember more positive moments from their life, and when they looked sad they were inclined to recall more negative ones.

Depressed people often tend to dwell on the aspects of their life that have not gone especially well, and this research suggests that their biased memory might be due, in part, to their behaviour. So, want to remember how great your life has been? Smile and sit up straight, and let your brain do the rest.

158

Activating the mind

The *As If* principle suggests that behaviour causes emotion, and helps to explain why some people experience anger-management issues, phobias and panic attacks. Can the theory also help to explain depression? Could it be, for example, that depressives do not just struggle to get out of bed in the morning because they feel down, but also feel down because they are spending too much time in bed? A large body of research now suggests this is indeed the case.

Much of the early work into the *As If* principle focused on facial expressions and emotion, and showed that smiling made people happy and frowning made them sad. Clinical psychologists have discovered a similar relationship between expressions and depression. In one study, for instance, Jessie Van Swearingen from the University of Pittsburgh recruited a group of patients suffering from facial neuromuscular disorder, and measured both the degree to which the patients were able to smile and their level of depression. As predicted by the *As If* principle, the less animated the patients' facial expressions, the more likely they were to be depressed.[33] Similarly, dermatologist Eric Finzi has evaluated whether Botox injections can minimize some of the facial expressions associated with sadness, and therefore help alleviate depression. In one small-scale pilot study, Finzi injected Botox into the frown lines of nine depressed women and then tracked their lives. The injections would have caused the women to frown less, but not prevented them from forming other facial expressions. As a result, the researchers predicted that the procedure would help prevent the women feeling sad and so help alleviate negative emotions. They were right – just two months after the injections none of the nine women showed signs of depression.

Other work has taken a more behavioural approach and looked at the effect of dance on depression. Driven by the notion that dancing is incompatible with feeling down, Sabine Koch from the University of Heidelberg and her colleagues examined the impact of dance on depression.[34] Koch assembled a group of people suffering from depression and had them dance to upbeat music. Worried that any effects might be due to the music or moving around, Koch had other groups of participants listen to the same soundtrack or spend time on an exercise bike. All three groups felt better after their sessions, but those who had been dancing the night away showed the most impressive improvements.

Psychologist Peter Lewinsohn wondered whether it might be possible to help change the way in which depressives thought and felt by altering their behaviour.[35]

Depressive behaviour is often about escape and avoidance. When some people encounter a negative life event, such as being made redundant or the break-up of a relationship, they withdraw from the world in order to prevent more pain in the future. This withdrawal can take many different forms, including spending large amounts of time in bed, avoiding their friends, comfort-eating, excessive drinking and drug-taking. In addition, the person may also try to avoid thinking about future events by, for instance, ruminating on the past ('If only things had been different') or watching soap operas and quiz shows on television. Unfortunately, all of this has unintended and negative consequences. Lying in bed and overeating might make them put on weight and so feel ashamed of themselves. Excessive sleeping and television watching might encourage their partner to criticize them. And not contacting their friends is likely to decrease the chances of being invited out, thus increasing the feeling of isolation.

To help reverse this downward cycle, Lewinsohn created a simple technique known as 'Behavioural Activation'. There are several versions of the treatment, but most involve two main phases.[36]

In the initial part people are encouraged to identify behaviours that are problematic and set some general goals (see overleaf). This can involve them indicating which aspects of their behaviour are symptomatic of depression and also identifying desired goals.

Rip it up

Behavioural Activation: Phase One*

In the first part of the process, psychologists use the following types of technique to identify behaviours that are problematic and set general goals.

1) Identifying problematic behaviours

Complete the following questionnaire.

Behaviour	Yes/No	
Are you avoiding seeing your friends and family?	❑	❑
Have you stopped taking part in activities that you enjoy, such as playing sport, going to the cinema, or eating out?	❑	❑
Have you stopped taking care of yourself by not eating properly or looking after your personal hygiene?	❑	❑
Have you stopped trying to do well at school, college or in the workplace?	❑	❑

---

* The exercises described here are designed to provide a general insight into the sort of techniques used by psychologists. If you believe that you have a serious and problematic phobia, consult a professional.

Behaviour	Yes/No
Do you tend to avoid thinking about the future by dwelling on your past?	❑ ❑
Have you lost interest in your relationship with your children or partner?	❑ ❑
Are you spending too much time watching television, playing computer games or lying in bed?	❑ ❑
Are you drinking heavily, comfort-eating or taking drugs?	❑ ❑

Look at the list of your selected behaviours – which of them would you like to change?

2) Identifying desired goals

Look at the following list of areas. Find one or two that you value and also one or two that you seem to be struggling with, and then answer the questions associated with the area(s).

Your relationships: Would you like to be in a relationship or improve an existing one? Perhaps increase the number of friends you have, or develop a better relationship with your parents or partner?

Work and education: Do you want to do well in college or improve your career? Perhaps run your own business, be promoted, or obtain a qualification or training?

Recreation: Do you want to get more enjoyment from your leisure time? What types of sports, interests and hobbies would you like to be more involved with?

Community: Would you like to do more for your community? Perhaps carry out some charity or voluntary work, or engage in some form of activism?

Physical health: Would you like to be healthier? Perhaps lose some weight, exercise more, or eat a more nutritious diet?

In the second phase of the process, people are encouraged to both engage in the type of activities that they have been avoiding and work towards desired goals (see box overleaf). The emphasis is on behaviour, rather than on what is going on between their ears. Gone are the days of asking people how they feel, and instead it is all about how they intend to change their behaviour.

People are asked to create a list of specific activities that, over time, will result in long-term behavioural change. For example, the general goal of spending more time with other people might involve having coffee with a friend once a week and going out to see a film with work colleagues once every fortnight. Similarly, the general goal of gaining a new qualification might involve several specific activities, such as using the Internet to find out about possible courses and having a meeting with a boss to talk about taking time off from work to study. During this phase, worksheets are created to help motivate and monitor these behavioural changes.

Rip it up

Behavioural Activation: Phase Two*

1) Identifying target behaviours

Look back at the behaviours that you want to avoid and your
desired goals. For each one, make a list of specific activities that
will help you avoid the former and achieve the latter.

Each of these specific activities should involve a small but real
step towards your goal. So, for example, spending less time in
bed might involve getting up at 9 a.m. every weekday and not
going to bed before 11 p.m. Similarly, starting a new relationship might involve registering with an online dating agency,
telling your friends that you are actively looking for a partner, and
joining a book club.

All of these specific activities need to be measurable, realistic,
and time specific. So writing 'be happier' wouldn't be acceptable
because it is difficult to measure and not time specific, whereas
'reading one new book every two weeks' would be much better.

A sample list of specific activities might include: Wake up each
day at 9 a.m. and get out of bed; Visit one museum or art gallery

---

* The exercises described here are designed to provide a general insight into the sort of techniques
used by psychologists. If you believe that you have a serious and problematic phobia, consult a
professional.

each week; Telephone my parents twice a week; Once a week, contact a friend and suggest that we meet for coffee; Each week, write 500 words of my novel.

2) Creating a plan

Use the table below to create a plan for each day of the week, noting which of the specific activities that you intend to achieve, and when you will achieve them.

MONDAY: Date:			
Time	Planned activity	Actual activity	Rating of how successful this was between 1 (not very successful) and 10 (very successful)
9 a.m.	Wake up and get out of bed.		
10 a.m.			
11 a.m.	Telephone my parents.		
12 p.m.	Produce 100 words towards my novel.		

At the end of the week, review the tables and identify which targets you did, and didn't, achieve. Carry the targets that you didn't achieve over to the next week. You might find the following tips helpful:

- Don't try to change all aspects of your behaviour at once. Instead, start with baby steps and build up gradually.
- Don't let your thoughts get in the way. If you find yourself thinking about failure, or feeling bad about yourself, just accept these thoughts and move on.
- Everyone fails once in a while, so if you don't manage to achieve all your goals, don't worry. Make up another activity sheet and try again.
- Moving out of your comfort zone may feel difficult at first, and it might feel better to fall back into your normal routine of avoidance by telling yourself 'I'll do it when I feel better', or 'I will wait for exactly the right situation'. Don't fall into these traps – try to change your behaviour no matter how you feel or what you are thinking.

According to the *As If* principle, this technique should be effective, but is that really the case?

In 2006, Sona Dimidjian from the University of Washington and her colleagues conducted a remarkable study.[37] Dimidjian recruited 200 outpatients suffering from major depression and randomly assigned them to one of four groups. Group One were given a course of a popular antidepressant drug called paroxetine, Group Two were given an inert placebo pill, Group Three attended cognitive therapy, and Group Four went through behavioural activation.

Following this, the research team then tracked the patients over a two-month period to discover which of the treatments worked best. The results revealed that for the most severely depressed patients, behavioural activation was significantly more effective than cognitive therapy. Perhaps most importantly, the study showed that behavioural activation was as effective as taking paroxetine.

Over the years a large number of studies have demonstrated this effect time and again.[38] When it comes to alleviating depression, trying to change what goes on in people's heads with drugs and cognitive therapy can be tricky. In contrast, changing their behaviour has far fewer side effects and is just as effective.

The *As If* principle is not just about producing happiness and love. It can also help eliminate pain and suffering and, in doing so, helps millions of people to live better and more productive lives.

Rip it up

Twenty Pieces: Part One

At some point before you finish reading the following chapter, I would like you to complete this exercise.

First, please tear out the following page and rip it into twenty pieces. Each of the pieces can be any size and shape you like.

It is a fairly boring task and will take about five minutes. You can either do it now or leave it until later on (I will remind you again before the end of the next chapter).

4. WILLPOWER

Where we learn why rewards punish, and discover
how to motivate others, beat procrastination,
stop smoking and lose weight.

'I prayed for twenty years but received no answer
until I prayed with my legs.'

Frederick Douglass

1. HOW REWARDS FAIL AND WHAT TO DO ABOUT IT

Psychologists have long tried to unpack the mystery of motivation. Why is it that some people are self-controlled and driven whilst others find it difficult to drag themselves out of bed in the morning? During the 1960s much of the work involved researchers placing pigeons into specially constructed cages and then carefully observing their bird-brained participants. The cages contained a button and a light, and the researchers attempted to train the pigeons to peck at the button whenever the light was illuminated. Extensive experimentation soon revealed that the pigeons learnt much more quickly when they were rewarded with small pellets of food. Assuming that people were much like large featherless pigeons, many researchers believed that the same type of reward system could be used to motivate humans. The idea was quickly embraced by organizations and governments across the globe, resulting in prisoners being allotted special privileges for good behaviour, school-children being offered sweets when they read books, and employees being awarded bonuses when they were especially productive.

Unfortunately, it soon became clear that laboratory-based pigeon research could not be generalized to humans living in the real world. Some of these reward systems either had no long-term effect or, in some instances, actually deterred the very behaviour that they were designed to encourage.

In his book *Punished by Rewards*, Alfie Kohn catalogues the wealth of evidence demonstrating the downside of incentives.[1] In one study, for example, researchers tracked more than 1,000 people as they attempted to give up smoking.[2] The investigators randomly split the smokers into two groups and asked everyone to take part in an eight-week course designed to help them quit. Participants in one of the groups were given various incentives to take part in the anti-smoking programme, including a free ceramic mug and an opportunity to win an all-expenses-paid trip to Hawaii. The smokers in the other group acted as a control and so were not given any incentives. Initially, the rewards worked well, with the participants who had been given the ceramic mug and dreams of sun-drenched beaches being especially enthusiastic about the programme. However, when the researchers re-visited the participants three months after the start of the study they discovered that the same percentage of people in both the control group and incentives group had abstained from smoking. After a year, more people in the incentivized group than in the control group had relapsed.

In another investigation psychologist E. Scott Geller from the Virginia Polytechnic Institute reviewed twenty-eight studies that had encouraged people to use seat belts.[3] After looking at the data from almost 250,000 people across a six-year period, Scott concluded that rewarding people with cash or gifts for buckling up was one of the least effective ways of encouraging long-term use of seat belts. Similar large-scale reviews of reward-based programmes designed to encourage schoolchildren to read also revealed no long-term benefits.[4]

Then there is the work on rewards for creativity. Offer artists big money and you might think they will soon get their creative juices flowing. But when Teresa Amabile from Brandeis University in Massachusetts asked a panel of professional artists to judge the artistic merits of both commissioned and non-commissioned creative work (without knowing which was which), she discovered that the non-commissioned projects were awarded higher ratings than the commissioned ones.[5]

Worried that this might not be due to the negative influence of rewards, but rather artists having their style cramped by the demands of financial backers, Amabile carried out a more controlled investigation.[6] She recruited a group of budding writers and asked them to write a haiku-style poem using the word 'snow' as the first and last line. The participants were then split into two groups. One group were asked to think about all of the riches that would flow from being a great writer, whilst the other group were requested to dwell upon the intrinsic pleasure that they derived from their work. Finally, everyone was asked to produce a second poem around the concept of laughter.

Amabile then assembled a panel of twelve poets, gave them the haiku poems about snow and laughter, and asked them to rate how creative the poems were. Both groups displayed the same amount of creativity when writing about snow. However, the group that was made to think about the rewards and riches that might flow from their writing displayed significantly less creativity when writing about laughter. Even thinking about rewards had had a detrimental effect.

Many psychologists were stunned by the results. Why

should the reward systems that worked so well in the laboratory frequently fail in everyday life?

Why rewards punish

Spend a significant amount of time with any social psychologist, and sooner or later they will tell you the story about the wise old man and the abusive teenagers.

According to the anecdote, there was once a wise old man who lived in a rough neighbourhood. One day, a group of surly teenagers decided to give him a hard time. Each day the teenagers would walk past the front of the old man's house and shout abuse at him. Many old men would have decided that the best way forward was to shout back at the teenagers, call the police, or hope that the group would eventually grow bored of their mean-spirited ways. However, the wise old man had a sound understanding of psychology, and so came up with a completely different, and altogether more cunning, plan.

He sat outside his house waiting for the teenagers to come along. When the group showed up the old man immediately handed a five-pound note to each of them and explained that he was happy to pay them to shout abuse. Bemused, the teenagers took the money and came out with their usual rude remarks. The old man repeated his actions each day for a week.

The following week was slightly different. When the teenagers came along, the old man explained that he had had a tough week financially, and so could only pay each of them a pound. Unperturbed, the teenagers continued to take his money and persisted with their childish chants.

At the start of the third week everything changed again. When the group arrived the old man explained that it had been another tough week, and so he could now only afford to pay the teenagers twenty pence each. Insulted at the small amount of money on offer, the teenagers refused to shout their abuse.

The story is almost certainly apocryphal, but it reflects a fundamental truth about why we do what we do. To fully understand the wisdom behind the old man's actions we need to travel back to the 1970s and discover what happened when a group of people were paid to solve a wooden puzzle.

Psychiatrist Edward Deci was a big fan of a commercially available puzzle called 'Soma'. The puzzle involved giving people several oddly shaped wooden blocks and asking them to arrange the blocks into specified shapes. Deci wondered if the puzzle could be used to discover whether the *As If* principle influences motivation.[7]

Deci invited volunteers into his laboratory and asked them to play with the puzzle for thirty minutes. Before starting, some of the volunteers were told that if they could solve the puzzle they would be given a financial reward, whilst the others weren't offered any incentive.

After thirty minutes, Deci told all the participants that their quality time with Soma was up. He then explained that he had left the paperwork needed for the next part of the experiment in his office, and so had to leave the laboratory to fetch it. As is so often the case with social psychology experiments, this 'I have to leave the laboratory now' ploy was a cover story. The important part of the experiment was just about to take place.

Deci left each participant alone for ten minutes. During this time, they were free to continue to play Soma, or read the magazines that had been strategically placed on a nearby table, or indeed neither. Their behaviour was being secretly observed all of the time by Deci.

Conventional pigeon-based reward theory predicts that those who had been paid to play Soma would have found the puzzle especially enjoyable, and so be more likely to carry on with it when Deci left the laboratory. In contrast, the *As If* principle makes a quite different set of predictions.

According to the *As If* principle, the participants who were offered the financial reward to play with the puzzle would have unconsciously thought, 'People only offer me money when they want me to do something that I don't want to do. I was offered money to play with the puzzle, so it can't be much fun.' Using the same logic, those who weren't offered any financial incentive would have unconsciously thought, 'People only offer me money when they want me to do something that I don't want to do. I wasn't offered any money to play with the puzzle, so it must be fun.' Seen in this way, those who had been offered the reward had been made to behave as if they didn't actually enjoy playing with the puzzle, whereas those who hadn't been offered any financial incentive were behaving as if playing with the puzzle was fun. According to the *As If* principle, Deci's payments would have turned play into hard work, and so the participants who were financially rewarded would be significantly more likely to leave the puzzle alone when he left the room.

Deci's results provided overwhelming support for the power of acting *As If*. Regardless of participants' success at completing the puzzle, those who had *not* been previously offered the financial reward were far more likely to play with the puzzle when left to their own devices.

Other researchers quickly conducted several similar experiments to discover whether this intriguing finding was genuine. In perhaps the best known of these studies Stanford psychologist Mark Lepper and colleagues visited several schools and asked schoolchildren to draw some pictures.[8] Before being allowed access to the crayons and paper, Lepper told one group of children that they would receive a 'good player' medal for drawing. A second group was not given the promise of any reward. According to the *As If* principle, the children who were offered the medals would have unconsciously thought, 'I am only offered rewards when adults want me to do something that I don't enjoy. I am being offered a gold medal for drawing, therefore I must not like drawing.' Similarly, the children in the other group would have thought, 'I am only offered rewards when adults want me to do something that I don't enjoy. I am not being offered any reward for drawing, therefore I must like drawing.'

A few weeks later Lepper and the teams returned to the school, handed out the drawing materials again, and measured how much the children played with them. Those who had received the medals a few weeks before spent significantly less time drawing than their classmates.

The message from the studies is clear. By rewarding the behaviour of schoolchildren, smokers and drivers you are encouraging them to behave as if they really don't want to read books, stop smoking or buckle up. As a result, the moment the rewards are removed, the desired behaviour runs the risk of grinding to a sudden halt or, worse, becomes even less frequent than before incentives were first introduced. In the short-term, reward systems can be effective. However, over the long haul most organizations struggle to maintain a continuous supply of special privileges, sweets, gifts and bonuses, and the moment the rewards stop, people's motivation often vanishes into thin air.

The man with X-ray eyes

Having established that the *As If* principle plays a key role in motivation, researchers began to explore other ways in which the effect could be used to encourage people to spring into action.

In the workplace, some business gurus argued for the importance of reconfiguring jobs to make them more intrinsically enjoyable by giving employees a greater sense of autonomy, purpose and fun. When it came to people's personal lives, some psychologists turned their attention to role-play. Take, for example, the work of Leon Mann from Harvard University and his groundbreaking study into giving up smoking.

Mann invited twenty-six very heavy smokers to his laboratory and randomly split them into two groups.[9] Those in one group were asked to behave as if they were going to give up smoking by role-playing someone who had been diagnosed with cancer. To make the pretence as realistic as possible, he created a fake doctor's office at the university. When the participants entered the room they were faced with a variety of medical equipment and an actor wearing a white coat. The actor played the role of a doctor and brought out the participant's alleged X-rays. It wasn't good news. According to a set of fictitious medical records, the participant had lung cancer. The participant was asked to respond by discussing how they now intended to give up smoking.

In contrast, the participants in the control group were shown the same highly emotional information about them having lung cancer, but were not asked to alter their behaviour by taking part in any form of role-play.

The results were remarkable. At the start of the study all of the participants were smoking around twenty-five cigarettes a day. Immediately after the experiment those in the control group cut down by an average of five cigarettes per day, whereas those who had been involved in the role-play showed an average reduction of ten cigarettes per day. Acting as if they were going to reduce the amount they smoked caused a significant change in the participants' actual behaviour. The researchers then tracked the participants over the next few years and discovered that the effect was not short-lived.[10] Two years after taking part in the study, those who had been involved in the role-playing were still smoking significantly less than those in the control group.

When they weren't injecting meaning into the workplace, or role-play in people's personal lives, psychologists were busy discovering that a little often goes a surprisingly long way.

Rip it up

Are you trying to give up smoking? Perhaps some emotional role-play will help. Have a good friend read the following few paragraphs about lung cancer, and also tear out the following page with the X-ray of a pair of lungs. Then, ask them to use the information and image to role-play a physician giving you some advice about smoking. You should try to become as fully involved in the role-play as possible, asking questions and explaining how you now intend to stop smoking.

Information and script outline

Your lungs are located in the upper part of your chest cavity. Each time you breathe in, they remove oxygen from the inhaled air and allow it to pass into your bloodstream. When you breathe out, your lungs remove the carbon dioxide from the blood and allow it to pass into your breath for exhaling.

Many smokers develop 'chronic obstructive pulmonary dis-ease' or emphysema. This condition diminishes your lungs' ability to convert oxygen and carbon dioxide, making breathing difficult and preventing much-needed oxygen from entering the body. Emphysema is one of the main causes of death in the Western world.

In addition, smoke contains several toxic chemicals and is associated with lung cancer. Physicians use X-rays to help deter-mine whether a patient has lung cancer. In an X-ray image, the dark parts show where the X-rays met little resistance, whilst the white parts indicate obstructions, such as dense tissue and bone.

Let me show you this X-ray of a patient with cancer in their left lung. The man was in his early sixties and for much of his life was a heavy smoker. His lung contains large amounts of scarring and cancer cells, which show up as large masses of white. The consequences of this cancer are dire. If, for example, a lung cancer is more than an inch in diameter, less than 50 per cent of patients will live for another five years. And that is with them using the most effective forms of therapy. This patient will probably be dead in less than a year.

How long have you been smoking? Are you already having problems breathing? Are you on your way to a serious health problem? If you carry on smoking, there is a strong likelihood that your X-ray will look like this one in a few years' time. How do you feel about that? What effect will that have on your own life and those around you?

That's the bad news. The good news is that the future is not set in stone. This doesn't have to be you. What do you intend to do to make sure this X-ray does not have your name on it in the future?'

2. WHY SMALL CHANGES HAVE A BIG IMPACT

Let's imagine that you are at home and suddenly hear a knock on the door. You peek through your lace curtains and see a young man standing on your doorstep. He looks harmless enough and so you decide to answer the door. The man explains that he is a volunteer working for the Canadian Cancer Society and wonders whether you would like to make a donation. You think about it and then decide that it is better to give than take, and so give a small amount of money to him.

This may seem like an innocent encounter. In reality, you may have just taken part in a psychology experiment. This type of 'would you mind contributing to charity' study was first carried out by Patricia Pliner from the University of Toronto, and demonstrated how the *As If* principle could be used to get people to spring into action.[11]

Pliner's results showed that 46 per cent of residents were prepared to put their hands into their pockets and money into the bucket. In the next stage of her experiment, the researchers had the volunteers approach a second set of houses and ask the residents to wear a lapel pin to help publicize their cause. The pin was small and almost all of the residents agreed. Two weeks later, the volunteers returned to these pin-wearing residents and asked for a financial donation. Amazingly, over 90 per cent of the residents agreed to give to the charity.

Known as the 'foot-in-the-door' technique, this approach works because the small initial request caused the residents to behave as if they were the type of people that give to charity. This encourages them to believe that they are altruistic individuals, and so motivates them to agree to the much larger request. Over forty years of research has shown that the technique works in many different situations.[12]

Some of the most interesting and practical work has been conducted by French researcher Nicolas Guéguen.

In one study, Guéguen travelled to Brittany and randomly split some of the residents into two groups.[13] He then telephoned the residents in one of the groups, pretended that he was from a local energy firm, and asked them to take part in a short telephone survey about energy conservation. A few days later Guéguen sent out a letter to all of the residents in his experiment. The letter came from the mayor of the town and asked them to participate in an energy conservation scheme. More than 50 per cent of those who had been asked to take part in the telephone survey agreed to participate, compared with just 20 per cent of those who hadn't been previously contacted.

In another study Guéguen emailed more than 1,000 people and asked them to visit a website that had been set up to support children who had been the victims of war.[14] When half of the people visited the website they saw a message inviting them to click another link if they wanted to make a contribution to the charity. In contrast, when the others came to the website they were asked to sign a petition against landmines, and then asked to click a link if they wished to make a financial contribution to the charity. Only 3 per cent of those who weren't asked to sign the petition clicked the donation link versus nearly 14 per cent of those who had signed the petition.

Finally, Guéguen has also used this foot-in-the-door phenomenon to help Cupid find his target.[15] Venturing out onto the streets, he arranged for experimenters to approach more than 300 young women and ask them out for a drink. Sometimes the experimenter asked for directions, or a light, before popping the question. Other times they took a more direct approach and asked the woman about the possibility of a drink straightaway. This small change made a big difference, with 60 per cent of those who had been asked directions saying yes to the drink, versus just 20 per cent of the women who had been asked directly.

In each instance people had seen themselves acting as if they were pro-energy conservation, anti-war or up for a drink, and so became motivated to act in a way that was consistent with their new-found identity.

This powerful principle is often employed by salespeople. Behavioural expert Robert Cialdini refers to it as the 'low ball' technique, and it involves a whole set of procedures that are designed to get people to behave as if they are interested in a certain product or service.[16] For example, a car showroom may advertise a vehicle at a very reasonable price in order to lure potential customers into their shop. It is only when they have enquired about a car, and therefore behaved as if they are interested in buying it, that the salesman explains about the various extra add-ons that will increase the price of the vehicle. Similarly, hotels may place online advertisements offering rooms at a low price. Once a potential customer has clicked on the ad, and so behaved as if they are going to book a room, they discover that the bargain rooms have all been sold but some higher-price rooms are still available.

Rip it up

Twenty Pieces: Part Two

Just before the start of this chapter, I asked you to complete Part One of the Twenty Pieces exercise. This exercise is all about procrastination. I pointed out that it was a fairly boring task, and that you didn't have to do the tearing there and then. Did you complete the exercise? If so, you are probably the type of person who doesn't have much of a problem in motivating yourself when the going gets tough. However, if you decided to leave the tearing until later then you are more likely to suffer from procrastination. The ability to procrastinate often stops people doing well in many aspects of their lives, and makes them feel tired and lacking in control (or, as William James put it, 'Nothing is so fatiguing as the eternal hanging on of an uncompleted task.').

If you do fall into the latter camp then fear not, the *As If* principle can help. Simply go back to the exercise and tear the page out of the book (no need to rip it into twenty pieces just now), and then read the following paragraph.

How do you feel about completing the rest of the exercise now? According to research, at this moment you will be experiencing a strange urge to finish off the job by ripping the page into twenty pieces. By working on an activity for 'just a few minutes' (that is, behaving as if you are a highly motivated person), you change the way you see yourself and make it far more likely that you will complete whatever it is you have to do.[17]

Whenever you have a mountain to climb, persuade yourself to spend just a few minutes taking those all-important first few steps.

The same principle can also cause people to radically change their behaviour for the worse. In the early 1970s, for instance, the military junta in Greece wanted to train ordinary soldiers to become sadistic torturers.[18] Using the foot-in-the-door technique, these soldiers were slowly persuaded to abuse prisoners. At the start of the process the soldiers were asked to stand outside cells whilst prisoners were tortured. In the next stage they were invited to come into the cells and witness the abuse. Then the soldiers were asked to provide a small amount of assistance inside the cells, perhaps holding the prisoner down as they were beaten. Finally, they were asked to carry out the beatings themselves, and so became the next generation of torturers as the newbie recruits stood outside the cells. Slowly but surely the foot-in-the-door technique motivated the soldiers to carry out actions that they would have originally considered completely unacceptable.

On a more positive note, some of the most recent research into the foot-in-the-door technique has explored whether the smallest of commitments can help make the world a better place.

The power of commitment

Americans generate more than 150 million tons of rubbish per year, enough to fill the New Orleans Superdome twice every day.[19] Psychologist Shawn Burn from the California Polytechnic State University decided to discover whether the foot-in-the-door technique might be able to promote recycling.[20]

Burn's experiment involved five separate areas in Claremont, a small affluent college town in eastern Los Angeles County. Just before the start of the experiment Burn and his colleagues secretly observed the recycling activity of the residents, identified about 200 households that didn't recycle, and set out to see if they could change the residents' behaviour.

Burn started off by enlisting the help of a local troop of Boy Scouts and spent three weeks training them for the study. First, he had the Scouts rehearse reading aloud a carefully created message stressing the need for recycling. Next, the investigators played the role of a Claremont resident, and asked the Scouts to knock on their imaginary door and deliver the well-rehearsed message. When the investigators were convinced that their highly trained group of crack Scouts were up for the job, they were let loose on the public.

After the Scouts were put into groups of three, the investigators took each group to Claremont, and asked the Scouts to knock on the door of an unsuspecting participant. When the door opened the Scouts would launch into their carefully prepared speech about the importance of recycling. A few moments later they would hand the resident a pledge card and a sticker. The pledge card simply said, 'I, _____ , pledge support for Claremont's Recycling Program. I will help win the war on waste!' The sticker was equally straightforward and just carried the message 'I Recycle to Win the War on Waste'.

For the next six weeks the research team again took to the streets and secretly observed the recycling behaviour of the residents. The results were remarkable. Those who had not been visited showed only a 3 per cent increase in recycling. In contrast, asking people to sign a pledge card and put a sticker up in their house resulted in a 20 per cent shift. Just spending a few moments behaving as if they intended to recycle had a dramatic impact on their subsequent motivation to go green.

Rip it up

Change4Life

In 2011, I teamed up with the British government to help promote a campaign that used the foot-in-the-door technique to encourage the public to lead healthier lives.

The work was part of a national campaign known as 'Change4Life', and involved getting people to make small alterations to their diet and level of exercise in the hope that these would then kick-start more significant changes.

In part of the work we asked people to change their behaviour whenever they encountered any of the following ten triggers. Try incorporating them into your life and see if they act as a catalyst for more significant changes.

Trigger	Instead . . .
When you find yourself reaching for some sweets, chocolate, or crisps . . .	. . . stop, and instead go for some fresh fruit (such as grapes, a banana, or raisins), mini rice cakes, or unsalted nuts.
When you are thinking about cooking a fry-up . . .	. . . make it a 'grill-up' instead. Try grilling your bacon and sausages, and scrambling or poaching eggs.

When you are just about to order a large glass of white wine . . .	. . . change it for a spritzer made with a smaller glass of wine and soda.
When you are out and about, and just about to take the lift or escalator . . .	. . . look around for some stairs and, if possible, use them instead.
If you are using public transport . . .	. . . see whether you can get off one stop early and walk the rest of the way.
When you are cooking for you or your family, and are about to serve up the food on a full-size plate . . .	. . . swap the plate for a smaller one, as this will encourage you to serve more modest portions.
When you're just about to put sugar into your tea or coffee . . .	. . . only put in half the amount of sugar.
When you are in a shop and just about to buy some white bread or white rice . . .	. . . boost the amount of fibre in your diet by choosing wholemeal bread and brown rice.
When you are about to order a sugary fizzy drink . . .	. . . change your mind and go for fizzy water, milk or pure fruit juice instead.
Instead of ordering a large main course . . .	. . . go for a smaller portion with a side order of salad or vegetables.

Rip it up

Pledge Cards

Would you like to volunteer for charity work, eat a healthier diet, be greener or take more exercise? Then the **Rip It Out** pledge cards can help. Please rip out the following page and cut out each of the pledge cards. Then, simply complete one of the cards and place it in a prominent place. Perhaps you can stick it to your fridge door, place it on your desk or next to your bathroom mirror.

By completing the card you are behaving as if you are motivated and driven, and so are more likely to obtain your goal. Once you have achieved your first target, use the remaining cards to change other aspects of your life.

I pledge to
_____

I pledge to
_____

I pledge to
_____

I pledge to
_____

Rip it up

Assessing your self-control

There is a secret message printed on the back of page 203. Please do not look at the message. Instead, carefully tear out the page and crumple it into a ball, but in such a way as to ensure that you don't see the secret message.

We are going to use the ball to discover whether you have an accurate insight into your level of self-control.

How long do you think you can go before you open up the ball and read the hidden message? A few minutes? A couple of hours? Perhaps a day or two? Maybe an entire week? Write your prediction on the line below . . .

Next, place the ball somewhere prominent in your house or office. Each time you look at the ball you will probably wonder about the secret message. Is it, for example, a hilarious joke? Or perhaps a quote that will change your life? Or maybe a really practical tip about how to increase your level of self-control. Unless you open the paper ball you will never know for sure.

When did you open the paper ball? Was your prediction accurate, or do you have less self-control than you first thought?

When most people start this exercise they are convinced that they will be able to avoid opening the paper ball for several weeks. However, as time passes curiosity quickly gets the better of them and they soon find themselves eager to read the secret message. Their unrealistic ideas about their powers of self-control illustrate the need for the various techniques described in this chapter.

'So, how did you do?'

3. LOSING WEIGHT WITHOUT TRYING

Levels of obesity are rising across the world. In the 1980s 15 per cent of Americans were considered obese. By 2003 this had risen to around 34 per cent, with a staggering 17 per cent of American children and adolescents being classified as overweight. Carrying too much weight increases the likelihood of various health problems, especially heart disease, type 2 diabetes and certain forms of cancer. It therefore isn't surprising that millions of people make a concerted attempt to lose weight at some point in their lives. Ironically, the chances of them being successful are slim.

Many people are attracted to the quick and easy results promised by proponents of very low-calorie diets. Such diets are usually based around low-calorie, nutritionally complete, liquid meals. The short-term impact of such diets is impressive, with several research studies suggesting that around half of those using these products quickly lose around 80 per cent of their excess weight. However, when the researchers followed the dieters for the next few years a very different picture emerged. After about three years most of the participants had returned to their pre-diet weight, and after five years only three remained slim.[21] This depressing pattern of results is not just limited to very low-calorie diets. After examining the results from hundreds of studies involving many different types of diet, one reviewer noted, 'It is only the rate of weight regain, not the fact of weight regain, that appears open to debate.'[22]

Rip it up

Pull me–push you

If you are sitting at a table, try this quick two-part exercise. First, close the book, put it down on the table and push it away from you. Second, pull the book towards you, pick it up, and give it a little hug and a kiss (if you are doing this in a bookshop, or another public place, you might want to smile at those around you in an 'It's OK, I'm not dangerous' kind of a way).

How did you feel about the book after each part of the exercise? Research suggests that pushing an object away from you (behaving as if you don't like it) makes you dislike the object, whereas pulling it towards you (behaving as if you like it) makes you feel far more positively about it.[23] As far as I am aware, no previous research has examined the impact of hugging and kissing an object, but I am assuming that makes you feel especially attached to the book.

Next time you are confronted with a plate of sugary snacks or chocolate biscuits, simply push the plate away from you and feel the temptation fade. Similarly, if you are in the sales game and want to make a client feel more positive about a product, place it on a table in front of them and encourage them to slide it towards themselves.

Other work that has tried to promote weight loss through physical exercise has faced similar problems.

In 2008 researcher Larry Webber from the Tulane University and his colleagues reported the results from a large-scale study examining whether it was possible to encourage physical exercise in middle school children.[24] The two-year experiment involved thirty-six schools, and thousands of children, from all across America.

In half of the schools the researchers did everything they could to encourage exercise and weight loss. Each week the children were told about the importance of physical activity and asked to carry out a specified amount of exercise. The researchers even encouraged the schools to team up with local health clubs and recreation centres, and stage special dance classes, gym sessions, and basketball matches. In contrast, the children in the other schools acted as a control and so were not subjected to such opportunities and encouragement.

To discover the effect of the programme the researchers fitted each child with an accelerometer to measure their movements, and also tracked their body mass index. What impact did the extensive programme of encouragement have? Almost zilch. The children who were given the opportunity to play more sport, and encouraged to exercise, ended up moving around very slightly more than those in the control group. Perhaps more importantly there was no difference in the average body mass index between the two groups.

Why? The study was based on the notion that changing minds causes people to change their behaviour. According to this approach, all you have to do is tell people about the importance of a healthy diet and regular exercise, and they will immediately jump into action. However, this approach has been shown to be flawed. Instead, an understanding of the *As If* principle provides a far more effective technique for long-term weight loss.

Eating with your eyes

In chapter 2 we learnt how the pioneering work of psychologist Stanley Schachter revealed the surprising relationship between the *As If* principle and attraction. In the 1960s Schachter also came up with a similarly daring hypothesis to explain why some people are obese.

According to Schachter, people start eating on the basis of two very different types of signal.[25]

The first set of signals comes from within your body. For example, after you have just consumed a large meal, your stomach might send you an 'OK, I couldn't even manage one more wafer-thin mint' message, and so you know that it is time to stop eating. Or maybe you feel your tummy rumble, experience a sudden drop in blood sugar, and know that you should head for the nearest eatery. Conceptually speaking, eating because you feel hungry is just like feeling happy because you are smiling. In both instances you decide how you are feeling on the basis of what your body is telling you.

Alternatively, your decision to eat might be influenced by signals from your surroundings. You might, for instance, see a great-looking cream cake in a patisserie window and decide that it has your name written all over it. Or you might glance at your watch, see that it is teatime, and head for the kitchen.

In these instances you are ignoring the signals from your body, and instead deciding how you should feel on the basis of what is happening around you.

Although everyone is influenced by both sets of signals, Schachter speculated that some people are more likely to listen to their body (he referred to them as 'internals'), whilst others are more likely to be affected by their surroundings ('externals'). He also hypothesized that when provisions are scarce neither group will become obese, as 'internals' will just eat when they are hungry and 'externals' will munch away on the rare occasions when they have access to food.

So far, so good. However, in most developed countries the supermarket aisles are jammed full of produce, fast-food chains encourage people to supersize, and cinemas offer huge buckets of popcorn. According to Schachter's theory, this excess of food will not present a problem to 'internals'. They will continue to listen to their bodies and munch away when they are hungry. In contrast, the 'externals' now have a problem. To them, each of the food-mountains that they encounter on a daily basis screams out 'eat me' and, unless these people can exercise an extraordinary amount of self-control, they will soon find themselves consuming everything in sight. As a result, Schachter predicted that in most of the developed world, internals tend to be on the slim side whereas externals tend to be overweight.

It is an elegant and clever theory, but is it correct? To help find out, Richard Nisbett from Yale University conducted an ingenious experiment.[26] Nisbett recruited a mixture of slim and overweight people, and invited them to his laboratory, one at a time. All of his participants were asked to arrive in the early afternoon, but not to eat after nine o'clock in the morning. After taking part in a boring experiment ('Can you count back from 1,000 in threes?') each of the participants was rewarded with some sandwiches. In reality, the tedious experiment was completely irrelevant, and Nisbett's experiment actually involved secretly observing the participants after they had been given the sandwiches (thus scientifically proving there really is no such thing as a free lunch). Each participant was presented with a plate containing either one or three tasty roast beef sandwiches and told that they were free to help themselves to more sandwiches in a nearby refrigerator.

Schachter's theory predicted that the slim participants would be internals, and so the amount of food they consumed would not be related to the number of sandwiches on the plate. If they felt hungry then they would start to consume the sandwiches, and they would stop eating the moment they felt that their stomachs were full. In contrast, the overweight participants would tend to be externals that were driven by their eyes, and so would eat far more when they were presented with the three sandwiches. Obviously, it was possible that the overweight participants felt hungrier than their more slim-line counterparts. To allow for this, the experimenters made an intriguing prediction – following the 'out of sight, out of mind' maxim, they predicted that the overweight participants wouldn't be any more likely than the slim subjects to raid the refrigerator.

What happened? When both groups of participants were presented with one sandwich they ate the same amount. However, when presented with three sandwiches the overweight participants quickly gobbled down far more than their slim counterparts. Not only that, both the slim and overweight participants were equally unlikely to raid the refrigerator.

In another cleverly designed study Ronald Goldman and his colleagues from Columbia University made good use of Yom Kippur.[27] Yom Kippur is one of the most sacred of the Jewish holy days, with those adhering to the Jewish faith undergoing twenty-four hours without food or water. Goldman knew that modern-day Jewish people vary in the degree to which they observe this tradition, with some spending almost all of Yom Kippur in the synagogue and others only going there for hour or so. Goldman speculated that those who spent lots of time in the synagogue would not be constantly reminded about food (in his paper describing the work, Goldman noted the main food-related reference during the religious rituals at Yom Kippur would be a 'passing mention of a scapegoat').

On the basis of Schachter's theory, Goldman speculated that slim people would be relying on their bodies to tell them whether they were hungry, and so feel the same amount of food-deprived discomfort regardless of the amount of time that they spent at the synagogue. In contrast, overweight people would be relying on their surroundings to tell them whether they should eat, and so feel significantly more comfortable at the synagogue. To find out if this was the case Goldman sent around a questionnaire to his Jewish students asking them for their height, weight, how many hours they spent at a synagogue during Yom Kippur, and how difficult they found fasting. The results from the slim students revealed no relationship between the number of hours they spent at the synagogue during Yom Kippur, and how difficult they found the fasting. In contrast, the longer the overweight students spent away from the synagogue during Yom Kippur, the more difficult they found fasting – exactly as Schachter had predicted.

Schachter's theory has huge implications for restaurants wanting to sell more food and people wanting to diet.

From a restaurateur's point of view, persuading customers to become less self-conscious, and so ignore the signals from their stomach, will be good for business.[28] For example, low lighting and soft music helps focus people's attention away from themselves, and also encourages diners to eat more. Similarly, tempting externals with photographs of food, or indeed the real thing, will also be good for business. Research shows that placing alluring images of delicious-looking dishes on a menu, or wheeling in the dessert trolley at the end of a meal, will tempt even the most self-controlled of externals. In one study, for example, researchers asked the staff at a French restaurant to classify their diners as either 'chubby' or 'normal' weight.[29] Then, at the end of the meal, a waitress approached their table clutching a pie and asked who would like dessert. Both the normal and overweight diners were equally likely to order dessert, but the overweight people showed a strong tendency to go for the pie that was sitting there right in front of their eyes.

If you do want to lose weight, Schachter's theory can help. Try to get in touch with your inner internal by focusing more attention on what your body is trying to tell you. Just before you order that cake, for example, ask yourself 'Am I really hungry?' Similarly, reduce the tempting sights that are leading you astray by keeping unhealthy food out of sight and staying away from supermarket isles packed with snacks and biscuits. Also, try to avoid situations that involve eating food and distracting your attention away from yourself. Don't watch television, listen to music, or even read whilst eating. Instead, focus your attention on the food itself and slowly chew each mouthful. If that fails, try to make mealtimes as self-conscious as possible by eating in front of a mirror,[30] switching your knife and fork for chopsticks (or vice versa), or using your non-dominant hand.[31]

Schachter's simple theory links the *As If* principle with eating. Slim people base the decision about whether to eat on the signals from their bodies. In the same way that people feel happy when their face forms a smile, so they eat when their stomach tells them that they are hungry. In contrast, people who are overweight tend not to base their decisions about eating on the signals from their body and are instead more influenced by external signals. By getting them to re-focus on behaving more in-line with the *As If* principle, they can quickly shed any unwanted pounds. Dieting does not have to involve struggling in vain to overcome temptation. Instead, it is a question of listening to what your body is telling you.

Rip it up

Monitoring yourself

Take a look at your computer monitor. Is the centre of the monitor above, below or level with your eye-line? According to research exploring the *As If* principle and motivation, the position of your monitor could be having a significant effect on your productivity.

In the 1980s, John Riskind from Texas A&M University decided to examine the effect of posture on persistence.[32] Riskind placed participants in one of two positions. Half of the participants were placed in a slumped position, such that their backs were stooped and hunched over, and heads dropped down. In contrast, the other participants were made to sit upright, with their shoulders pulled back and heads held high. After sitting stooped or upright for about three minutes, each participant was sent to another room and asked to try and solve several geometric puzzles that involved tracing over a diagram without lifting their pencil off the page. In fact, many of the puzzles were impossible to solve and Riskind was only interested in how long the participants kept going in the face of failure. Describing his findings in a paper entitled 'They Stoop to Conquer', Riskind noted how the participants who had previously been sitting up straight persevered for almost twice as long as the slouchers.

More recently, other psychologists built on this work by asking participants to sit at a computer and work on a complex problem.[33] Some of the time the computer monitor was placed in a low position, causing participants to slump down. Other times it was placed slightly above their eye-line, causing participants to sit up straight. Once again, those with their head held high persevered for longer.

To ensure maximum motivation, place the centre of your monitor slightly above your eye-line.

Creatures of habit

Schachter's theory is fascinating, but it is not the only work to link the *As If* principle and eating.

I have worked at the University of Hertfordshire for many years. Throughout my time there I have been fortunate enough to have brushed shoulders with many energetic and creative colleagues. Professor Ben Fletcher is one of those people.

Despite nearly always dressing in black, Ben is a happy man, who shares my passion for quirky psychology that is relevant to everyday life. Ben's background is in business psychology, and much of his early work involved examining stress in the workplace. Whilst carrying out this research, he discovered the downside of being a creature of habit.

Some people think and behave in highly inflexible ways. They might, for example, always try to solve problems using the same type of solutions, hold meetings in highly formulaic ways, and find comfort in the certainty that comes with their daily routines. In contrast, others embrace the unpredictable, enjoy lateral thinking, and are open to new ideas. Ben speculated that people who struggle to be flexible might be fine when they are working in an environment that is highly stable, but struggle when faced with the need to change and adapt.

To find out if his hunch was correct, Ben created a questionnaire to measure the degree to which a person's level of flexibility ('Do you sometimes behave in a way that your colleagues consider unconventional?', 'Do you get bothered when people change plans at the last minute?', 'You enjoy being presented with questions followed by a limited range of options – True or false?'*). He then went to several different types of companies, and asked the employees there to complete the questionnaire, rate how well they coped with change, and indicate how anxious they felt. The results revealed that inflexible people did indeed find change difficult, tended not to enjoy their jobs, and were especially anxious.[34]

Ben then wondered whether the same concept also applied to people's lives outside of their workplace. He speculated that many of the problems that people have in life are caused by them being inflexible and so tied to certain habits. Overweight people have got into the habit of eating too much and exercising too little. Smokers habitually reach into their pocket and light cigarettes. Many of those struggling to find a new relationship have got into the habit of going to the same sort of places and chatting to the same sort of people. What would happen, wondered Ben, if these people were encouraged to behave as if they were not creatures of habit?

---

* I made up the last one.

Rip it up

Muscle magic

People who are highly motivated often tense their muscles as they get ready to spring into action. But is the opposite also true? Can you boost your willpower by tensing your muscles?

Ris Hung from the National University of Singapore and his colleague decided to find out.[35] Hung assembled several groups of participants and asked them to keep their hands submerged in an ice bucket for as long as possible, consume a healthy but terrible-tasting vinegar drink, or visit a local cafeteria and buy healthy food rather than sugary snacks. Every time, half of the participants were asked to tighten certain muscles by making their hand into a fist, sitting down and lifting their heels off the floor, holding a pen by tightly weaving it between their fingers, or contracting their bicep. Each of these exercises was designed to make the participants behave as if they were trying hard to exert self-control. The results showed that those carrying out the exercises were more likely to keep their hand in the bucket of ice for longer, down more vinegar or buy healthier food.

Next time you feel your willpower draining away, try to tense a muscle. Consider, for example, making a fist, contracting your bicep, pressing your thumb and first finger together, or gripping a pen in your hand.

If all else fails, try crossing your arms. Another study, conducted by Ron Friedman and Andrew Elliot from the University of

Rochester, involved asking people to tackle difficult anagrams with either their arms crossed or resting on their thighs.[36] By folding their arms people were acting as if they were persistent. The volunteers with their arms folded continued to persevere for nearly twice as long as those with their hands on their thighs.

To find out what happens when people are encouraged to alter their habits, Ben teamed up with another university colleague, Karen Pine, and together they developed a technique known as 'Do Something Different' (or DSD for short). DSD consists of a series of exercises that encourage people to behave as if they have a flexible approach to life. They might, for example, be asked to stop watching television for a day, pen a poem, get in touch with an old friend, or travel to work using different routes (see box overleaf). Over the years Ben and Karen have monitored the effects of these simple techniques on many different areas of people's lives.

Take, for example, Ben and Karen's work on weight loss.[37] In several studies they recruited people who wanted to lose weight and randomly allocated them to different groups. One of the groups was encouraged to carry out the DSD techniques for a month. These participants were not told to eat a healthier diet or get more exercise. Instead, they were encouraged to vary their ways of thinking and behaving, such as going to bed an hour earlier or turning off their mobile phones for a day. In contrast, some of the other groups were either not given any instructions or followed a diet of their own choosing.

After tracking the groups over several months the results suggest that DSD helps people lose weight. Similar research has shown that the same technique can also help them stop smoking and increase their chances of finding a job.

Many undesirable behaviours, such as smoking and overeating, are the result of people behaving as if they are creatures of habit. By getting them to behave in a far more flexible fashion they begin to see themselves in a completely different way. Suddenly they are no longer someone who just mindlessly repeats old behavioural patterns, but rather a person who is able to take control their life and respond to their surroundings. To them it may seem like magic. In reality, it is another example of the *As If* principle at work.

Rip it up

Habit busting

Ben Fletcher and Karen Pine have created a large series of exercises designed to encourage people to change their habits.[38] The following techniques are based on their work and are designed to give you a flavour of this approach. Both of these exercises are designed to help motivate you by breaking old habits and getting you to behave as if you have a more flexible approach to life.

Exercise One: Try to break old habits by doing one of the following every few days:

- Tune into a television programme that you haven't seen before, listen to a new type of music, or read a different newspaper/news-site.
- Go to work using a new route.
- Try an unusual form of food.
- Visit a new art gallery or museum.
- Go to a shop that you have never visited before.
- Make time to see a film that you don't think you will enjoy.

Exercise Two: Complete the following questionnaire by ticking a box to indicate the extent to which you agree or disagree with each statement.

	Disagree strongly	Disagree moderately	Neither agree nor disagree	Agree moderately	Agree strongly
I see myself as . . .					
1) Moody	❑	❑	❑	❑	❑
2) Critical of others	❑	❑	❑	❑	❑
3) Bossy	❑	❑	❑	❑	❑
4) Self-centred	❑	❑	❑	❑	❑
5) Impatient	❑	❑	❑	❑	❑
6) Mature	❑	❑	❑	❑	❑
7) Stingy	❑	❑	❑	❑	❑
8) Messy	❑	❑	❑	❑	❑
9) Secretive	❑	❑	❑	❑	❑
10) Uncreative	❑	❑	❑	❑	❑

Which traits resulted in you ticking the 'Agree moderately' or 'Agree strongly' columns? Every few days, choose one of these traits and try to act in the opposite way. For example, if you indicated that you are a tad stingy, spend a few days trying to be more generous. Or if you said that you were critical of others, spend more time praising those around you.

The *As If* principle provides a new and exciting way of looking at the thorny issue of motivation. This principle explains why rewards often fail and, more importantly, provides the basis for several motivational tools that are both quick to implement and highly effective. If you carry out the smallest of commitments you are far more likely to engage with much bigger changes. Cross your arms, tense your muscles and sit up straight, and you will persevere longer when the going gets tough. Behave as if you are no longer a creature of habit and suddenly you will find it much easier to give up smoking and lose weight. These simple and quick techniques encourage you to change one small aspect of your behaviour. In so doing, the *As If* principle springs into action, and makes you feel like a new, and far more motivated, person.

5. PERSUASION

Where we explore the problems of changing people's minds, find out what really manipulates the masses, and discover how cooperation can shape society.

'How can I tell what I think till I see what I say?'

E. M. Forster, *Aspects of the Novel*

1. THE PROBLEMS OF PERSUASION

The Korean War saw two major conflicts. The first involved American and other pro-democracy forces fighting fierce battles with communist troops drawn from China and North Korea. The second conflict was fought behind the barbed wire fences of North Korea's prisoner-of-war camps, and was a battle for the hearts and minds of American service personnel captured during the fighting.

Hostilities officially came to an end in July 1953, with both sides agreeing to divide Korea into two separate countries. In January the following year the prisoner-of-war camps were shut down and captured service personnel released. It was only then that the full extent of the second conflict became apparent.

After the camps were closed, twenty-one American soldiers chose to remain in communist Korea, openly denouncing their own country and siding with an enemy that had killed over 30,000 of their comrades. In addition, a surprisingly large number of the American service personnel who did return home enthusiastically expounded the strengths of communism.

The family and friends of the servicemen who chose to remain in Korea were stunned, with one set of parents telling *Time* magazine: 'I won't believe anything except that my boy wants to return home.'[1] The world's media flocked to Korea to report the story, and asked psychologists to explain the soldiers' seemingly incomprehensible decision. Some researchers suggested that the Koreans had brainwashed the American soldiers with flashing lights and white noise. Others speculated that they had used advanced forms of hypnosis or mind-altering drugs. They were all wrong.

Understanding exactly what happened to the American soldiers reveals how the *As If* principle can be used to change the world. Our journey begins by venturing deep into the psychology of persuasion.

'When I read about the evils of drinking, I gave up reading'*

Governments spend large sums of money trying to persuade the public to stop smoking, avoid excessive drinking, and eat a healthier diet. These well-meaning campaigns often rest on one assumption: Tell people that their lifestyle is bad for them and they will soon change their ways. Let the public know, for instance, that smoking causes cancer and they will stop lighting up. Show them how alcoholism ruins lives and they will curb their drinking. Point out how fatty foods clog up the arteries and they will start eating more fresh fruit. There is, however, one small problem with this sensible approach: much of the time it doesn't work.

Irish comedian Andrew Maxwell recently made a television programme in which he went on a road trip with five people who firmly believed in various 9/11 conspiracy theories. One of the believers, Rodney, was certain that the Twin Towers were not destroyed by two hijacked aeroplanes but

---

* Attributed to comedian Henny Youngman.

instead collapsed because of a government-controlled explosion. Another member of the group, Charlotte, was equally sure that terrorists with such a limited amount of training would not have been able to fly the planes into the Twin Towers.

Maxwell took Rodney and Charlotte to meet several experts who presented overwhelming evidence against their cherished theories. In one sequence a demolition specialist showed just how difficult it would be to prepare charges to bring down buildings the size of the Twin Towers. Then, in another instance, a flight instructor demonstrated how easy it is to pilot modern-day aircraft. Did these experiences change Rodney and Charlotte's beliefs? Not at all. At the end of the programme they remained unmoved by the evidence and explained that they continued to believe that the events of 9/11 were the work of the American government.

Similarly, in 1997 members of the Heaven's Gate cult convinced themselves that they would soon be transported away from earth via a spaceship travelling behind the Hale-Bopp comet. A few weeks before the comet was due to come close to the earth some of the Heaven's Gate members visited a shop that sold scientific apparatus and purchased a sophisticated telescope. When the group looked through the high-powered lens they could clearly see the comet but not the spacecraft. It would be reasonable to think that the experience might have caused the group to question their beliefs. Instead, they returned to the shop the following day, explained that the telescope was faulty, and asked for their money back.[2]

It would be nice to think that when it comes to the rocky

relationship between evidence and belief, there is something rather special about Rodney, Charlotte, and the saucer-seeking members of the Heaven's Gate cult. Nice, but wrong. Although very few people think that the American government destroyed the Twin Towers or that spaceships lurk behind comets, we all hold other beliefs with similar levels of conviction. And when maintaining those beliefs in the face of disconfirming evidence, we are all capable of performing the type of mental gymnastics displayed by conspiracy theorists and cult members. Like them, we seek out the company of like-minded souls, avoid information that doesn't support our point of view, and question the integrity of those who dare to disagree with us. Despite our desire to be creatures of logic, if the facts don't fit our beliefs, we all find it surprisingly easy to ignore the facts.

One study, for example, tracked the public reaction to a comprehensive scientific report pointing out the strong link between smoking and cancer. An impressive 90 per cent of non-smokers said that they found the report convincing, compared to just 60 per cent of smokers.[3] In another study, participants were first asked to say whether they were pro or anti an important issue, such as climate change.[4] Then everyone was presented with various arguments about the topic, with some of the arguments being especially plausible ('Climate change is most probably due to the greenhouse effect') whilst others were extremely implausible ('Large numbers of scientists have been bribed to say that climate change is a reality'). The participants were asked to read each of the arguments and then remember as many as possible. If they were rational human beings then the participants should have remembered a mixture of plausible and implausible arguments. In fact, a clear pattern emerged, with those on both sides of the debate remembering the plausible arguments that supported their position and the implausible ones against it.

This 'I have made up my mind, don't confuse me with the facts' approach creates a major hurdle for governments wanting to change hearts and minds. Print 'Smoking Kills' in big black letters on packets of cigarettes and smokers will still find a way of convincing themselves that lighting up can't be all that bad. Tell heavy drinkers about the horrors of alcoholism and they will continue to believe that they will be fine. Run a campaign about the importance of healthy eating and the obese will still scoff impressive quantities of burgers and chips.

To make matters worse, this is just the tip of the iceberg.

On saying and doing

Psychologists have spent decades investigating the relationship between how people say they will behave and how they actually behave, not least the work of Leonard Bickman and his colleagues from Smith College in Massachusetts.[5]

Bickman wanted to discover the connection between people's beliefs and behaviour with something as simple as littering. He and his team found a busy high street and strategically placed crumpled-up pieces of paper several feet away from a rubbish bin, ensuring that the paper was in the direct path of pedestrians. Next, the experimenters moved across the street and secretly recorded the percentage of pedestrians who picked up the litter and placed it in the bin. It turned out that the good folk of Massachusetts weren't too tidy, with only 2 per cent of pedestrians picking up the paper and putting it in the bin.

In the next phase of the study the experimenters stopped hundreds of the pedestrians after they had walked past the litter and asked them one question: 'Should it be everyone's responsibility to pick up litter when they see it, or should it be left for the people whose job it is to pick it up?' What percentage of the pedestrians said that everyone should do their bit to keep the streets clean? Ten per cent? Forty per cent? Sixty per cent? In fact, a remarkable 94 per cent of the people who had just walked past the crumpled ball of paper said they firmly believed that it was everyone's job to pick up litter.

Bickman's research suggested that with littering, people are highly skilled at a kind of Orwellian double-think that allows them to think one thing but behave in a completely contradictory way.

Eager to discover whether this strange inconsistency applied to other areas of life, researchers turned their attention to a variety of important topics, including morality. Would you describe yourself as a moral person? Someone who generally tries to do the right thing, to settle arguments in a fair way, and to behave in an ethical fashion? Faced with this type of question almost everyone repeatedly ticks the 'Yes, that's me' box. But do people actually tend to *behave* in a moral and ethical way? Psychologist Daniel Batson from the University of Kansas decided to find out.[6]

Batson was interested in whether people who claim to be highly moral behave in a moral way, or whether they just rather like the idea of appearing moral but aren't so keen on the associated costs (a phenomenon that he has labelled 'moral hypocrisy'). In one study, Batson first asked a group of people to rate how moral they were by answering several questions about their ethics. Did they believe in a just world? Did they generally try to do the right thing? Were they selfish, or concerned for the welfare of others?

A few weeks later Batson invited the same group of people to his laboratory, one at a time and asked them to take part in an experiment. Each participant was told that the study involved a second person who was currently secreted in an adjoining room. He then explained that one of them would be given a raffle ticket that could result in them winning a large prize, whilst the other would spend thirty minutes adding up a series of numbers.

Next, Batson suggested that the allocation of the raffle ticket and number-adding task should be made on the basis of a coin toss, and asked the participant if they thought this was a fair approach to the issue. When the participant agreed, Batson explained that if the coin landed heads side up then they would get the raffle ticket and the person in the next room would be given the number list. If, however, the coin landed tails side up then the participant would be handed the number list and the person in the next room would get the raffle ticket.

Finally, Batson handed the coin to the participant and explained that they should step into the corridor, flip the coin, and then return to the laboratory and report whether it had come up heads or tails. He explained that he had no way of knowing the actual outcome of the coin toss and so was relying on the participant to tell the truth.

The results revealed something deeply strange. By chance, the coin should have come up heads half the time. However,

90 per cent of the participants returned to the laboratory grinning like a Cheshire cat, explained that the coin had come up heads, and claimed their raffle ticket. In short, there was evidence that a large number of the participants were being a tad economical with the truth. Were the participants who had previously rated themselves as being highly moral more honest than the others? When push came to shove even those who had previously claimed to hang out on the moral high ground couldn't bring themselves to tell the truth.

Batson's findings show that even for something as deep-seated and important as our sense of morality, often beliefs do not predict behaviour.

Manufacturing a lack of consent

The findings from the research on littering and morality are not an exception. Time and again, psychologists have discovered that people are highly skilled at holding one belief but behaving in a completely contradictory way.[7] Given the problems associated with changing beliefs and behaviour, it is not surprising that many government campaigns have struggled to make a difference, and a good example is 'The Hutchinson Smoking Prevention Project'.[8]

In the late eighties and early nineties the National Cancer Institute in the United States spent around 15 million dollars creating and assessing a large-scale campaign designed to prevent children from smoking. Part experiment and part public education programme, more than 4,000 children from twenty randomly chosen school districts in Seattle were bombarded with information designed to prevent them lighting up. For months these children attended special lessons and were given all sorts of helpful anti-smoking advice, including how to resist peer pressure and ignore tobacco advertising. Another 4,000 children in a different twenty districts weren't given this information and so acted as a control group.

The researchers then tracked down the vast majority of the children two years after they had left high school and asked them whether they smoked. Worried that they might not tell the whole truth about their smoking habits, the investigators even went to the effort of measuring the amount of nicotine-based chemicals in the teenagers' saliva. The results were as dramatic as they were disappointing. Had the anti-smoking campaign produced the intended effect? Of the children who came from the districts that had run the campaign 29 per cent smoked, versus 28 per cent of children from the control districts. Spending millions in an attempt to prevent children from smoking had had almost no impact.

Unfortunately, this is not an isolated example. Another American national anti-smoking campaign encouraged parents to try to dissuade their children from smoking using the slogan 'Talk. They'll Listen'. The result? Children displayed an age-old tendency to disobey authority figures, with the campaign ads making them *less* likely to believe that smoking was dangerous and *more* likely to say that they intended to smoke ('Don't Talk: Otherwise they'll do the complete opposite').[9] In Britain, the Department of Health spent more than 3 million pounds encouraging the public to eat five portions of vegetables a day, only to see vegetable consumption drop by around 11 per cent.[10] And between the late 1990s and 2004 the US Congress gave almost 1 billion dollars to fund an extensive anti-drug media campaign, only to discover that the ads had failed to persuade teenagers to avoid smoking marijuana and might have actively encouraged some to try it.[11]

Realizing that the conventional approaches to changing hearts and minds frequently failed to produce results, researchers started to examine other ways of transforming attitudes and beliefs. Eventually, a young psychologist fresh out of graduate school came up with a radical idea that changed the entire course of behavioural science.

Rip it up

Manufacturing consent – Part One

Please complete the following questionnaire by giving each statement a rating between 1 (strongly disagree) and 5 (strongly agree).

Statement	Rating
1 I leave the tap running while I clean my teeth.	1 2 3 4 5
2 I catch a flight when I could have travelled by car or train.	1 2 3 4 5
3 The light bulbs in my house and office are not energy efficient.	1 2 3 4 5
4 I don't place my rubbish in recycling bags.	1 2 3 4 5
5 I buy new goods rather than second-hand ones.	1 2 3 4 5
6 I leave lights on when I leave a room.	1 2 3 4 5
7 I strongly support the idea of green living.	1 2 3 4 5

Many thanks. More about this later.

2. WHY SAYING IS BELIEVING

Around the turn of the last century sociologist William Graham Sumner argued that certain beliefs are biologically ingrained in the human brain. Sumner referred to these beliefs as 'folkways' and declared they were extremely difficult to change. In 1896 the United States Supreme Court was required to rule on the legality of racial segregation. Many of those in favour of segregation argued that the notion of one race being superior to another constituted one of Sumner's folkways, and thus any attempt to legislate against it would be futile. The Supreme Court was swayed by the argument and, citing the maxim that 'law-ways cannot change folkways', ruled that all American citizens should have access to the same public services but that there could be separate facilities for each race. In reality, the facilities available to African -Americans were usually of a much lower quality than those available to others.

From the middle of the 1940s onwards the American Civil Rights movement worked hard to overturn the racial segregation laws, and in the early 1950s the Supreme Court was required to re-examine the legality of segregated schools. Lawyers in favour of desegregation argued that the 1896 'separate but equal' doctrine was unconstitutional, in part because it created a sense of inferiority among African-American children. The legal teams supported their case by citing the work of several behavioural scientists, including psychologists Kenneth and Mamie Clark.

In a series of now-classic studies the Clarks had asked African-American children to select either a white or black doll, and then describe the chosen doll's character.[12] Almost all of the children preferred the white doll and attributed positive characteristics to it, and the Clarks argued that the results provided a vivid demonstration of how segregated schools caused African-American children to suffer low self-esteem. The arguments proved persuasive, and in 1954 the Supreme Court unanimously ruled that separate educational facilities were unconstitutional. Other similar rulings quickly followed, including the courts coming down against racial segregation on buses and other forms of public transport.

At the time of the rulings, social psychologist Daryl Bem was a graduate student at the University of Michigan. Although originally intending to study physics, Bem had become fascinated by the impact of the Civil Rights movement on public belief, and switched to psychology. He decided to analyse the results of surveys examining the attitudes of white Americans towards racial segregation before and after the 1954 Supreme Court ruling. His analysis soon revealed a rather curious pattern.

Before the landmark decision only a minority of white Americans supported desegregation. For instance, in a survey undertaken in 1942, only 30 per cent of white Americans were in favour of school integration, 35 per cent approved of residential integration and 44 per cent supported integrated transport. However, just two years after the Supreme Court's decision the numbers had significantly increased, with a 1956 survey showing 49 per cent now supporting school integration, 51 per cent approving of residential integration, and 60 per cent favouring integrated transport.[13]

For years the American Civil Rights movement had struggled to gain public support for desegregation. Now, within just a few years of the Supreme Court ruling, far more white Americans supported the idea than ever before. Eager to explain this curious effect, Bem searched through various psychology textbooks and eventually came across William James's work on behaviour and emotion.

As we discovered in chapter 1, according to the *As If* principle, behaviour causes emotion. When, for example, people smile they feel happy, and when they frown, they feel sad. Bem wondered whether the principle does not just determine how people feel, but also affects what they believe. Common sense suggests that thoughts create behaviour. Imagine, for example, that you want to go out one evening and have the choice of seeing a film or a play. You know that you prefer films to plays, and so head for the cinema. In this example your thought ('I prefer films to plays') caused your behaviour (going to the cinema). Following in James's footsteps, Bem turned this common-sense view of the human psyche on its head, and suggested that your behaviour influences what you believe. So if, for instance, you want to go out for the evening and are subtly persuaded to go to the theatre you would look at your behaviour and unconsciously think 'Hold on, here I am watching a play. I guess I must enjoy the theatre more than the cinema.' As a result, you would end up feeling surprisingly positive towards the theatre (see diagram, overleaf).

Common sense suggests that the chain of causation is:

I like films ⟶ Go to the cinema

The *As If* theory suggests that the reality is:

Go to the cinema ⟶ I must like films

This extension of the *As If* principle into the heady world of thought control could explain why the Supreme Court's ruling about desegregation caused a sea change in public belief. The legal ruling required people to behave as if they supported desegregation. This, in turn, caused them to unconsciously think 'Hold on, here I am behaving as if I support desegregation. I guess I must believe that racial equality is a good idea'. As a result they then developed a new and much more positive view about desegregation.

Although the surveys before and after racial desegregation supported the *As If* principle, they did not provide conclusive proof as the seismic shift in public opinion could have been due to other factors, such as the extensive campaigning by the Civil Rights movement. Eager to discover whether the *As If* principle really did affect what people believe, researchers retreated to their laboratories and conducted a series of systematic experiments.

Comment and commitment

The Vietnam War cost the lives of more than 50,000 American soldiers. To bolster public support during the war the American government frequently attempted to put a positive spin on the conflict, arguing that the Communist North of the country would soon be defeated or that the South would soon become sufficiently strong enough to defend itself. President Lyndon B. Johnson was responsible for sending more troops to the country than any other leader. From time to time Johnson became aware that members of his administration were privately expressing concerns about the war. Did Johnson pull these politicians into his office and try to explain his point of view? Not at all. Instead, he used a far more unusual tactic. He sent the doubters on a 'fact-finding' mission to the country, along with a group of reporters.[14]

Johnson was well aware that members of his administration would be unlikely to express their private doubts in public, and would instead be forced to give high-profile speeches defending the government's policies. The *As If* principle predicted that the doubters would hear themselves giving pro-Johnson speeches and eventually come to believe their own remarks.

Researchers used the same approach in their laboratory tests to examine whether the *As If* principle influenced what people believed. To find out, researchers invited participants into the laboratory and asked them to complete questionnaires about their political beliefs.[15] Next, half of the participants were asked to give a short speech in which they argued in favour of a political party that they opposed, whilst the others watched these speeches through a two-way mirror. Two weeks later all of the participants completed another questionnaire about their views.

The *As If* principle predicts that those who had given the speeches would have seen themselves supporting a political party, and so come to believe that perhaps this party wasn't so bad after all. In contrast, those just hearing the speeches would have received exactly the same information but, because they didn't see themselves arguing the point, would not have changed their beliefs. The results supported the theory, with just a few minutes of role-play achieving what a constant bombardment of campaigning and political ads had failed to do.

Over the years the same procedure has been used in many different contexts. People have been filmed presenting talks in favour of a whole host of issues such as abortion, the dangers of drink-driving, and greater police powers. On each occasion, behaving as if they believed a certain argument achieved what a hundred rational reasons couldn't; quickly changing their attitudes in favour of the position they were asked to support.[16]

Indeed, the depth of change is such that the participants often deny ever holding their original opinions, and if they are shown their original questionnaires they argue the forms have been faked or claim they misread the questions.[17]

This mechanism also accounts for many otherwise inexplicable shifts in belief. At the start of this chapter, I described how, at the end of the Korean War, a large number of the servicemen decided to remain in Korea, and many of those who did return home enthused about the benefits of communism.

Extensive interviews with those who had survived the harsh conditions of the camps revealed that these beliefs had not been instilled with the help of hypnotism, drugs or physical punishment.[18] Instead, the Chinese authorities had deliberately employed the *As If* principle to alter the minds of the American prisoners of war.

This unusual form of mind control often started the moment the prisoners entered the camps, with the guards shaking the hands of the new detainees and saying, 'Congratulations, you've been liberated.' During the next few weeks the prisoners were required to attend long lectures on the benefits of communism, and then asked to discuss the talks in small groups. A member of the Chinese Communist party was often assigned to each group to help ensure the prisoners reached the 'correct' conclusions. If anyone in the group openly displayed any anti-communist sentiments then all of the prisoners had to endure the lecture and discussion again.

Shortly after capture, the Chinese guards also asked the servicemen to jot down a few short pro-communist statements ('Communism is wonderful', 'Communism is the way of the future', and 'Communism is the most enlightened form of government'). Many of the Americans were happy to oblige because the request seemed so trivial and compliance was often rewarded with a small bar of soap or some cigarettes. A few weeks later the guards upped the ante and asked the prisoners to read the statements aloud to themselves. Once again, most agreed. A couple of weeks later the Americans were asked to read the statements out to their fellow prisoners, and finally to engage in mock debates arguing why they believed the statements to be correct.

In addition, highly valued goods, such as fresh fruit or sweets, were offered to any soldiers who were prepared to write pro-communist essays for the camp newsletter. When the essays were published the authors were asked to wear a Mao Tse-tung badge and excused unpleasant camp chores. Many of the prisoners were again happy to oblige.

Over time such behaviour caused many of the American prisoners to change their attitudes towards communism, and even persuaded some to stay in Korea rather than return home. The *As If* principle helps explain this dramatic change in belief: the Chinese did not have to resort to physical punishment or arcane brainwashing techniques, all they had to do was ensure that the prisoners saw themselves repeatedly saying they supported communism, and then leave them alone to develop beliefs that were consistent with their comments.

The same effect can be used to influence entire populations.[19] Saying 'Heil Hitler' every day would have encouraged many ordinary Germans to become more open to Nazi ideology. Having people repeatedly sing a national anthem will make them more patriotic. Making children pray every morning increases the likelihood of them adopting religious beliefs.

In each instance, saying becomes believing. Intrigued by this research, some people started to examine if other types of behaviour also had the power to persuade. Perhaps the two best-known examples focused on eye colour and the creation of the 'Third Wave'.

Rip it up

One finger, one thumb, keep moving

The *As If* principle has the power to radically change people's ideological beliefs. This same 'behaviour creates belief' process can also be used to shape people's thoughts about many aspects of their everyday lives.

It's time for a quick experiment. Please hold out your thumb as if you are giving a 'thumb's-up' sign and then read the following paragraph:

> Donald was faced with a difficult situation. For the past few months he had been renting a flat, but now wanted to move out. His contract had expired but his landlord was refusing to return his deposit. After repeatedly asking for his money back, Donald became more and more angry. One day, he finally lost the plot, picked up the telephone, and shouted a stream of abuse at his landlord.

What do you think of Donald? Do you approve of his behaviour in this particular instance? Now extend your middle finger as if you are giving someone the 'bird' and then read the paragraph again. What do you think of Donald and his behaviour this time?

In most Western countries, raising your middle finger towards someone is usually a sign that you don't like them, whereas giving them the 'thumbs-up' is a far more positive signal. In each instance, whether you like or dislike a person influences your behaviour. But could the opposite also be true? Could your gestures change the way you think about a person?

This mini-experiment is based on a study conducted by Jesse Chandler from the University of Michigan.[20] Chandler invited a group of participants into his laboratory and explained that they were going to take part in an experiment about gestures and language. The participants were first asked to either extend their middle finger or hold out their thumbs, and then read about Donald and his landlord. At the end of the story participants were asked to rate how much they liked Donald. When people read the story with their middle finger raised they thought that Donald was an aggressive man. In contrast, when they read the story with their thumb raised they found him far less aggressive and much more likeable.

Two key implications flow from the work. First, on a theoretical level it demonstrates how just a few seconds behaving 'As If' can influence what you think about someone. Second, on a more practical level, if you're struggling to get on with a work colleague, try giving them the 'thumbs-up' on a regular basis.

When it comes to everyday persuasion, this is just the tip of the iceberg.

In another study, for example, students were asked to listen to a discussion suggesting their tuition fees should be increased.[21] Some of the students were asked to nod their heads up and down whilst they listened to the discussion (causing them to nod as if they agreed with the arguments), whilst others moved their heads from side to side (resulting in them shaking their heads as if they disagreed). The students were then asked how much their annual tuition fees should be. Those who had been shaking their heads from side to side produced much lower estimates than those who had been happily nodding away. Want to encourage someone to agree with you? Then subtly nod your head as you chat with them. They will reciprocate the movement and find themselves strangely attracted to your way of thinking.

Then there is the issue of chairs. In another study experimenters had participants sit on either a hard wooden chair or a soft cushioned chair, and then asked them to role-play negotiating for a new car with a stranger and rate the personality of the stranger. Those in the hard chairs were more inflexible in their negotiations and saw the strangers as less likeable. In short, evidence that hard furniture creates hard behaviour, emphasizing the importance of soft furnishings in your home and office.

3. MANIPULATING THE MASSES

In the late 1960s Jane Elliott was working as a primary school teacher in Riceville, Iowa. On 4 April 1968 Martin Luther King Jr. was assassinated and Elliott decided to hold a class discussion about racism. She was disappointed with the impact of the lesson, and began to think about other ways of getting her pupils to engage with the topic. That evening, she devised a daring plan.[22]

The following day, Elliott told her class that children with blue eyes were superior to those with brown eyes. At first many pupils were sceptical, and so the quick-thinking Elliott created some pseudoscience to support her claim, explaining that blue eyes were the result of melanin and that research had shown that the same chemical was linked to higher intelligence.

The majority of the pupils bought the pseudoscience and she proceeded with the next phase of the exercise. Because the blue-eyed children were superior, explained Elliott, they would be given special privileges, including second helpings at lunch, extra long breaks, and the opportunity to sit at the front of the class. In contrast, the brown-eyed children were treated like second-class citizens. They were encouraged to play only with other brown-eyed children and not allowed to drink from the blue-eyed children's water fountain. To make the difference between the blue-eyed and brown-eyed pupils especially obvious, Elliot also had each group of children wear different-coloured scarves.

Suddenly the *As If* principle kicked in and the enforced changes in behaviour resulted in a dramatic shift in the children's personalities. The blue-eyed children became arrogant and bossy, whilst the brown-eyed children became timid and subservient. As a result, the blue-eyed children started to outperform the brown-eyed children on various tests.

A few days later Elliott told her class that she had made an error, and that actually it was the brown-eyed children that were superior to the blue-eyed children. Suddenly, the children's sense of identity flipped, with the blue-eyed children becoming much more reserved, and the brown-eyed children acting in a far more assertive way. On the final day of the exercise, she revealed that there was no difference between blue-eyed and brown-eyed children, explained that the exercise had been designed to help the class understand what it feels like to be the subject of discrimination, and told the children to take off their scarves. Many of Elliott's children cried and hugged one another.

The media caught wind of Elliott's exercise and she was eventually invited onto Johnny Carson's *Tonight Show*. Although viewers across America were touched by the story, many Riceville residents thought the item gave the impression that their town was a hotbed of racism. As a result, many of Elliott's colleagues refused to speak to her, and her family was subjected to verbal and physical abuse.

Unperturbed, Elliott repeated the exercise many times over the following decades. Time and again, the same results emerged, with the children's behaviour quickly affecting their beliefs about one another. As adults, many of those who took part in Elliott's exercise describe how the experience completely changed the way they viewed the disenfranchised and powerless in society.

Elliott eventually left teaching in the mid-1980s to become a full-time diversity trainer.[23]

Around the same time Elliott was handing out privileges on the basis of eye colour, another teacher was attempting to use the same technique to create a microcosm of Nazi Germany.

In 1967, a charismatic twenty-five-year-old history teacher and basketball coach named Ron Jones was working at a senior high school in Palo Alto, California.[24] Ever keen to explore new methods of teaching, Jones decided to employ an unusual hands-on approach to explaining some of the factors that contributed to the formation of Nazi Germany.

At the start of one of his lessons, Jones lectured about the beauty of discipline and self-control. In order to emphasize his point, he had his students repeatedly sit up straight, put their feet flat on the floor, and place their hands flat across the small of their backs.

On the following day, he spoke about the value of community and had his class repeatedly recite the phrase 'Strength through Community'. At the end of the lesson he also created a 'class salute', explaining how his students needed to bring their right hand up to their right shoulder in a curled position. When the end of lesson bell sounded Jones slowly carried out the action and saw his entire class return the salute.

The next day Jones gave each of his students a 'membership card', and asked them to help enlist other students into a newly formed organization called the 'Third Wave'. Every member was also encouraged to report anyone openly expressing scepticism about the project.

Word about the Third Wave quickly spread throughout the school, with some students creating banners and leaflets to promote the cause. Soon, Jones's organization boasted over a hundred members, with many students developing highly authoritarian characteristics and demanding strict obedience of the rules. Jones decided that his experiment was getting out of hand and decided to call an end to the project. He announced that all members of the Third Wave should meet in the school's auditorium for a special announcement.

Over 200 students gathered at the appointed hour, with many wearing white shirts and home-made armbands. Jones turned on a projector, and showed the group images depicting the history of the Third Reich and the Nuremberg rallies. As the final frame faded, he announced that the exercise was designed to show how easily people's behaviour and beliefs can be manipulated, and to emphasize the need for everyone to take responsibility for their actions. Many of the students started crying as the reality of the situation hit them.

A few years after Jones conducted his experiment he was refused tenure, and has since spent over thirty years writing, speaking and working with people with mental disabilities. His work was subsequently described in the novel *The Wave*, which became required reading in many German schools. In 2008 the experiment acted as the inspiration for the German film *Die Welle*, and in 2010 Jones staged a musical about his project.

Rip it up

Manufacturing consent – Part Two

Please complete the following questionnaire by giving each statement a rating between 1 (strongly disagree) and 5 (strongly agree).

Statement	Rating
1 I don't leave the tap running whilst I clean my teeth.	1 2 3 4 5
2 I rarely catch a flight when I could have travelled by car or train.	1 2 3 4 5
3 Few of the light bulbs in my house and office are not energy efficient.	1 2 3 4 5
4 I place my rubbish in recycling bags.	1 2 3 4 5
5 When I can, I buy second-hand goods rather than new ones.	1 2 3 4 5
6 I don't leave lights on when I leave a room.	1 2 3 4 5
7 I strongly support the idea of green living.	1 2 3 4 5

Please look at the answer that you have just given to Question 7. Next, flick back to page 236 and look at the answer that you gave to the same question during Part One of the exercise. According to research conducted by psychologist Shelly Chaiken from New York University, it is likely that you will have given a lower rating first time around.[25]

Chaiken's work shows that the relationship between the *As If* principle and belief also applies to the way in which people think about the past. The questionnaire in the first part of the exercise asked about times when you *didn't* act in an environmentally friendly way by, for example, not turning off the tap when you cleaned your teeth or took a plane when you could have gone by train. In contrast, the questionnaire in the second exercise asked about times when your behaviour was much more green, such as when you recycle or turn off the lights when you leave a room.

The *As If* principle causes people to complete the first questionnaire and think, 'Well, I don't behave as if I am an environmentally-friendly person, so I don't support green living', whilst the second questionnaire makes them think: 'Well, my behaviour seems very pro-environment, so I must hold green views.'

By reminding people of specific aspects of their past and present behaviour, questionnaires like this can be used to manufacture, rather than simply measure, belief.

4. ON THE JUSTIFICATION OF ACTION

In 2004 the American magazine programme *60 Minutes* broadcast a shocking report about the terrible abuse being inflicted on prisoners held at Iraq's Abu Ghraib prison. According to the report, American soldiers had carried out a range of physical and psychological abuse, including beating, rape and torture. The world was shocked to see photographs of prisoners being pulled around like dogs, being led to believe that they were about to be electrocuted, and being piled naked in prison corridors. The United States Department of Defense responded by removing several soldiers from duty, with many of them subsequently charged with a range of offences. One question weighed heavily on the public's mind: how did the soldiers come to commit such terrible atrocities?

A key part of the answer centres around the *As If* principle.

One of Aesop's best-known fables concerns a fox and a bunch of grapes. According to the story, a fox is strolling through an orchard when he happens to see a lovely-looking bunch of grapes hanging from a lofty branch. Realizing he is thirsty, the fox draws back a few paces and takes a running jump at the grapes. Unfortunately he misses the bunch. Never one to give up easily, the fox tries a second jump, but once again misses the grapes. Throughout the afternoon the fox repeatedly attempts to reach the branch, but fails each time.

Eventually he gives up, walks away from the orchard empty-mouthed, and convinces himself that he doesn't want the grapes because they are probably sour.

In addition to providing the basis for the popular idiom 'sour grapes', the story provides a perfect illustration of the *As If* principle. The fox started off believing that the grapes looked great, but when he was forced to leave the orchard without them he formed a new and negative view of them. In short, the fox looked first at his actions and then created a new belief to justify them.

A small group of researchers decided to discover whether the same process influences people's beliefs. Would they, for instance, decide they disliked objects that they couldn't obtain, and become especially fond of those within their grasp?

In one series of studies participants were first asked to rate how much they liked several products, such as a coffee maker, sandwich grill, toaster, portable radio and so on.[26] Next, the experimenters selected two items that had received the same rating, showed them to the participant, and asked them to choose one of the items as a gift. The chosen item was then put in a box, securely tied with string, and placed next to the participant's coat. All of this was designed to give the participant the impression that they would be taking the object home with them (in reality the experimenters were on a tight budget and so reclaimed their 'gift' the moment the study had finished). Finally, the participant was asked to rate the desirability of both items a second time.

Before making their decision the participant had indicated that both objects were equally appealing. However, according to the *As If* principle, the moment people behave as if they like one item more than the other they justify their actions by convincing themselves that they are especially fond of the chosen object. The results confirmed the theory – the participants suddenly found their chosen item significantly more desirable than before.

In another study, researchers left their laboratories and headed for the racetrack.[27] They randomly selected a group of people who were just about to place their bets and asked them to rate the chances of their horse winning the race. On average people said that their horse had a 'fair' chance. The research team then approached another group of people seconds after they had placed their bet and asked them the same question. According to conventional theories of belief, their confidence should be the roughly the same pre- and post-bet. However, the *As If* principle predicts that people unconsciously think 'Well, I have just seen myself placing my bet, so I must be pretty certain that my horse will win', and so feel more confident about their decision. As the researchers discovered, participants who had just handed over their betting slips now rated their chosen horse as having an 'excellent' chance of being first past the post.

Rip it up

The power of warm

From an early age we associate the feeling of warmth with safety and security (think hugs and open fires), and coldness with unfriendliness (think 'getting the cold shoulder' and 'icy stare'). Inspired by this notion, psychologist Chen-Bo Zhong from Northwestern University decided to discover whether being excluded from the group really does make people feel a little chilly.[28] For example, in one experiment Zhong gathered together a group of people, asked one half of them to think about a time in their lives when they had felt rejected by others, and the other half to remember an experience in which they had been accepted as part of a group. Everyone was then asked to estimate the temperature of the room they were in. Remarkably, those who had simply thought about a time when they were alone rated the room as significantly colder than those who had imagined themselves being part of a group. It seems that loneliness does indeed make people feel physically cold. Zhong believes this association between warmth and social inclusion may start early in life, with children who are hugged by their parents feeling a sense of belonging and physical warmth.

Given that lonely people feel physically cold, the *As If* principle predicts that warming people up should make them feel far more friendly. Research conducted by University of Colorado psychologist Lawrence Williams suggests this is indeed the case.[29]

Williams conducted an experiment in which participants were handed either a hot cup of coffee or a cold drink, asked to read a short description of a stranger, and then asked to rate the stranger's personality. The participants who had been warmed up by the coffee thought the stranger seemed much friendlier than those who had been clutching the iced drink.

The implications are obvious – if you are trying to befriend someone, skip the frozen cocktails in an air-conditioned bar and instead opt for a steaming mug of tea in front of a roaring fire.

This effect emerges in many other situations. Imagine, for example, going shopping for a winter jacket and seeing an entire rack of great-looking coats. All of the jackets are very attractive and it takes you hours to decide which one to buy. However, the instant you pass your credit card over to the cashier you suddenly start to justify your behaviour by thinking about all the reasons why your coat is obviously so much better than the ones you left on the rack. Within moments your behaviour has caused you to form a new belief and now you become certain that you have made the right decision. Unfortunately, the effect can create unhealthy levels of overconfidence, causing politicians to doggedly pursue failing policies, companies to continue promoting unsuccessful products, and investors to carry on supporting poor initiatives.

The *As If* principle does not just explain how people's behaviour can cause them to become overconfident. It also accounts for some of the surprising effects that can emerge whenever people decide to do something that deep down they really don't want to do.

In the 1960s psychologist Jack Brehm from Duke University in the United States carried out work to explore whether the *As If* principle can be used to change the way children view vegetables.[30] Brehm first asked about fifty children to rate the degree to which they liked each item on a long list of vegetables. A few weeks later he told the children that he was interested in whether their perception of vegetables would change after they had eaten them, and asked them whether they would mind tasting a randomly selected vegetable. In reality, the vegetables were not randomly selected. Instead, Brehm had gone shopping and bought the very vegetables that each of the children disliked. Each child was presented with a serving of their despised vegetable, and asked to try and eat three portions of it each week for the next few weeks. A month later Brehm tracked down the children, presented them with the long list of vegetables, and again asked them to rate each of the items. The *As If* principle predicts that the children would have seen themselves eating the vegetables and justified their behaviour by convincing themselves that they must quite like the food after all. And this is what happened. The message from Brehm's study is clear – persuade someone to do something they don't enjoy and often they will end up justifying their actions by convincing themselves it is not so bad after all.

This curious phenomenon helps explain why legislation often results in a significant shift in public opinion. When smoking in public places was banned in Britain, many smokers found it much harder to light up and so came to adopt an anti-smoking attitude. Similarly, when the British government passed a law that made wearing a seat belt compulsory, opinion polls showed that many people started to believe that buckling up was a good idea. In each instance, as the *As If* principle suggests, people's behaviour caused them to adopt certain beliefs.

However, whilst some changes can be positive, the same idea can also cause pain and suffering.

A few years ago psychologist David Glass from Ohio State University conducted a remarkable experiment.[31] Glass invited people to his laboratory one at a time and introduced them to another participant (actually a stooge working for the experimenters). The participant and stooge were allowed to chat for a few minutes and then the participant was asked to answer a few questions about their new-found friend, including whether they would admit the person into their circle of close friends and whether they would like to share a flat with them.

Next, honouring a long-held tradition in social psychology experiments, the experimenter explained that the two participants would now carry out a study in which one of them would attempt to learn a long list of words and the other would give them an electric shock every time they made a mistake. The experimenter flipped a coin to assign the two tasks and yes, you guessed it, the genuine participant was asked to administer the shocks. Following this, the participant then went into the room containing the controls to the shock machine and the stooge went into an adjoining room.

The two rooms were connected with an intercom that allowed the participant to hear the stooge. Each time the stooge made a mistake (which turned out to be surprisingly frequent) the participant thought that they were delivering a hundred-volt shock (in reality, the machine was disconnected and the stooge was quietly sitting next door enjoying a sandwich).

After administering several shocks the participant was asked how they felt about what they had done and to again rate the degree to which they liked the stooge. They could have concluded that they were a bad person or were following orders. However, most participants were reluctant to think badly of themselves, and justified their behaviour by saying that their fellow participant was not such a nice person after all and so was deserving of the shocks. As the *As If* principle predicts, the participants formed a new belief on the basis of their behaviour. In this situation, they behaved as if they didn't like a person and so ended up believing that that person was dislikeable and deserving of punishment.

At the start of this section I described how American soldiers abused prisoners in Iraq's Abu Ghraib prison. Glass's research illustrates how the *As If* principle helps explain the atrocities. If a guard with high self-esteem administers a small but illegal punishment to a prisoner, the guard may convince himself that the prisoner is a bad person and so deserving of such treatment. This may then cause him to believe that they are justified in carrying out more abuse that, in turn, causes them to believe the prisoner is deserving of even greater punishment. If this process remains unchecked over time it can feed on itself, resulting in a situation that quickly spirals out of control and creates the type of shocking behaviour seen in Abu Ghraib.

Fortunately, not all of the research into how the *As If* principle affects what people think is so gloomy. On a more positive note, other research has shown how the principle can also be used to bond people together and even saves lives.

Rip it up

Charisma, empathy and the *As If* principle

Please rate the degree to which you agree with the following statements by assigning each of them a rating between 1 (strongly disagree) and 5 (strongly agree).

Statement	Rating
1 I often find myself tapping my feet along to music.	1 2 3 4 5
2 I feel sad when I see someone who looks lonely.	1 2 3 4 5
3 I enjoy hugging people.	1 2 3 4 5
4 I care a great deal about animals.	1 2 3 4 5
5 I find it easy to make others laugh.	1 2 3 4 5
6 I quickly become anxious if people around me become nervous.	1 2 3 4 5
7 I find it very easy to 'catch someone's eye'.	1 2 3 4 5
8 I often cry when I see a romantic film or hear a love song.	1 2 3 4 5
9 People often describe me as the life and soul of the party.	1 2 3 4 5
10 I enjoy giving people presents and looking at their faces when they open them.	1 2 3 4 5

Ask people to name a charismatic figure and they are likely to come up with the likes of Martin Luther King, Nelson Mandela, John F. Kennedy, and Barack Obama. However, ask them to explain why these people possess the X-factor and they will struggle to define this elusive quality.

We all mimic the facial expressions and body language of those around us.[32] This process happens unconsciously, automatically, and in the blink of an eye. When you see someone smile, the sides of your mouth start to move towards your ears. Similarly, if you are faced with a frown, your brow begins to furrow. This process allows emotions to spread from one person to another, and has evolved to promote group empathy and cohesion.

Some people are naturally skilled at using their face, body and voice to induce their own emotions in others. Research conducted by psychologist Howard Friedman from the University of California shows that such people are seen as highly charismatic.[33] These individuals are able to induce in those around them the passion and energy that they feel, often initiating a wave of emotional contagion that spreads from one person to the next. This process can make an entire room feel highly energized and transfix an audience of thousands. Charismatic communicators bypass the normal paths to persuasion, making people feel rather than think, and so speak directly to the heart.

Similarly, other people will be especially good at 'catching' other people's emotions. In one experiment, Per Andréasson from the Uppsala University in Sweden first asked a group of participants to rate how empathic they were, and then showed them photographs of people who were either happy or angry.[34] When the highly empathic participants saw a happy face, the muscles around the sides of their mouth suddenly burst into action. In contrast, the participants who had indicated that they had a low sense of empathy showed almost no reaction. Similarly, when the highly empathic participants saw an angry face their eyes instantly started to narrow, whereas the low empaths kept a straight face. By behaving as if they are experiencing the emotions of those around them, highly empathic people literally feel the pain and joy of others.

The questionnaire at the start of this section measures the degree to which you are able to send and receive emotions.[35] To discover your charisma score, add up your responses to the *odd* numbered questions (Questions 1, 3, 5, 7, and 9). To find out your empathic score, add up your responses to the *even* numbered questions (Questions 2, 4, 6, 8, and 10).

Charisma score:

Scores between 5 and 15 are classified as Low, scores between 16 and 25 as High.

Empathy score:

Scores between 5 and 15 are classified as Low, scores between 16 and 25 as High.

5. FROM BEHAVIOUR TO BONDING

Muzafer Sherif was born in Turkey in 1906. When Sherif was a teenager he witnessed some of the atrocities carried out by the Greek Army during the Greco-Turkish War. Appalled at seeing innocent Turkish citizens robbed, tortured and killed, Sherif wanted to understand why people sometimes behave in such savage ways. He enrolled for a degree in psychology, then emigrated to America to continue his education at Harvard University, and eventually went on to enjoy a highly successful academic career.

During his time in America, Sherif conducted a highly controversial experiment to help explain some of the terrible scenes that he had witnessed as a teenager.[36] In so doing, he also inadvertently carried out an impressive test of whether the *As If* principle can be used to move people emotionally closer to one another.

Sherif first needed to find some unsuspecting volunteers to take part in his experiment. He hung around several school playgrounds, secretly observing groups of twelve-year-old boys ('And that, m'lord, rests the case for the defence'). He was on the lookout for boys who seemed psychologically stable, reasonably popular, and of normal intelligence. Whenever Sherif saw a boy who seemed to fit the bill, he scurried away and checked his school reports to ensure that he was not prone to temper tantrums and had a good attendance record. Over time, he assembled a list of possible pupils and moved on to the second stage of the selection process. Sherif arranged to meet the boy's parents, explained what he was up to, and asked whether he could whisk their son away for a three-week psychology experiment. Eventually he assembled a group of twenty-two boys. None of them knew they were about to take part in a research project. Instead, they were told that they had been selected to attend a summer camp.

The next step involved Sherif building an artificial world in which he could manipulate and monitor his carefully chosen group of boys. After checking several possible locations, he eventually came across an isolated State Park in Oklahoma. Located over forty miles from the nearest town, the park consisted of 200 acres of forest. Hidden from civilization, it was the perfect place for Sherif's project.

The park housed two separate camps hidden from one another by dense greenery. Each camp consisted of cabin accommodation, a food hall, a swimming pool, and a boating lake. The camps also had shared access to a large baseball pitch.

Sherif randomly allocated each of the boys to one of two groups, ensuring that neither group knew about the existence of the other, and then bussed one of the groups to the first camp and the other group to the second camp.

Throughout the experiment he played the role of the park janitor and his research team acted as camp coordinators. Although they all often appeared disinterested in what was happening, in reality Sherif and his team made copious notes about the boys' daily behaviour, secretly recorded their conversations, and took over a thousand photographs.

During the first part of the experiment Sherif wanted each

group of boys to bond together, and so arranged for them to participate in various joint activities, including hiking, playing baseball, and swimming. He also asked each group to come up with a name for their gang and create their own flag. One group labelled themselves the 'Rattlers' and the other went with the 'Eagles'.

Sherif's plan worked, and within just a few days the twenty-two strangers had transformed into two close-knit communities. Pleased with the progress, he moved on to the second phase of his study: the experimental production of hatred.

On an agreed morning the researchers told the Rattlers about the existence of the Eagles, and the Eagles about the Rattlers. Both groups had enjoyed playing baseball, with each group thinking that it had sole access to the baseball pitch and so considering it part of their territory. The researchers decided to use this situation to create a sense of competition, and so told the Eagles that the Rattlers had also been using the pitch and vice versa. Both groups felt threatened and said they wanted to challenge the other group in some type of competition. The researchers suggested they organize a tug of war or a game of baseball, and offered to reward the winning team with medals and trophies.

The following day both groups agreed to stage a game of baseball. It was a testosterone-charged affair right from the very start. The Eagles arrived waving their flag and singing the somewhat menacing theme tune to the film *Dragnet*. Almost as soon as the game was underway the Eagles started to chant 'Our pitcher is better than yours', causing the Rattlers to engage in a spot of name-calling. Enraged by the labels 'Fatty' and 'Tubby', the Eagles responded by getting out some matches and setting fire to the Rattlers' flag. Understandably upset by its demise, the Rattlers then decided to head back to their cabin and plot a raid on the Eagles' camp.

At ten thirty that night the Rattlers put dark paint on their faces and arms, and carried out a commando-style attack on the Eagles' cabin. Minutes later the Eagles awoke to the sound of their beds being turned over and mosquito netting being ripped from their windows. Angry, they decided to mount a counter-attack later that night, but the experimenters banned the assault when they saw the Eagles preparing to use rocks as weapons. Ever resourceful, the Eagles agreed to cancel the evening attack, and instead carried out their retaliatory raid the following morning. Arming themselves with sticks and bats, they ransacked the Rattlers' cabin, and then returned to their own cabin and filled their socks with rocks in preparation for a possible return raid.

Within days the previously peaceful camps had come to resemble a scene from the William Golding novel *Lord of the Flies*. Sherif's careful selection process had ruled out the likelihood of the boys having any psychopathic tendencies. However, he later noted that if someone had observed the two groups at this point in the experiment they would have concluded the boys 'were wicked, disturbed, and a vicious bunch of youngsters'.

How had this dramatic transformation come to pass? Sherif's experiment was designed to discover whether certain situations possess the power to make level-headed and normal people behave in a highly aggressive way. Before starting the study he had examined the atrocities carried out by the Greek Army during its invasion of Turkey, and concluded much of the aggression arose from each community having a strong sense of identity and competing for limited resources. To test his hypothesis, Sherif had created a small-scale version of the same situation during his experiment by getting the boys to bond together and then compete over access to the baseball pitch. All hell was let loose, with the trouble quickly escalating in a series of tit-for-tat responses. Sherif argued that regardless of whether a dispute is over land, power, money, or jobs, the same process quickly turns one group against another.

Disturbed by the level of experimentally induced aggression, he decided to move into the final phase of the study: the experimental production of bonding.

At the start of this phase the experimenters asked the boys to describe specific members of their own and the opposing group. The boys tended to see the people in their own group as brave and tough, and those in the other group as sneaky and untrustworthy.

Sherif first wanted to discover whether it was possible to change the boys' beliefs about one another by bombarding them with information. He asked both groups to attend Sunday religious services, and had the minister give pointed appeals for forgiveness, cooperation and brotherly love. The boys quietly left the services and within minutes were plotting their attacks on one another.

With the information campaign a failure, Sherif adopted another approach and explored the impact of getting them to help one another.

When people feel that they have bonded with one another they often act in unison. Those who share a religious belief come together to pray, troops march around in step, sports fans cheer for their team, and those attending political rallies applaud speeches. But can behaving as if you are part of such a group help to bond people together?

To find out, Sherif staged a series of fake emergencies that encouraged both the Rattlers and Eagles to stand shoulder to shoulder. In one instance both groups were told that some vandals had damaged the water supply, and that they needed to work together to solve the problem. In reality, there were no vandals and the experimenters had caused the damage themselves by placing two large boulders on one part of the supply. The groups realized that they would both benefit from having drinking water and so worked together to remove the boulders.

In another instance, a 'camp attendant' (actually one of the research team) offered to drive to the nearest town and get both groups some nice food. However, his truck suddenly developed a fault and the Eagles and Rattlers needed to work together to help start the truck.

The results were dramatic. Within just a few days much of the animosity between the Eagles and the Rattlers vanished into thin air, and the two groups started to bond. On the final night of the project one of the Eagles took out his ukulele and played a song to entertain the Rattlers. In return, one of the Rattlers performed his Donald Duck imitation, with Sherif's research notes revealing '. . . this performance was received with great enthusiasm'.

The findings from the final phase of Sherif's remarkable experiment demonstrated how the *As If* principle has the power to change people's beliefs about one another for the better. By getting the Rattles and Eagles to collaborate, he had managed to get both groups to see each other in a far more positive light.

Inspired by the success of these types of studies, one researcher began to explore whether the same effect could be used in the real world to bring children closer together.

Rip it up

All together now

Want to get a group to quickly bond and believe in a single cause? Then get them to act in unison.

A few years ago Scott Wiltermuth and Chip Heath from Stanford University gathered together groups of three students.[37] Some of the groups were asked to walk around the campus normally, whilst others were formed into a mini-army and asked to march around the same route in step. In another part of the study groups were asked to listen to a national anthem, and others asked to sing along and move in time to the music. The people in each of the groups were then asked to play a board game in which they could choose to either help or hinder one another. Those who had been walking in synchrony and singing in unison quickly bonded, and were significantly more likely to help one another during the game.

People who have bonded together often act in unison. Similarly, acting in unison helps people bond together.

The jigsaw man

In the early 1970s psychologist Elliot Aronson from the University of Texas was contacted by a superintendent from a local school. The superintendent explained that many of the schools in Austin had recently been desegregated, and so children from a variety of racial backgrounds were sharing a classroom for the first time. Unfortunately, the deep-seated feelings of suspicion and distrust between the different racial groups had resulted in a hostile atmosphere and even violence.

The school superintendent asked Aronson whether there was anything he could do to help solve the problem. Aronson visited a few schools and noticed that most of them were producing a strong sense of competition among the students. In the same way that Sherif had created conflict by getting the Rattlers and the Eagles to argue over ownership of the baseball field, so teachers were inadvertently encouraging their classes to compete against one other for good grades. Mindful of the success that Sherif had had by getting his guinea pigs to work together, Aronson invented a new type of learning that has come to be known as the 'Jigsaw Method'.

Let's imagine that a teacher wants their class to learn about the life and ideas of Martin Luther King. The teacher would first divide the students into small groups of five or six pupils, ensuring that each group consisted of a diverse mix of gender, race, and ability. Next, the teacher would divide the different elements of the lesson into several different parts. In the case of Martin Luther King, this might, for example, include information about his childhood, the influence of other leaders on his life, his early protests, his rise to power, his assassination and his legacy.

One student in each group is then asked to learn about just one of these elements. After they have spent some time finding out what they can, the pupils rearrange themselves so that all those who have learnt about one particular element sit together. Each of these new groups then discusses what they have learnt. So, for example, one group of pupils might share their knowledge about Martin Luther King's early life whilst another group might discuss his legacy. At the end of these discussions the class goes back into their original groups, and each pupil presents what they have discovered to the group. At the end of the lesson, the teacher then gives a short quiz on the material so that the pupils have a chance to discover what they have, and haven't, learnt.

Aronson introduced the Jigsaw Method into several randomly selected classrooms. Even though the pupils in these classrooms only spent a small amount of time using the method, they quickly became far less prejudiced and significantly more self-confident. Not only that, but the children using the method showed a drop in absenteeism and performed better in their end-of-year exams.

In his seminal book on social psychology, *The Social Animal*, Aronson discusses the impact of the Jigsaw Method on a Mexican-American pupil named Carlos. At the time of the study Carlos did not speak English well and years of education in a substandard, racially segregated school had left him feeling shy and insecure. When Carlos used the Jigsaw Method he was forced to speak to his group. He stammered his way through the material and his fellow pupils quickly started to ridicule him. When one of Aronson's researchers heard the exchange she focused the group's attention on the need to cooperate, pointing out that it was vital that they helped Carlos speak to the group if they all wanted to do well in the forthcoming exam. After a few weeks, Carlos's group became skilled interviewers who were able to ask helpful questions and elicit clear answers. In short, they were behaving as if they liked Carlos and he quickly became one of the group. As a result, his self-esteem and performance improved.

Many years later he came across Aronson's book and recognized himself. By that time Carlos had just gained admission to Harvard Law School. He reminisced about Aronson visiting the school ('you were very tall . . . had a big black beard and you were funny and made us all laugh') and how the Jigsaw Method had converted enemies into friends. In his final paragraph Carlos explained why he was writing to Aronson:

> My mother tells me that when I was born I almost died. I was born at home and the cord was wrapped around my neck and the midwife gave me mouth-to-mouth and saved my life. If she was still alive, I would write to her too, to tell her that I grew up smart and good and I'm going to law school. But she died a few years ago. I'm writing to you because, no less than her, you saved my life too.

6. CREATING
A NEW YOU

Where we learn how to feel more confident, change our
personality, and slow down the effects of ageing.

'No man, for any considerable period, can wear one face
to himself and another to the multitude, without finally
getting bewildered as to which one is true.'

Nathaniel Hawthorne

1. THE PROBLEM WITH PERSONALITY

Imagine that you go to a job interview and are asked to distil the essence of your personality into just three adjectives. What would you say? Would you, for instance, describe yourself as outgoing or shy? Creative or down-to-earth? Go-getting or laid-back? If the interviewer asked you what has made you the person you are today, how would you reply? Do you believe, for example, that your personality is due to genetics, childhood experiences, or events that have happened during your adult life?

Many of the world's greatest thinkers have wrestled with these issues. The Victorian scientist Sir Francis Galton was convinced that your character could best be determined by carefully studying the bumps on your skull and the shape of your nose. Sigmund Freud thought that Galton's approach was deeply strange, and instead argued that your personality is based on the bodily orifice from which you derived greatest pleasure as a child (thus giving rise to the idea of 'oral' and 'anal' people). Psychiatrist Carl Jung believed that both Galton and Freud were badly mistaken, and instead thought that your identity was determined by the position of the stars when you were born (there again, Jung was a Leo, and so was predisposed to come up with silly ideas).

Perhaps not surprisingly, most modern-day psychologists would not categorize you on the basis of the bumps on your head, preferred bodily orifice, or star sign. Instead, they would see you in terms of your key personality traits.[1]

A few thousand years ago the eminent Greek philosopher Hippocrates had two interesting thoughts. First, he suggested that all physicians should take the so-called 'Hippocratic oath' and pledge to always act in the best interests of their patients (unless the money was really good). Second, he speculated that differing amounts of blood, phlegm, black bile, and yellow bile caused people to develop one of four personalities: 'melancholy' (the anxious introvert), 'phlegmatic' (the relaxed introvert), 'sanguine' (the relaxed extrovert) and 'choleric' (the anxious extrovert). Although Hippocrates' thoughts about bodily fluids quickly fell out of favour, the idea of trying to fit the apparent complexity of personality into a simple structure has stood the test of time.

In the 1930s Harvard psychologist Gordon Allport came across Hippocrates' work and wondered whether science could help uncover the structure of personality. Allport laboriously worked his way through a large dictionary and noted down all the adjectives that could be used to describe a person's personality. After identifying around 4,000 words, Allport (studious, hard-working, bored) had had enough and handed the work over to his colleague Raymond Cattell. Cattell (compassionate, caring, empathic) carefully went down Allport's immense list and eliminated all of the words that described the same general characteristic. Eventually Cattell (compassionate) ended up with a list of about 170 core adjectives.

Several research teams then asked thousands of people to rate themselves with these adjectives, and used a sophisticated statistical technique known as 'Factor Analysis' (don't ask) to analyse the structure in the data. The results suggested that Hippocrates was wrong to think that everyone's personality falls into one of four boxes. Instead, a small number of personality 'dimensions' appear to exist, and everyone falls somewhere along each of them. For example, rather than everyone being either 'extroverted' or 'introverted', there exists a sliding scale, with 'Yippeee, it's time to party!' at one end and 'Oh Christ, I'd rather stay in with a good book' at the other. Each of these fundamental dimensions of personality is referred to as a 'trait'.

For the next fifty years or so psychologists repeatedly locked horns about exactly how many traits were needed to describe fully a person's personality. Cattell, for instance, was convinced that there are sixteen core traits, whilst the British psychologist Hans Eysenck opted for just three. In the early 1990s the majority of researchers agreed to split the difference and settle on the existence of five fundamental dimensions: 'Openness' (the need for new and unusual experiences), 'Conscientiousness' (the tendency for organization and self-discipline), 'Extraversion' (the need for stimulation from the outside world and other people), 'Agreeableness' (the tendency to care about others), 'Neuroticism' (the tendency for emotional instability), and 'Innumeracy' (the tendency to struggle with even basic arithmetic).

Many researchers believe that your scores on each of the five personality traits are due, in part, to your genetic make-up. Take the introvert–extrovert dimension. According to conventional personality theory, your DNA has created a brain that has a certain pre-set level of arousal, in the same way that your television set may have a pre-set volume when you first turn it on. If you are an introvert, then your brain is naturally aroused and so you will try to avoid situations that further excite your already stimulated brain. As a result, no matter what situation you are in, you will tend to avoid bright lights and noisy groups of people, and instead gravitate towards much more tranquil activities such as reading and quiet chats. If you are more of an extrovert, your brain will have a much lower pre-set level of arousal and so you have a need for continuous stimulation. Because of this, no matter what situation you encounter, you will be attracted to the stimulating effects of large groups of people, risk-taking and impulsive behaviour.

According to this point of view, your personality is hard-wired into your brain, causes you to behave in the same way in many different situations, and doesn't change during your lifetime. Although all of this may sound reasonable, it is far from the full story.

Psychologists have frequently tested the notion that people's personalities cause them to exhibit consistently the same behavioural patterns in a variety of situations. In one study, for example, counsellors working at a summer camp for teenage boys were asked to secretly note down the degree to which the boys displayed various forms of extroverted behaviour, such as talking during mealtimes, seeking the limelight, and initiating conversations.[2] The researchers then carefully analysed the data by comparing the boys' level of extraversion on odd and even days. The 'personality causes behaviour' theory predicts there would be a high level of consistency in the boys' actions, with the extroverted teenagers constantly chatting away and the introverted ones repeatedly hiding away in the corner. In fact, the results failed to show any evidence of such consistency. On one day, one of the boys would be full of beans and very chatty, whilst on the next day the very same boy was quiet and withdrawn.

In another experiment psychologists visited several schools and set up highly realistic situations in order to test the honesty of schoolchildren.[3] The research team presented the children with an opportunity to steal some money that had been 'left' on a table, then lie about stealing it to avoid trouble, and finally gave them the chance to change their exam scores. Each time the children's behaviour was secretly recorded and compared in the different situations. The 'personality causes behaviour' theory would predict that the same children will tend to steal, lie and cheat, but the results failed to show such consistency, with a child behaving dishonestly in one situation but then getting in touch with their inner angel in another.

Disillusioned with the notion that personality causes behaviour, a small number of researchers started to develop a completely different view of human identity.

In previous chapters, I have presented a large amount of research showing how your behaviour can create your emotions, thoughts and willpower. Smile and you feel happier. Hold hands with another person and you find them strangely attractive. Tense your muscles and you develop greater self-control. Inspired by this work, some researchers wondered whether the same process might also explain the relationship between behaviour and identity. Rather than your personality causing you to behave in a particular way, could your behaviour cause you to develop a particular personality?

Common sense suggests that the chain of causation is:

Extroverted personality ⟶ Outgoing behaviour

The *As If* principle suggests that the reality is:

Outgoing behaviour ⟶ Extroverted personality

If true, this topsy-turvy approach to personality opens up the possibility of you being able to alter your sense of identity at will. Just by changing the way you behave, you could, for example, quickly become less aggressive, especially likable, and far more confident.

For the past forty years researchers have examined whether the *As If* principle can indeed make you feel like a completely new person. Our journey into this real-world version of *Pygmalion* starts with an unusual experiment involving a set of weights and several earthworms.

2. HOW TO BE MORE CONFIDENT

Do you trust your own judgement, even when others are questioning your decisions? Are you able to put your mistakes behind you and not spend too much time worrying about what will happen in the future? Do you think that you will do well in most situations? If you have just answered 'Yes' to all of these questions then you probably have fairly high self-esteem, whereas a series of 'No's suggests you are a tad insecure.

According to the conventional 'personality causes behaviour' theory, very low self-esteem has several disadvantages, including encouraging people to endure humiliating and demeaning experiences. However, the *As If* principle turns this idea on its head. Rather than low self-esteem causing people to put up with demeaning experiences, it suggests that it is the taking part in demeaning experiences that causes them to develop low self-esteem. Psychologist James Laird set out to discover if this was indeed the case.[4]

In chapter 1, I described how Laird had conducted the first test of the *As If* principle, and discovered that smiling makes people feel happy. Excited by the positive findings from this initial work, Laird has devoted most of his academic career to exploring the power of the principle.

Imagine that you have signed up to participate in a study of Laird's. You are invited to the laboratory and asked to complete a self-esteem questionnaire. The experimenter then takes you into another room and asks you to sit down at a small table. On the table are some cooking weights, a knife and fork, and a live worm. The experimenter explains that you will have to take part in one of two tasks. One will involve you lifting each of the weights and ordering them according to heaviness. The other involves you cutting up and eating the worm.

The researcher then flips a coin and explains that unfortunately you have been assigned to the worm-eating task. You sit down in front of the wriggling worm and look at the wee beast for a few moments. The experimenter then asks you to complete a second self-esteem questionnaire before tucking in.

This experiment was carefully designed to discover whether the *As If* principle applies to self-esteem. Laird considered that if people saw themselves about to carry out a demeaning and humiliating experience (that is, behaving as if they had low self-esteem) they would be likely to conclude that they did indeed have low self-esteem. As predicted, the self-esteem of the worm-eaters crashed and burnt. In the same way that smiling caused people to be happy, so taking part in a demeaning experience caused them to develop low self-esteem.

But the study did not end there. Imagine that you have finished the second questionnaire and, just as you pick up the knife and fork, the experimenter rushes across the room and explains he has made a terrible mistake. You should have been given a choice about which task to complete. Do you choose to continue to consume the worm or switch to the weights?

Laird knew that people with low self-esteem often believe

that they deserve bad experiences, and he wanted to discover whether the laboratory-induced low self-esteem would alter their behaviour. None of the volunteers who were randomly assigned to the weights switched to the worm-eating. However, and remarkably, only 20 per cent of those assigned to eating the worm switched to the weights. Even though these people now had the option to switch to a more pleasurable task, their experimentally created low self-esteem caused the vast majority of them to choose to eat the worm (although just as the participants were about to tuck in the experimenters rushed across the room and stopped the study).

When Laird's study was published some psychologists criticized the method, arguing that perhaps the participants were merely role-playing, safe in the knowledge that the researchers would never allow them to actually eat a worm. As a result, other researchers repeated the study, but this time using large edible caterpillars.[5] In this second study the participants actually consumed the caterpillars, and the results replicated Laird's original findings.

This effect helps explain why people who have had the ill fortune to experience a random, but negative, life event often end up with low self-esteem and even blame themselves for it. Those who have been the victims of a random violent assault often feel that they somehow caused the attack, and those suffering from a terminal illness wonder what they have done to deserve their fate. As predicted by the *As If* principle, their sense of identity is the direct and unfortunate result of having been forced to endure an unpleasant event.

Unfortunately, once the process has started, it feeds on itself. Those low in self-esteem endure more negative events that, in turn, cause an even greater decline in their esteem.

The good news is that the same idea can be used to quickly boost self-esteem and confidence.

Power posing

Most courses designed to improve self-esteem are based on the notion that low self-esteem and poor confidence are a result of the way people think about themselves, and therefore encourage participants to focus on instances in their life when they have done well or ask them to visualize themselves being more assertive. In contrast, the *As If* principle suggests that it would be much quicker and far more effective to ask them to change their behaviour.

In one early study, experimenters assembled a group of participants to apparently examine whether a newly developed pair of plastic glasses might affect people's perception.[6] The participants were split into two groups and both groups were given the same intelligence and personality tests. Half were asked to complete the tests as normal, whilst the others were given a pair of glasses with clear lenses. Because we associate glasses with intelligence, the experimenters speculated that merely wearing them would make people suddenly feel more confident and clever. They were right: the actual scores on the intelligence tests didn't differ between the two groups, but when wearing the glasses the participants rated themselves as more stable, competent and scholarly.

Then there is the issue of posing. Researcher Dana Carney from Columbia University knew that confident people tend to feel good about themselves, take more risks, have higher levels of testosterone (a chemical associated with dominance) and lower levels of cortisol (a chemical associated with stress). What would happen, wondered Carney, if a group of people were asked to behave in a dominant way? To find out, Carney and her colleagues gathered together a group of participants, told them that they were there to help assess a new heart monitoring system, and split them into two groups.[7]

The participants in one group were placed in one of two power poses (see photos below). Some were seated at a desk, asked to put their feet up on the table, look up, and interlock their hands behind the back of their head. Others were asked to stand behind a desk and lean forward, placing both hands palms down on the desk.

Those in the other group adopted one of two poses not associated with dominance (see photos opposite). Some of these participants were asked to place their feet on the floor, with hands in their laps and look down at the ground. Others stood up, and crossed their arms and legs.

After just one minute of posing each participant was asked to rate how 'powerful' and 'in charge' they felt. The posing had a significant effect on their self-esteem, with those who had been placed in the 'power poses' giving higher ratings than the others. But this was just the tip of the iceberg.

Participants were then given a quick risk-taking test. They were handed two dollars and told that they could either keep the money or gamble it on the flip of a coin. If they won the toss they would double their money and get four dollars, but if they lost the toss they would go home with nothing. In line with the 'power posing makes you more of a risk-taker' hypothesis, over 80 per cent of those put in the dominant position took the gamble compared with just 60 per cent of others.

In the final part of the study, the researchers turned their attention to the chemicals coursing through the volunteers' veins. Both before and after adopting the experimental posing, the researchers asked all of the participants to chew on gum for a few minutes to build up a ready supply of saliva (noting that this technique was just as good as 'passive drool procedures'), and then spit into a test tube. After analysing the contents of the tube the researchers could see that compared to those sitting with their hands in their laps, those power posing had significantly higher levels of testosterone and lower levels of cortisol than before the test. In short, just a minute behaving as if they were more dominant had changed the chemical make-up of their bodies.

Finally, if you haven't got time to strike a powerful pose, just make a fist.[8] Psychologist Thomas Schubert asked a group of men to rate how confident they felt, then to form their hand into a fist for a few seconds (under the guise of playing 'rock-scissors-paper'), and then to re-rate their confidence. The participants' bodies influenced their brains, with the men enjoying a significant boost in confidence because they had spent a few moments forming a fist.

Rip it up

The confidence trick

To take part in this exercise you will require a pen, a piece of paper and two hands.

First, rate how confident you feel about yourself on a scale between 1 (not at all confident) and 7 (very confident).

Second, take a look at the list of adjectives below and choose three words that reflect your best traits and three that reflect your worst qualities.

loyal, affectionate, aloof, ambitious, unmotivated, secretive, caring, callous, cheerful, grumpy, considerate, thoughtless, cooperative, unhelpful, courageous, rude, indecisive, enthusiastic, apathetic, flexible, stubborn, unforgiving, focused, frugal, generous, grateful, hard-working, lazy, honest, dishonest, humble, arrogant, jealous, immature, modest, optimistic, pessimistic, punctual, self-confident, insecure, sincere, disorganized, pretentious, ostentatious

Third, place the pen in your *non-dominant* hand and slowly write the three *negative* traits that you selected on the paper.

Fourth, place the pen in your *dominant* hand and slowly write the three *positive* traits you selected on the piece of paper.

Finally, rate how confident you feel about yourself on a scale between 1 (not at all confident) and 7 (very confident).

Did the exercise make you feel more confident?

This exercise is based on work conducted by psychologist Pablo Briñol from the Universidad Autónoma de Madrid.[9] Briñol told participants that they were taking part in a study about graphology, and asked them to write down their best or worst qualities using either their dominant or non-dominant hand. Immediately afterwards all of the participants rated their self-esteem and confidence.

The experimenters knew that when the participants used their non-dominant hand they would see themselves produce very shaky handwriting, and so were behaving as if they didn't have much confidence in their words. As a result, the researchers predicted that listing positive traits with their non-dominant hand would decrease the participants' self-esteem, whereas writing their negative traits with their non-dominant would make them feel more confident and motivated. This is exactly what their results revealed.

If you want a quick and effective way of increasing your confidence, the message is clear – use the write stuff.

3. WHY CLOTHES MAKETH THE MAN

John Howard Griffin lived a remarkable life. Born in Texas in 1920, he travelled to Europe at a young age and trained as a musicologist specializing in Gregorian chanting. When the Second World War broke out he worked for the French Resistance and helped smuggle Austrian Jews to safety. After the war was over he returned to America, became an investigative journalist, and decided to highlight the plight of African-Americans living in the Southern States.

Rather than simply write about racism, however, he decided to carry out an extraordinary experiment in order to experience it first-hand. Working closely with a skilled dermatologist, Griffin used a mixture of artificial pigments, drugs, and sunlamp treatments to darken his white skin. Once the transformation was complete, he shaved off his hair and so, to the casual observer, appeared to be an African-American. He then toured around several Southern States by bus and hitchhiking, experiencing the hatred and discrimination faced by genuine African-Americans on a daily basis.

At the start of his bestselling book about the project,[10] Griffin described how he only looked at himself in a mirror once the transformation was complete, and presents a vivid account of the impact that this reflection had on his sense of self:

I had expected to see myself disguised, but this was
something else. I was imprisoned in the flesh of an
utter stranger, an unsympathetic one with whom I felt
no kinship . . . I looked into the mirror and saw
reflected nothing of the white John Griffin's past. No,
the reflections led back to Africa, back to the shanty
and the ghetto, back to the fruitless struggles against
the mark of blackness . . . I had tampered with the
mystery of existence and I had lost the sense of my
own being. This is what devastated me. The Griffin
that was had become invisible.

By changing the colour of his skin, Griffin felt like a different
person. Throughout his life, he would have looked in the
mirror and seen a Caucasian man. Assuming that skin colour
was an important part of his self-identity, he would have seen
himself as possessing the background and traits associated
with his appearance. After his dramatic transformation he
saw himself as resembling an African-American, and unconsciously used this image to construct a new sense of identity.
Within seconds he experienced his old self crumbling away,
and a new identity forming.

Most people are unlikely to follow in Griffin's footsteps
and try to change their skin colour. However, the same
principle applies to something that is much easier to alter –
your clothing. We frequently judge other people on the basis
of the clothes they are wearing. If you see a man in an expensive suit then you tend to automatically assume that he
is successful and competent. See the same person dressed in
a kaftan and flowery shirt, and you might assume that they
are the creative type. Bump into the man wearing large shoes,

a red nose and hooped trousers, and you know it is time to run.

These differences in perception often cause us to behave in very different ways. For example, Nicolas Guéguen from the Université de Bretagne Sud dressed up men in either civilian clothing or a fireman's outfit and had them approach more than 200 randomly chosen women on the street.[11] Each time the man caught the woman's eye, he came out with the same pre-prepared script:

> Hello. My name's Antoine. I just want to say that I think you're really pretty. I have to go to work this afternoon but I wonder if you would give me your phone number. I'll phone you later and we can have a drink together.

Guéguen carefully analysed the percentage of women who were happy to give out their telephone number, and discovered that the uniform had a remarkable effect. When the men were dressed in civilian clothing just 8 per cent of the women gave their number. However, when exactly the same men were dressed as firefighters they enjoyed a 22 per cent success rate.

In a similar study, John Marshall Townsend from Syracuse University dressed the same group of actors in either a Burger King outfit or a smart suit, showed photographs of the actors to women, and asked them to rate whether they would be willing to have sex with them.[12] Clothes maketh the man, with more women indicating that they were willing to sleep with the man when he was sporting a suit as opposed to a Burger King uniform.

Other research shows that even the smallest changes can

have a big effect. In another study a psychologist posing as a market researcher approached various people and asked whether they would mind taking part in a survey.[13] Half the time the man wore a tie, and the rest of the time he was tieless. This small difference had a huge effect, with more than 90 per cent of people agreeing to carry out the survey when he was sporting a tie compared with just 30 per cent when he wasn't.

In the same way that the clothes people wear clearly affects our perception of them, do the clothes that you wear influence the way in which you see yourself? Most proponents of the 'personality causes behaviour' theory would argue that your sense of self has slowly developed over a period of years, and is not going to be influenced by something as transitory as putting on a new shirt or changing your shoes. In contrast, the *As If* principle predicts that dressing as if you are a certain type of person will affect your sense of identity. To discover which theory was correct, Mark Frank from Cornell University conducted a series of strange studies.[14]

Frank knew that people tended to associate black clothing with authoritarian and aggressive behaviour, and wondered whether simply wearing such clothing might change the way in which they behaved. Luckily for him, the data needed to test his hypothesis was already available. Frank searched through the records of the National Football League, comparing the data from teams who wore black outfits with others. He identified the five teams that wore black outfits – including the Los Angeles Raiders, Pittsburgh Steelers and Cincinnati Bengals – and started to look at their behaviour on the field.

In American football, infringements can be punished, with

the offending team being moved back by five, ten or fifteen yards. Frank calculated the average number of yards each team were moved back during each game, and discovered a remarkable pattern. The teams dressed in black were moved back significantly more than the others, suggesting that they did tend to engage in especially aggressive behaviour.

Encouraged by these early results, Frank moved on to the records from the National Hockey League and again compared teams wearing black uniforms with others. In hockey, violations can result in players having to sit out for either two, five or ten minutes depending on the severity of the violation. Frank discovered that those in black spent significantly more time on the bench.

The hockey data also allowed Frank to conduct an especially clever test of his hypothesis because two of the teams – the Pittsburgh Penguins and the Vancouver Canucks – switched from non-black to black uniforms. The 'wear black – become aggressive' effect emerged. Before switching to black, the players from both teams rarely frequented the benches. However, afterwards they became a near-permanent fixture.

Most researchers would have left it there. However, Frank knew that other researchers would be sceptical of his idea and perhaps argue that aggressive players were attracted to teams with black outfits. The only way to settle the matter was to conduct an experiment. He assembled a group of willing volunteers and randomly split them into two groups. One of the groups was dressed in black and the other in white. Both were then told that they were going to be split into small teams and asked to play a variety of games. The experimenters then presented the participants with a list of games and asked them which ones they would like to play. Unknown to the participants, the games had been specially chosen to vary in aggressiveness. Some of the games, like the 'dart gun duel', were highly aggressive whilst others, such as the 'putting contest' were much more passive. The people who had dressed in black chose far more aggressive games than those wearing white.

Other research suggests that this effect is far from a black-and-white issue.

Another study conducted by Robert Johnson from Arkansas State University assembled a group of participants and explained that they were going to be given an opportunity to give another person electric shocks.[15] The experimenter described how each participant was to be photographed before giving the shocks, but it was important that their clothing was covered up in the photograph. And how was this anonymity to be achieved? The helpful experimenter had brought along two types of outfit. Half of the participants were asked to wear a robe resembling a Ku Klux Klan outfit, with the experimenter justifying the clothing by mumbling, 'I'm not much of a seamstress – this thing came out looking kind of Ku Klux Klannish.' In contrast, the other participants were given outfits that made them look like nurses ('I was fortunate the hospital recovery room let me borrow these nurses' gowns to use in the study.')

In the next stage the experimenter said that there was a person in the next room trying to learn a list of words, and asked the participants to administer an electric shock to them whenever they made a mistake. In reality, the person in next room was a stooge, and the electric shock apparatus was entirely fake. Whenever the participant heard the person in the next room make a mistake they could choose to either increase or decrease the alleged shock. Participants dressed in outfits resembling those of the Ku Klux Klan chose to deliver significantly higher shocks than those wearing the nurse outfits, exactly as predicted by the *As If* principle.

The same effects have been observed beyond the laboratory. In 1969, the police in Menlo Park, California, decided to try and improve community relations by getting rid of their navy-blue paramilitary-style uniforms and changing into a more relaxed look.[16] The officers were asked to wear a forest green sports blazer, black slacks, a white shirt, and a black tie. They were also asked to conceal their weapon under the blazer. Word soon spread and over 400 other American police departments experimented with the same informal uniform. Eighteen months into the experiment researchers had the officers complete various tests, with the results showing that when stripped of their symbols of authority the officers gradually adopted a new role of policeman as 'public service officer'. In line with this new identity, the police officers displayed fewer authoritarian characteristics compared with their colleagues in more formal attire. During the same period injuries to civilians by the police dropped by 50 per cent.

The message is clear – the way you dress directly influences who you think you are. Don a black shirt and you start to become an authoritarian and aggressive person. Slip into something far more comfortable and you turn into a more tolerant and giving individual. For years psychologists have urged job candidates to 'suit up and boot up' before an important interview in the belief that smart clothing will have a positive impact on the interviewer. The *As If* principle suggests that such attire will also have a profound and perhaps even more important effect on the candidate. By putting on a smart outfit he will see himself as a more successful person and this, in turn, will help him perform far better. Clothes do not just maketh the man: they maketh every man, woman and child.

Rip it up

Thinking outside the box

Want to instantly become a more creative person? Then try this two-part experiment.

First, I would like you to think of as many uses for a pencil as possible. For example, you could use a pencil as a magic wand or dowel. However, before you start writing down your ideas, please spend sixty seconds walking around your room, ensuring that your path forms a rectangle or box (that is, walk in straight lines and perform ninety-degree turns).

Now spend the next sixty seconds jotting down your alternative uses for the pencil in the space below:

For the second part of the experiment, I would like you to think of as many uses for a piece of paper as possible. For example, you might fold up the paper and use it as a hat or doorstop. However, before you start writing down your ideas, please spend sixty seconds walking around your room, but this time ensure your path is far more curvy and unpredictable than before (that is, avoid walking in straight lines and instead trace out whatever shape you like).

Now spend the next sixty seconds jotting down your alternative uses for the piece of paper in the space below:

Research carried out by Angela Leung and her colleagues at the Singapore Management University suggests that your behaviour directly influences your level of creativity.[17] In one experiment the researchers asked some participants to sit inside a five-foot square box, whilst others sat outside the box. In another study some participants walked around a room in straight lines, whilst others walked along far more random and curvy paths. After completing the exercises, all the participants were asked to carry out various creativity tasks. Those who had literally been thinking outside the box and walking in a more free-flowing way obtained significantly higher creativity scores than the other participants. Behaving in a creative way directly influenced the way the participants thought.

According to these findings, you should have found it much easier to produce alternative uses for the paper than the pencil. Want to get your creative juices flowing? Then forget about expensive lateral-thinking courses and go for a long, unpredictable and meandering walk.

For an extra boost, try acting as if you are creative. Tear out the blank sheet of paper over the page and spend a few moments thinking about how you can transform it into a work of art. Before deciding on your final course of action, study the list below and see if anything appeals.

Use the paper in a creative way by . . .

. . . cutting out a silhouette of a skyline or person

. . . folding it into a box or model-building

. . . making a random squiggle on the paper and then converting this squiggle into a picture

. . . screwing it up and making a sculpture

. . . using it to add a 'pop-up' element to this book

. . . using it to create an interesting shadow

. . . turning it into a copy of a famous painting or work of art

. . . turning it into a motivational poster

. . . making an origami figure, such as a frog, bird, paper aeroplane or swan

. . . making a picture by simply placing creases in the paper

. . . folding it up and ripping out pieces to make a snowflake design

. . . folding it up and tearing parts away to create a chain of people

. . . making a flick book

. . . pleating the paper to make your very own accordion

. . . tearing it into tiny pieces and rearranging them to create a work of art

. . . using it to make an item of clothing or jewellery (such as a hat, ring or badge)

. . . making a rubbing of a surface

. . . creating your own paper currency for a magical kingdom

. . . making a 'rip it up' bookmark

. . . poking two holes in it and wearing it as a mask

4. THE NEW YOU

By law, any contract for a book about the history of social psychology has to contain Clause 4.6.8.3.2. This clause explicitly states that at some point in the book the author is legally obliged to describe the Zimbardo prison experiment. As a result of this clause, many authors are forced to crowbar in the study, often placing it between a lurid description of Milgram's infamous electric shock study and a closing paragraph on the apparent banality of evil. Fortunately, I am not faced with a similar dilemma because Zimbardo's classic experiment plays a central role in our journey into the surprising relationship between the *As If* principle and identity.

Philip Zimbardo was born into poverty in New York City's South Bronx ghetto during the Depression. Fascinated by the impact that people's surroundings had on their behaviour, he studied psychology throughout the 1960s and eventually joined the faculty at Stanford University, where he conducted his now infamous experiment.[18]

Prior to starting the study, he converted the basement rooms of Stanford's Psychology Department into a mock jail. Several of the smaller rooms were turned into cells by replacing their doors with steel bars. Other areas were converted into guards' living quarters and a prison 'yard'. The mock prison also contained several two-way mirrors and hidden cameras that allowed the experimenters to observe and record the participants' behaviour.

Zimbardo then placed an advertisement in a local newspaper appealing for men to take part in a two-week study examining prison life. Each applicant was sent an extensive questionnaire about their background, psychological health, and any prior history of criminal activity. Zimbardo carefully examined the replies and invited the twenty-four applicants who showed the highest levels of psychological stability, and lowest levels of previous antisocial activity, to take part. He randomly assigned half of them to play the role of the 'prisoner' and the other half to be the 'guards'. Zimbardo himself decided to adopt the role of the prison superintendent (a move that he later described as 'a serious error in judgement').

Just prior to the study there had been violent clashes between police officers and anti-war protesters on the Stanford campus, and Zimbardo found out that the city police chief was eager to improve his relationship with the university. He asked the chief whether he might be able to assign some officers to help with the initial part of the study and the chief agreed. On the first morning of the experiment nine of the 'prisoners' were unexpectedly arrested in their homes by the Palo Alto City Police Department. Each of them was charged on suspicion of burglary or armed robbery, handcuffed and driven to their local police station. The officers then searched and fingerprinted the prisoners, blindfolded them, and drove them to Zimbardo's mock prison.

Meanwhile, the volunteers playing the role of the 'guards' were dressed in khaki uniforms, and given a whistle, mirror sunglasses and a wooden baton. They were asked to look after the prison by working in three-man shifts, with each shift lasting eight hours.

Life was not much fun for the prisoners. When they arrived, the guards gave each of them an identification number, strip-searched them, took away their clothing and made them wear an ill-fitting smock. The prisoners were not allowed to wear any underclothes, and had a chain attached to one of their ankles. They lived in the prison twenty-four hours a day, had three bland meals each day, and were only allowed to visit the toilet three times in any twenty-four-hour period.

The guards quickly started to behave in a way that was consistent with their role. Often they became highly authoritarian, referring to the prisoners by their identification numbers and making verbal threats of violence. If the prisoners refused to obey, the guards repeatedly forced them to cite their identification numbers, refused permission to visit the toilet, and removed bedding from their cells. On the second day of the experiment some of the prisoners decided to stage a revolt by blockading their cell doors and ripping off their identification numbers. In response, the guards attacked the prisoners with fire extinguishers (ironically, the University Ethics Committee had insisted on the extinguishers to safeguard the prisoners), and punished those involved by stripping them naked, placing them in solitary confinement, and forcing them to do push-ups.

At the time of the study Christina Maslach was a psychology postgraduate at Stanford University, and involved in a romantic relationship with Zimbardo. Curious to discover how her partner's experiment was progressing, Maslach visited the prison and briefly chatted to one of the off-duty guards. The man came across as friendly and affable. A few moments later one of the experimenters asked Maslach if she would like to see one of the guards in action. They explained that they had labelled the guard 'John Wayne' because of the aggressive way he handled the prisoners. When Maslach looked, she was stunned to see that 'John Wayne' was actually the friendly guard she had met earlier. When he wasn't in the prison environment the guard seemed to be pleasant and placid. Inside the mock prison he appeared to become a completely different person, shouting at the prisoners and treating them poorly.

After visiting the mock prison Maslach had a heated argument with Zimbardo. She thought that the situation had spiralled out of control and should be stopped. Normally gentle and sensitive, Zimbardo appeared distant and keen to let the project continue. Maslach was stunned, realizing that Zimbardo had adopted his role as the prison supervisor, and was no longer standing outside the study but had instead become an integral part of it. As the argument continued Zimbardo realized what had happened and decided to call a halt to the study. Although originally planned to run for two weeks, the experiment was abruptly terminated after only six days.

A key part of Zimbardo's experiment involved exploring whether acting as if they were a prisoner or guard would influence participants' identities. The results were as fast as they were dramatic. After the experiment one of the guards noted:

> I really thought that I was incapable of this kind of
> behaviour. I was dismayed that I could have acted in
> a manner that is so absolutely unaccustomed to any-
> thing that I would really dream of doing. And while I

was doing it I didn't feel any regret or any guilt. It was
only afterwards when I began to reflect on what I had
done that it began to dawn on me and I realised that
this was part of me that I hadn't really noticed before.

Similarly, those playing the role of the prisoners also changed
their identities, with most of them becoming extremely passive and far more submissive. These rapid changes often had
an extremely negative effect on the prisoners. Doug Korpi
('Prisoner 8612') suffered one of the more extreme emotional
reactions and was released during day two of the study (fascinated by his behaviour during the study, Korpi went on to
study forensic psychology and work in Californian prisons).
A few days later four other prisoners were released early due
to evidence of anxiety, depression and anger.

Zimbardo's classic study illustrates the power of acting *As
If*. People's sense of unique identity comes from their name,
clothing and appearance. In the prison study all of these were
removed, causing them to lose their own sense of identity and
replace it with the role they had been assigned.

Dressing and acting as if they were prisoners or guards,
the participants had started to think in ways that they considered consistent with their roles. One group quickly became
aggressive and authoritarian, the other passive and conform-
ing.

Zimbardo conducted his study inside a mock prison, and
used the *As If* principle to create aggression and anxiety.
Other research has shown that same principle operates in
everyday life and applies to many aspects of identity. In one
study, for instance, researchers tracked the lives of a group of
women over the course of several years and discovered that

those who were given extra responsibilities in the workplace developed more assertive personalities.[19] In another study employees who were given more demanding work became more flexible and confident.[20] A large part of people's personalities are not fixed. Instead, they often accept the roles they have been assigned by themselves and others, behave accordingly, and then develop an identity that matches this role.

Perhaps most intriguing of all, other psychologists have explored how this effect can be used by people to transform their lives for the better.

Lights, camera, action!

George Kelly was born in 1905 on a Kansas farm. After high school, he received a degree in physics, moved to Minnesota and taught public speaking. Then he stopped teaching public speaking, enrolled at the State University of Iowa, and was eventually awarded a doctorate in psychology. Recognizing the difficulties of farming families during the Depression, Kelly decided to take his psychology on the road and act as a travelling psychotherapist.

At first he adopted a Freudian approach, asking farmers to lie down on his couch and describe their dreams. However, he soon found Freudian theory too esoteric for the down-to-earth farmers, and so started to develop more practical ways of tackling their problems.

One of Kelly's first creations has come to be known as 'mirror time'. During these sessions people would be encouraged to spend thirty minutes sitting in front of a mirror looking at their reflection and thinking about what they saw.

Did they like or dislike the person in front of them? What were the differences between the person in the mirror and the person they wanted to be? What did they see in their face that others missed?

Although people often enjoyed staring longingly into their own eyes, Kelly wasn't convinced that these moments of deep reflection were proving especially helpful, and so decided to draw on his experience of teaching public speaking to encourage people to explore other ways of seeing the world.

His extensive therapeutic experience led him to believe that people's personalities were not fixed, and in the same way that an actor plays many different roles during their career, so people can change their identities throughout their lifetime. Moreover, Kelly was convinced that the way in which people saw themselves was often at the root of their problems, and effective therapy involved helping clients adopt a less problematic identity. He christened this approach 'fixed-role therapy' and, over time, developed a series of effective techniques for getting people to adopt a new identity.[21]

The first stage of fixed-role therapy usually involves various exercises that are designed to help you understand how you currently see yourself. One of the most popular exercises involves comparing yourself to several other individuals that you know in order to identify the core psychological dimensions that you use to classify people. Another exercise might involve you writing a short description of yourself from someone else's perspective (*see also* pages 316–22).

On the basis of the results, you would then design a new identity for yourself. This might entail a radical overhaul of your personality or just involve tweaking a few small aspects. You then spend some time thinking about how this 'new you' would behave in the type of situations you encounter every day, and possibly involve some role-playing to help solidify these new behavioural patterns.

In the next part of the process you 'play' your new role for about two weeks. Kelly's research revealed something strange. After spending a few weeks behaving in a completely different way, many people started to forget that they were playing a role and began to develop a new identity. Many of Kelly's clients reported that the new role seemed as though it had always been their real self, and that it was only now they were becoming fully aware of it.

People had created a new sense of identity by behaving like the person that they wanted to be, exactly as predicted by the *As If* principle.

The same principle can also help bring people together by getting them to see how the world looks to others. In one study, for example, one group of students was asked to behave as if they had recently been paralysed in a road accident and were now confined to a wheelchair.[22] The students spent twenty-five minutes working their way around a pre-specified route in a wheelchair, and so had to navigate several lifts, ramps and doors. Another group of students walked behind the wheelchair and witnessed everything that happened. Both groups were then asked about their attitudes towards issues related to disability, including, for example, whether public funds should be spent on a new rehabilitation centre. A remarkable difference emerged between the groups, with those that had spent time in a wheelchair showing far greater empathy for the disabled. The same principle is often used in a form of therapy known as 'psychodrama'. By getting clients to adopt different personas, and sometimes even role-play friends and colleagues, they are able to see their life from several very different perspectives.

Kelly's research has provided new and improved identities for tens of thousands of people across the world. New technology has taken the idea to previously unimaginable heights.

Rip it up

Who do you think you are?

PART ONE:

Do you want to find out how you see yourself and others? The following two exercises are based on the work of George Kelly and will give you an insight into how you perceive your current personality.*

Exercise One: Your constructs

This four-stage exercise usually takes about twenty minutes to complete, and is designed to give you an insight into the core dimensions that you use to see yourself and others.

Stage 1) Think of five people that you know well – perhaps your mother, your father, your closest friend, your boss, your partner, a work colleague, or a past lover. Write the names of these people below.

Person 1:
....

* The exercises described here are designed to provide a general insight into the sort of techniques that are used by psychologists. If you believe that you have a serious problem in your life, consult a professional.

Person 2: ....

Person 3: ....

Person 4: ....

Person 5: ....

Stage 2) Now look at the first row of the table below. The columns marked 'Person 1' and 'Person 2' contain 'X's. Think of one way in which Person 1 and Person 2's personalities differ from you. Perhaps, for example, Person 1 and Person 2 are outgoing, and you are shy. Or perhaps they are both somewhat stingy, and you are more giving? Write down the way in which Person 1 and Person 2 are similar in the column marked 'Way in which they are similar', and the opposite trait (which should describe your personality) in the column marked 'Me'.

Person 1	Person 2	Person 3	Person 4	Person 5	Way in which they are similar	Me
X	X					
	X	X				
		X	X			
			X	X		
X		X				
	X		X			
		X		X		
X			X			
	X			X		

Stage 3) Move into the next row and repeat the same process. Once again, think about how Person 2 and Person 3 are similar, and how they differ from you. Carry on like this down the table, each time trying to come up with different traits.

Stage 4) Look at the resulting list of traits in the 'Me' column, and try to identify some commonalities. Do words like 'anxious' and 'relaxed' appear a lot? Or perhaps the words 'outgoing' and 'shy' make regular appearances? These are the core psychological constructs that you use to see yourself and others.

Here is a typical completed exercise:

Person 1: John

Person 2: Katie

Person 3: Jenny

Person 4: David

Person 5: Erica

Person 1	Person 2	Person 3	Person 4	Person 5	Way in which they are similar	Me
X	X				Like detail	Bigger picture thinker
	X	X			Highly artistic	More down-to-earth
		X	X		Anxious	Relaxed
			X	X	Pessimistic	Optimistic
X		X			Disorganized	Organized
	X		X		Conscientious	Less reliable
		X		X	Agreeable	More hard-headed
X			X		Shy	Outgoing
	X			X	Neurotic	Relaxed

Exercise Two: The description

Spend about twenty minutes writing a brief description of yourself. This description should be written from the third person perspective, perhaps as you think a close friend or work colleague sees you.

PART TWO:

The following stages are designed to help you create, and adopt, new aspects of your identity.[23]

Stage 1) Take a look at the constructs that you used to describe yourself in Exercise One. Do you think that any of these constructs are negative or problematic? Now take a look at the description that you produced in Exercise Two. Does that contain any clues about which aspects of your identity you would like to change? Perhaps, for example, you don't think that you are very confident, are struggling to make friends, are overly aggressive, or seem a bit selfish.

Stage 2) Use this information as a basis for the new you. If you are struggling to think about how you want to change, perhaps draw on elements that you admire in friends, colleagues, role-models, and even fictional characters from books, films and plays. Alternatively, look at the list of character strengths described in the table below and choose one or more that appear especially appealing.[24]

Character strength	Brief description
Creativity	Good at thinking of novel ways to do things.
Curiosity	Having an interest in exploring and discovering.
Open-mindedness	Being willing to examine issues from several perspectives.
Bravery	Not running away from a threat or challenge.
Persistence	Keeping with it when the going gets tough.
Vitality	Approaching life with zest and energy.
Love	Being able to form close relationships with others.

Kindness	Enjoying giving to other people.
Citizenship	Being a team player and supporting those around you.
Leadership	Taking responsibility and moving forward.
Forgiveness	Being able to forgive those that have done wrong.
Humility	Not drawing attention to your achievements.
Prudence	Expressing self-control and not being overly impulsive.
Gratitude	Being thankful for the good things in your life.
Hope	Expecting that good things will happen and being prepared to work to achieve them.
Humour	Seeing the funny side of life and being light-hearted.

Next, write a short description of the 'new you', focusing on how you will behave differently in everyday situations. For example, let's imagine that you tend to be overly aggressive and are frequently getting into arguments with your friends and colleagues. The 'new you' might be a lot more relaxed and fun to be with. If that were the case, how would you behave? Would you joke around? Would you ask other people for their thoughts and opinions, and accept these comments rather than use them as the basis for an argument? Would you make a special effort to give praise and encouragement?

Alternatively, let's imagine that a few people have remarked upon the fact you are overly stingy, and that you have decided to change this part of your character. Would the new you contribute to charity, give generous gifts to others, and go out of your way to help those around you?[25]

Or maybe you would like to be more confident. If so, do you

have an especially assertive friend or colleague who could act as an inspiration for the new you? How do they behave in the type of situations that you struggle with? Can you pretend to be them and act differently in these situations?

Stage 3) Spend around two weeks role-playing your new identity. Focus on changing your behaviour rather than trying to change the way you think. To help with this process you might also ask a close friend or family member to role-play a few common situations with the 'new you'. Also, rather than seeing yourself as undergoing a permanent change, it might be helpful to think of your old personality as being on holiday for two weeks, and so you have an opportunity to act like a different person. It is important, however, that you play out your new role twenty-four hours a day, even when you're alone. The *As If* principle will cause you to feel like a new person and the 'new you' will soon become part of your actual identity.

Orcs and elves

Jeremy Bailenson runs the Virtual Human Interaction Lab at Stanford University. Much of his work involves creating computer-generated representations of humans (referred to as 'avatars'), and having them move around virtual worlds. Bailenson came across the *As If* principle and wondered whether it would also operate in the imaginary worlds that he created. Would, for instance, people who were given a tall avatar in a computer game feel more assertive in real life? Or would those who were given an avatar dressed in black become more aggressive?

The possibilities seemed endless, but first Bailenson had to discover whether the principle operated in the virtual world. To find out, he turned to the international phenomenon that is 'World of Warcraft'.

World of Warcraft is a hugely popular online fantasy game in which millions of people across the globe fight against one another in a virtual land. The game involves taking part in 'epic sieges' and 'a host of legendary experiences', with each player trying to make their way through sixty levels of increasing difficulty. Before starting the game, players have to create their own avatar. These virtual identities are based on one of eight different 'races' (including Gnomes, Night Elves, Orcs, Trolls, and Humans), with each race having a predetermined height (for example, Gnomes are somewhat short whilst Trolls are much taller).

Jeremy Bailenson and his colleague Nick Yee knew that in real life taller people are more assertive than shorter people, and wondered whether the same effect would emerge among the World of Warcraft avatars.[26] To find out they examined the data from over 76,000 players, looking at the relationship between the height of each player's avatar and how far they had progressed in the game. The virtual world mimicked the real world, with players having relatively tall avatars (think Trolls and Orcs) outperforming those with shorter virtual selves (think Dwarfs or Gnomes). These results have two important implications. They suggest the *As If* principle functions in virtual worlds and, on a more practical level, if you want to gain the edge in World of Warcraft, become a Troll rather than a Gnome.

Although Bailenson and Yee were excited by their results, they realized that there were two problems. Critics might argue that more competent or assertive players had simply chosen taller avatars at the start of the game. Also, even if the height of a person's avatar did change the way they behaved online, there was no guarantee that it would affect them in the real world. Bailenson and Yee tackled both issues in a second experiment.

In this study, a group of students were asked to wear virtual reality glasses that allowed them to see a virtual version of themselves on a computer screen. To make the situation as realistic as possible, the research team attached high-tech sensors to the students' faces, arms and legs, and ensured that the virtual figure copied their movements. If the student looked to the left, so did their avatar. If the person started to jog, their avatar trotted along too. The close match-up between the participants' actual movements, and those of their virtual self, resulted in the students quickly believing they were the figure on the screen.

At the start of the experiment the researchers randomly assigned a tall or short avatar to each participant. Then, after the students had spent some time in the virtual world, they were asked to remove their headsets, come back into the real world, meet another participant, and play a game called 'Ultimatum'.

In this game one player has just one shot at proposing a way of dividing a hundred dollars between both players. If the second player accepts the offer then the cash is divided. If, however, the second player rejects the offer then neither player gets anything. The test has been used in psychology departments across the world for years, with the first player's opening offer being seen as a good reflection of how assertive and aggressive they are.

Players who had been given a tall avatar made more assertive opening offers than those who had been assigned a short avatar, as predicted by the *As If* principle. The difference was far from trivial, with those with taller virtual selves offering, on average, a 60/40 split, whilst those with shorter avatars offered a 50/50 split. Not only that, but those with taller avatars were also more assertive when it came to accepting or rejecting the offers of others. Around 60 per cent of those with tall virtual selves rejected a 75/25 split in favour of the other player, compared with just 30 per cent of those with short avatars.

Bailenson and Yee's work paved the way for an explosion of similar studies. In one study some volunteers saw their avatars run on treadmills whilst another group saw their virtual selves lounging around.[27] When the researchers tracked the participants over time they discovered that those who had seen themselves running around in the virtual world were far more likely to exercise for real. In another experiment, people who inhabited a physically older avatar were subsequently more likely to agree to contribute more to their pensions.[28]

Time and again the research has shown that the *As If* principle does indeed operate in the virtual world, and that seeing an avatar look and behave in a certain way affects how people think and behave in the real world. Bailenson has labelled the phenomenon the 'Proteus effect', after the Greek god who can change his shape and identity at will. The effect opens up the *As If* principle to new worlds, limited only by our imaginations.

5. TURNING BACK TIME

Born in the Bronx, psychologist Ellen Langer began her college career studying chemistry at New York University. Realizing that a life among the test tubes wasn't for her (she later noted that 'I practiced Jewish chemistry – a little is good, more is better'), she enrolled in an introductory psychology course being taught by Philip Zimbardo and became hooked. Langer eventually became a professor at Harvard University, with much of her work attempting to unravel the mysteries of ageing.

She has conducted many high-profile studies during her career. In one classic experiment, some of the residents in a nursing home were given a houseplant to look after, whilst the others were given an identical plant but told that the staff would take responsibility for it.[29] Six months later, the residents who had been robbed of even this small amount of control over their lives were significantly less happy, healthy, and active than the others. Even more distressing, 30 per cent of the residents who had not looked after their plant had died, compared with just 15 per cent of those who had been allowed to exercise control.

In a similar study Langer examined the effect of encouraging elderly people to behave as if they are still mentally active.[30] In this experiment the researchers visited one group of residents each week and asked them various questions, such as the names of the nurses and the nature of the activities that would be taking place in the nursing home on particular days. If the residents were uncertain about the answers, the experimenters encouraged them to find out by the next visit. The effects were dramatic. Compared with a control group of residents who were not presented with such challenges, those asked to remember simple questions developed superior short-term memories and appeared far more alert. The researchers revisited the homes two and a half years later and found that only 7 per cent of the group had passed away, compared with nearly 30 per cent of the control group.[31]

However, perhaps Langer's most striking study involves getting people to use the *As If* principle to travel back in time.[32] In 1979 she recruited a group of men in their seventies and eighties for what was described as a 'week of reminiscence' at a retreat outside Boston. Before the study started, Langer asked all the men to take part in a series of tests measuring their physical strength, posture, eyesight and memory.

She then randomly split the men into two groups, and told one group (the 'time travellers') that the experiment was about the psychological impact of actually reliving the past and the other group that it was all about the effects of reminiscing. Langer had decided to try and turn back the hands of time by twenty years, and so encouraged the participants to either relive, or reminisce about, their lives during 1959.

Next, she arranged to bus the group that would be reliving the past to a ten-acre country retreat. To get them in the mood for the study, Langer played 1959 radio broadcasts throughout the trip. She was keen to encourage the participants to act as if they were twenty years younger throughout the experiment. When the time travellers arrived at the retreat, for instance, there was no one there to help them off the bus and they had to carry their suitcases inside. In addition, the retreat had not been equipped with the type of rails and other movement aids they had at home.

Participants had been asked to supply photographs of themselves from 1959, and when they first went to their bedrooms each participant found copies of all of those photographs, along with 1959 issues of *Life* magazine and the *Saturday Evening Post*.

After unpacking, everyone was assembled in the main room of the retreat. Surrounded by various objects from the era, including a black-and-white television and a vintage radio, Langer informed the participants that for the next few days all of their conversations about the past had to be in the present tense, and that no conversation must mention anything that happened after 1959.

Each day the participants took part in various carefully orchestrated activities and discussions. During one activity, for example, they were asked to write an autobiographical sketch in the present tense, ending in 1959. Other times they were taken to a makeshift cinema to watch *Anatomy of a Murder* starring James Stewart, took part in discussions about the launch of the first American satellite, played games such as *The Price is Right* using old prices, heard a speech by President Eisenhower, and sat around the radio listening as the horse Royal Orbit won the 1959 Preakness.

For the control group, life was very different. They heard present-day music on the bus, were asked to reminisce about 1959 in the past tense, were given current photographs of one another, and watched present-day films.

Within days, Langer could see the dramatic effect of behaving *As If*. The time-travelling participants were now walking faster and were more confident. Moreover, within a week several of these participants had decided that they could now manage without their walking sticks. Langer took various psychological and physiological measurements throughout the experiment and discovered that the time-travelling group now showed improvements in dexterity, speed of movement, memory, blood pressure, eyesight and hearing. Interestingly, over 60 per cent of those in the time-travelling group showed an improvement on intelligence tests, compared with just 40 per cent of those in the other group. Acting as if they were young men had knocked years off their bodies and minds.

To discover if Langer's original work could be repeated, the BBC recently re-ran her experiment. Six elderly British celebrities agreed to try and turn back the clock to their heyday during the 1970s. The BBC uncovered photographs of the celebrities' bedrooms during that decade and reconstructed the rooms in minute detail, complete with psychedelic wallpapers and swirling carpets. During the week, each celebrity was given the opportunity to relive an important moment in their lives, with, for example, dancer Lionel Blair returning to the stage of the Palladium to choreograph a routine.

Within just a day or two, many of the celebrities showed an improvement in their memories, physical strength, energy and mood. The eighty-eight-year-old actress Liz Smith had had three immobilizing strokes, but soon showed that she was able to get around without her walking stick. Prior to the experiment cricket umpire Dickie Bird had become solitary, but within days was the life and soul of the party. Tests assessing the participants' biological age suggested that two of the group had the brain of a person twenty years their junior, and overall the group showed significant improvements in memory and intelligence.

This is not the only set of experiments to show that it is possible to slow down the effects of ageing by acting like a younger person.

In another experiment, Langer asked people to role-play air force pilots and examined the impact on their vision.[33] Nineteen air force cadets had their eyesight tested and were then split randomly into two groups. An instructor invited each of the cadets in one of the groups to go into a flight simulator and attempt to fly a plane. Those in the other group were also asked to climb into the pilot's seat, but were told the simulator was broken. All of the participants were then asked to read the letters on the sides of aeroplanes they saw through the cockpit window. Those acting as if they were fighter pilots improved their vision by 40 per cent, whilst those not behaving in this way showed no change at all.

Other work examined whether being around children really does keep you young. In one study, Langer examined the life expectancies of women who had children later in life compared to those who had them in their younger years.[34] You might think that running around very young children when you are in your forties is not such a great idea but you would be wrong. In fact, the women who had children later in life had significantly longer life expectancies than others. In a similar vein, Langer looked through the marriage registers searching for couples that differed in age by more than four years. She hypothesized that the younger partner will be likely to behave as if they are older than they actually are, and the older partner as if they are younger. This had a significant effect on their life expectancy, with the younger ones having significantly shorter lifespans.

Then, not for the first time in this book, there is the power of dance. Researchers at the Albert Einstein College of Medicine in New York City followed a group of more than 500 participants between 1980 and 2001.[35] When they first joined the study everyone was to indicate the degree to which they carried out various activities that stimulated their brains (reading, writing for pleasure, solving crosswords, playing board games, taking part in discussions, and playing a musical instrument), or bodies (playing tennis or golf, swimming, bicycling, dancing, walking, climbing, doing housework). When 500 of the participants were over seventy-five years old, the researchers monitored the degree to which they had developed dementia. Those who were readers showed a 35 per cent reduced risk of dementia, whilst doing crossword puzzles for at least four days a week showed a 47 per cent drop. Interestingly, almost none of the physical activities, such as bicycling and swimming, had any impact at all. The exception to the rule was dancing, with the regular dancers in the group exhibiting a massive 76 per cent drop. By consistently dancing the night away these people were acting as if they were young and, over time, this helped slow down the effects of ageing.

As the playwright George Bernard Shaw once wisely remarked, 'We don't stop playing because we grow old; we grow old because we stop playing.'

Rip it up

How to slow down ageing

Here are five tips, based on the research of Ellen Langer, to help you to slow down the effects of ageing:

– **Maintain a sense of control in your life:** Do not associate old age with helplessness and reliance on others. Instead, try to exert control over as many aspects of your life as possible. Langer's work suggests that even the smallest amounts of control make a big difference. Shop for yourself, look after a houseplant, tend to your garden, get a pet, take charge of your finances, and get out and about under your own steam.

– **Keep mentally active:** There is a great deal of debate about whether so-called 'brain training' affects your mental well-being. However, acting as if you are interested in the world around you is beneficial. Keep up with world news, find out what is happening in your area, start a blog, set goals, remain curious, maintain hobbies and interests, and stay in touch with friends and family.

– **Young at heart:** Langer's work shows that those who spend time with children and younger people stay young. Make room in your life for grandchildren and young friends and neighbours.

– **Actively active:** Try to move like a younger person. Keep as physically active as you can, continue to be involved in sport, put a spring in your step, and remember that by far the most psychological benefit is derived from dancing.

– Make an effort: The way that you look influences how you feel. In one study, Langer measured the blood pressure of women before and after they had their hair dyed.[36] Women who thought that they looked younger after the appointment showed a significant reduction in blood pressure. Make an effort to look and dress a few years younger than you actually are.

CONCLUSION

Where we hypnotize a woman, saw a brain in
half, and discover why you really are in two minds
about everything.

'Everything we have seen indicates that the surgery
has left these people with two separate minds. That is,
two separate spheres of consciousness.'

Roger Sperry, neuroscientist

Our journey has revealed the remarkable truth about your body and brain. For thousands of years people have assumed that the relationship between their brain and body is much like that of a rider to a horse. In the same way that a rider determines how a horse behaves, so our minds decide what our bodies do. Because of this, those wishing to change their lives have spent vast amounts of time and money trying to alter how they think. Encouraged by self-appointed gurus and life coaches, these people have attempted to visualize their perfect self, think like a millionaire, and adopt a positive mindset. Unfortunately, this approach to change is difficult, time-consuming and frequently ineffective.

A century ago Harvard philosopher William James turned the conventional view of the human psyche on its head. James suggested that your actions influence how you think and feel, and argued that it should be possible to easily alter your thoughts and emotions by changing your behaviour. Eighty years after James first proposed his strange-sounding theory, a small number of maverick researchers carried out the first experiments to discover whether he was right. Their positive findings inspired other scientists to conduct similar research, and over time this work has revealed that the *As If* principle can help explain people's emotions, levels of motivation, beliefs, and personalities.

The message from this remarkable body of research is

clear – it is not just that the mind influences the body, but rather that the body also influences the mind. This simple idea has given rise to a series of quick, easy and effective techniques that can help people become happier, avoid anxiety and depression, fall in love and live happily ever after, beat procrastination and even slow the effects of ageing. None of these techniques involve trying to change the way you think. Instead, they all entail ripping up the rules about self-development, changing the way that you behave and are based on William James's century-old maxim 'If you want a quality, act as if you already have it.'

This work has important consequences for anyone wishing to understand the mysteries of the mind. Since its inception around the turn of the last century, psychology has struggled to find a single concept that can be applied to the many different facets of the human psyche, including emotion, thought and behaviour. For example, research into the psychology of motivation has produced several theories that help explain what makes people get up and go, but these ideas do little to further our understanding of happiness. Similarly, other work has tackled what happens when people feel sad, but these theories have nothing to say to those interested in understanding the psychology of persuasion. The *As If* principle does not suffer from such limitations. From passion to phobias, confidence to creativity, and persistence to personality, the same simple notion provides a remarkable insight into a diverse range of phenomena and, in doing so, offers the very real possibility of being psychology's first unifying theory.

Although such theoretical considerations are fascinating, the *As If* principle also has important practical consequences.

As we have seen throughout this book, this deceptively simple idea provides the basis for a diverse range of self-development techniques that are quick, easy and highly effective. Clench your muscles and you develop instant willpower, force your face into a smile and you feel happier, stand up straight and you become far more confident. The same principle has also inspired other exercises that pave the way for more long-lasting and large-scale change, including those that help people shape their personality, lose weight, and alter the beliefs of entire nations.

New experiments into the *As If* principle are now being regularly reported at scientific conferences and published in academic journals. Just over a hundred years after James came up with his controversial theory, the principle has come in from the cold and is now accepted as part of mainstream psychology. Indeed, some researchers are convinced that the *As If* principle is not just a fascinating quirk of the human mind, but is instead operating each and every moment of your waking life. To support their case, they point to a strange body of work involving post-hypnotic suggestion, live brain surgery and a picture of a chicken's claw.

Dr Zomb and the people with two brains

When I was a child I developed a strong interest in conjuring, and have worked as a professional magician. In my early twenties I thought that it might be fun to learn how to become a hypnotist, and so I visited my local magic shop and bought a book entitled *The New Encyclopedia of Stage Hypnotism* by Ormond McGill.

McGill was an experienced hypnotist who had worked

under the stage name 'Dr Zomb', and his book claimed to present a step-by-step guide to placing people in a deep trance. Inspired by Dr Zomb's authoritative tone, I read his encyclopedia from cover to cover, learnt the various induction procedures, and decided to give it a go. Rather than risk making a fool of myself on stage, I thought it best to try out my new-found skills on Claire.

Claire and I had been sharing a house for about a year, and so she was used to being asked to choose cards and think of the first number that came into her head. I asked Claire whether she would like to be my very first hypnotism guinea pig and she kindly agreed. About ten minutes later she was lying on our old comfy sofa and I was sitting in a nearby chair. I recited one of Dr Zomb's most powerful induction procedures, asking Claire to close her eyes and drift away from consciousness. After a few minutes she was laying motionless on the sofa.

Everything seemed to be going well, and so I asked Claire to imagine that the number 'six' didn't exist, and then to count from one to ten. A few moments later she started her count and I was thrilled to hear her confidently come out with the numbers '. . . four, five, seven, eight . . .'.

After working my way through several other standard hypnotic exercises, I decided to add one of Dr Zomb's post-session suggestions. I told Claire that when she awoke, she wouldn't remember anything about the sessions, but would feel a strange urge to wander across the room and open a window.

A few moments later I counted to ten and Claire suddenly opened her eyes. Slightly dazed, she asked how the session had gone. I said that all was well and explained about the mystery of the missing six and the other exercises. At the end of the discussion Claire stood up, walked across the room, and opened the window. Bemused, I casually asked her why she had opened the window on what was quite a chilly day. Claire confidently explained that she felt hot and so needed some fresh air.

Many proponents of hypnosis would argue that it is as if there are two people inside Claire's head – one of them controlled her behaviour (let's call him or her 'The Boss') and the other observes these actions and tries to work out what is going on ('The Observer'). According to this theory, in everyday life The Boss is actually the one in charge but people are only aware of The Observer. So, for example, The Boss might head to a restaurant and The Observer would look at what was going on and conclude they must be hungry. Or The Boss might look longingly at their husband or wife and The Observer might conclude they are in love.

However, when people are hypnotized The Observer takes some much-needed time off, and it is possible to talk directly to The Boss. When I hypnotized Claire I told The Boss to open the window when the session had ended. After Claire came out of the trance The Observer woke up again and all seemed well. Then, as instructed, The Boss opened the window, and The Observer saw what was going on and assumed Claire must feel hot.

Psychologists have long debated the nature of hypnosis. Some have argued that people can indeed enter a strange trance-like state and that during a hypnotic session it is indeed possible to talk to other aspects of a person's psyche. In contrast, others have argued that hypnosis is just an elaborate form of role-play.[1] It is a long and complex debate, and so my experience with Claire does not constitute strong proof for the existence of The Boss and The Observer. Fortunately, this is far from the only evidence that you have two people inside your head.

During some brain operations patients can be fully conscious and able to report their thoughts and feelings. During the late 1960s brain surgeon José Delgado thought that it would be interesting to see how his patients felt when he stimulated different parts of their brain during an operation.[2] In several operations Delgado applied a tiny electrical pulse to the part of the brain that controlled head turning. On cue, each of the patients slowly rotated their head to the right and then the left. However, when Delgado asked why they were behaving in this way, most of them quickly justified their actions, explaining, for example, that they were looking for their slippers, had heard a noise or just generally felt restless. Once again it seemed that the patients had looked at their actions and created a plausible narrative to explain what was going on.

By far the most profound work into this notion was carried out in the early 1970s by the American neuropsychologist Roger Sperry.

Sperry and his colleagues originally set out to devise a new treatment for epilepsy. They knew that the brain consists of two large hemispheres connected by a thick band of nerve fibres called the corpus callosum, and that previous work had revealed some epileptic fits were the result of excessive electrical activity in one of these two hemispheres quickly spreading to the other. Sperry wondered if it might be possible to prevent this electrical 'storm' by cutting the tissue that connected the two hemispheres. To find out, he operated on several epileptic patients, severing the entirety of their corpus callosum. This dramatic procedure proved a considerable success, with the majority of the patients going on to lead normal lives. However, it was Sperry's additional experiments with these so-called 'split brain' patients that yielded a remarkable insight into who we are.

Each of the hemispheres controls muscles on the opposite side of the body. The right hemisphere controls muscles on the left side of your body, for instance, and the left hemisphere controls muscles on your right side. The same process also applies to the images entering your eyes, with images from the left-hand side of your visual field going to the right hemisphere and images from the right going to the left. Normally, the corpus callosum ensures that this information quickly flows between the hemispheres, and so is available to both sides of the brain. Sperry realized that this sharing of information couldn't happen in his 'split brain' patients, and thus it should be possible to work with them to investigate the different abilities of the hemispheres.

The research team constructed a laboratory inside a camper-trailer, hitched the trailer up to a van, and toured around the country testing their participants.

In one series of studies, each participant was asked to focus on a dot in the centre of a screen. Sperry then flashed up images on either the right or left of the dot. These flashes were deliberately so fast that the patients did not have time to move their eyes, which in turn ensured that the image went to just the right or left hemisphere.

Your language and self-awareness tends to be located in the left hemisphere and so when Sperry flashed up a picture of an object on the right of the screen the patient could easily name the object. However, when the same picture was flashed on the left-hand side of the screen it was fed to the right hemisphere, and the patient felt as if they had seen nothing. Nevertheless, the images influenced the patients' behaviour. For example, when the word 'smile' was flashed up on the left of the screen the patient would smile. When an image of a nude woman was flashed up to male patients an appreciative grin would sometimes spread across their faces.

These patients had no insight into the real cause of their behaviour, and so when asked to explain their actions they would say that they were smiling because they found the experiment funny, or said they looked 'appreciative' because they found the experimenter attractive. Once again, it was as if The Observer was watching their actions and trying to explain what was going on.

In another study the researchers showed the split-brain patients two pictures, presenting one picture to each hemisphere. The participants were then asked to look at an assortment of other pictures, and chose an image most closely related to the original pictures. For example, in one instance a patient had a picture of a chicken claw flashed to their left hemisphere and a snow scene to their right hemisphere. Shown the ensuing selection of other images, the patient correctly selected a shovel with his left hand and a chicken with his right hand. When the researchers asked the patient to account for his actions, he explained that the chicken claw was obviously associated with a chicken, and that you needed a shovel to clean out a chicken shed. Once again, it was as if The Observer saw how the patient behaved, had no insight into why this was the case, and made up a story to account for his actions.

Sperry's work strongly suggests that one part of your brain decides whether to eat, sleep, laugh or cry, and another observes your actions and then tells you a story in an attempt to explain what is going on. Seen in this way, the *As If* principle is not simply a fascinating quirk of the human mind, but instead underlies every thought and feeling that you have experienced throughout your entire life.

Over a century ago William James proposed that behaviour causes emotion. It was a simple idea that changed everything. A hundred years of research has revealed that James's theory applies to a remarkable range of psychological phenomena, from persuasion to procrastination, fear to phobias, and passion to personality. In addition, it provides a profound insight into the fundamental nature of the human mind, and has the power to change lives and shape societies. The time has come to jettison out-of-date ideas about the human psyche and adopt William James's radical theory. To use the power of the *As If* principle to help people improve their lives and to change the world. To Rip It Up and start again.

Rip it up

Ten ways in which your body instantly changes your brain

The preceding chapters contain a series of quick and effective exercises that will help change the way you think and behave. Here is a one-stop description of ten of the most effective techniques that we have encountered.

Motivation: Pull me – push you

Pushing an object away from you (and so behaving as if you don't like it) makes you dislike the object, whereas pulling it towards you (behaving as if you do like it) makes you feel far more positively about it. Next time that you are confronted with some sugary snacks or chocolate biscuits, simply push the plate away from you and feel the temptation fade.

Dieting: Using your non-dominant hand

When you eat with your non-dominant hand you are acting as if you are carrying out an unusual behaviour. Because of that you place more attention on your action, do not simply consume food without thinking about it, and so eat less.

Willpower: Tensing up

Tensing your muscles boosts your willpower. Next time you feel the need to avoid that cigarette or cream cake, make a fist, contract your bicep, press your thumb and first finger together, or grip a pen in your hand.

Persistence: Sit up straight and cross your arms
In several experiments researchers have presented volunteers with tricky problems and measured how long they persevered. Those who sit up straight and fold their arms struggle on for nearly twice as long as others. Make sure your computer monitor is slightly above your eye-line and, when the going gets tough, cross your arms.

Confidence: Power posing
To increase your self-esteem and confidence, adopt a power pose. If you are sitting down, lean back, look up and interlock your hands behind your head. If you are standing up, then place your feet flat on the floor, push your shoulders back and your chest forward, and hold out your hands in front of you.

Procrastination: Make a start
To overcome procrastination, act as if you are interested in what it is that you have to do. Spend just a few minutes carrying out the first part of whatever it is you are avoiding, and suddenly you will feel a strong need to complete the task.

Creativity: Move outside the box
If you want to come up with new ideas, act in a novel way. Spend some time walking around, but ensure that your path is curvy and unpredictable. If that doesn't get your creative juices flowing, try acting as if you are artistic by drawing, painting or making some form of sculpture.

Persuasion: Getting the nod

Researchers have found that when people nod their heads up and down whilst they listen to a discussion (causing them to nod as if they agree with the arguments) they are more likely to agree with the points being made. When you want to encourage someone to agree with you, subtly nod your head as you chat with them. They will reciprocate the movement and find themselves strangely attracted to your way of thinking.

Negotiation: Warm tea and soft chairs

When people think that they are connected to others they feel physically warm. And it is also true that by warming someone up with a nice mug of tea they become far friendlier. Similarly, hard furniture is associated with hard behaviour. In one study researchers had participants sit on either soft or hard chairs, and then negotiate over the price of a used car. Those in the hard chairs offered less and were more inflexible.

Guilt: Wash away your sins

If you are feeling a tad guilty about something, try washing your hands or taking a shower. In several experiments, people who carried out an immoral act and then cleaned their hands with an antiseptic wipe felt significantly less guilty than others.

Acknowledgements

First and foremost, I wish to thank the University of Hertfordshire for supporting my work over the years. I would like to thank Clive Jefferies and Emma Greening for reading earlier drafts of the manuscript. This book would not have been possible without the guidance and expertise of my agent Patrick Walsh and editors Jon Butler and Millicent Bennett. Special thanks also to my wonderful colleague, collaborator and partner, Caroline Watt. Finally, I would like to thank the many academics who dedicated their professional lives to creating and exploring the *As If* principle, including Daryl Bem, James D. Laird, Stanley Schachter, Arthur Aron, and, of course, that adorable genius William James.

Notes

1. HOW TO BE HAPPY

1 Miller, G.A. (1993). *Psychology: The Science of Mental Life*. New York: Harper & Row.

2 Much of the information in this section is based upon: Hunt, M. (1993). *The History of Psychology*, Doubleday: New York. Richardson, R.D. (2006). *William James: In the Maelstrom of American Modernism*. New York: Houghton-Mifflin.

3 Miller, G.A. (1962). *Psychology: The Science of Mental Life*. New York: Harper & Row.

4 Cited in Myers, G.R. (1986). *William James: His Life and Thought*. New Haven: Yale University Press.

5 James, W. (1892). *Psychology: Briefer Course*. New York: Henry Holt.

6 William J. (1890). *The Principles of Psychology*, Volume 1. New York: Henry Holt & Co.

7 Snyder, P.S., Kaufman, R., Harrison, J., & Maruff, P. (2010). 'Charles Darwin's Emotional Expression "Experiment" and His Contribution to Modern Neuropharmacology'. *Journal of the History of the Neurosciences*, 19, 158–170.

8 James, W. (1899). *The Gospel of Relaxation*. Scribner's, 499–507.

9 Much of the information in this section is based on: Laird, J.D. (2007). *Feelings: The Perception of Self*. New York: Oxford University Press.

10 Zajonc, R.B., Murphy, S.T., Inglehart, M. (1989). 'Feeling and facial efference: implications of the vascular theory of emotion'. *Psychological Review*. 96(3), 395–416.

11 Larsen, R.J., Kasimatis, M., & Frey, K. (1992). 'Facilitating the furrowed brow: An unobtrusive test of the facial feedback hypothesis applied to unpleasant affect'. *Cognition and Emotion*, 6, 321–38.

12 Strack, F., Martin, L.L., and Stepper, S. (1988). 'Inhibiting and facilitating conditions of the human smile: A nonobtrusive test of the facial feedback hypothesis'. *Journal of Personality and Social Psychology*, 54, 768–77.

13 Levenson, R.W., Ekman, P., & Friesen, W.V. (1990). 'Voluntary facial action generates emotion-specific autonomic nervous system activity'. *Psychophysiology*, 27(4), 363–84.

14 Levenson, R.W., Ekman, P., Heider, K., & Friesen, W.V. (1992). 'Emotion and autonomic nervous system activity in the Minangkabau of West Sumatra'. *Journal of Personality and Social Psychology*, 62(6), 972–88.

15 Feinstein, J.S., Adolphs, R., Damasio, A., and Tranel, D. (2010). 'The Human Amygdala and the Induction and Experience of Fear'. *Current Biology*, 21, 34–8.

16 Lee, T.W., Josephs, O., Dolan, R.J., & Critchley, H.D. (2006). 'Imitating expressions: Emotion-specific neural substrates in facial mimicry'. *Social Cognitive Affective Neuroscience*, 1, 122–35.

17 Hill, A., Rand, D., Nowak, M., & Christakis, N. (2010). 'Emotions as infectious diseases in a large social network: the SISa model'. *Proceedings of the Royal Society B: Biological Sciences*, 277 (1701), 3827–35.

18 Snodgrass, S.E., Higgins, J.G., and Todisco, L. (1986). 'The Effects of Walking Behavior on Mood'. Paper presented at the American Psychological Association convention.

19 Koch, S.C. (2011). 'Basic body rhythms and embodied

intercorporality: From individual to interpersonal movement feedback'. In W. Tschacher, & C. Bergomi (eds.), 'The implications of embodiment: Cognition and communication' (pp.151–71). Exeter: Imprint Academic.

20 Velten, E. (1968). 'A laboratory task for induction of mood states'. *Behaviour Research and Therapy*, 6, 473–82.

21 Larsen, R.J. , & Sinnett, L.M. (1991). 'Meta-analysis of experimental manipulations: Some factors affecting the Velten mood induction procedure'. *Personality and Social Psychology*, 17, 323–34.

22 Hatfield, E., Hsee, C.K., Costello, J., Weisman, M.S. & Denney, C. (1995). 'The impact of vocal feedback on emotional experience and expression'. *Journal of Social Behavior and Personality*, 10, 293–313.

23 Neuhoff, C.C. and Schaefer, C. (2002). 'Effects of laughing, smiling and howling on mood'. *Psychological Reports*, 91, 1079–80.

24 Kim, S. and Kim, J. (2007). 'Mood after various brief exercise and sport modes: aerobics, hip-hop dancing, ice skating, and body conditioning'. *Perceptual and motor skills*, 104, 1265–70.

25 Lovatt, P. (2011). Personal communication.

26 Clift, S., Hancox, G., Morrison, I., Hess, B., Kreutz, G. and Stewart, D. (2010) 'Choral Singing and Psychological Wellbeing', *Journal of Applied Arts and Health*, 1, 19–34.

27 Kreutz, G., Bongard, S., Rohrmann, S., Grebe, D., Bastian, H., and Hodapp V. 'Does singing provide health benefits?'. Proceedings of the 5th Triennial ESCOM Conference, 216–19.

2. ATTRACTION AND RELATIONSHIPS

1 Riley, J. (1967). 'The saga of the Barefoot Bag on Campus'. *Life* magazine, 17 March, 72–3.

2 Cited in: Berscheid, E. and Walster, E. (1978). *Interpersonal*

Attraction. Reading, Massachusetts: Addison-Wesley Publishing, p.149.

3 Clark, R.D., III & Hatfield, E. (1989). 'Gender differences in receptivity to sexual offers'. *Journal of Psychology and Human Sexuality*, 2, 39–55.

4 For a review of this work, see: Sternberg, R.J. and Weiss, K. (2006). *The New Psychology of Love*. New Haven: Yale University Press.

5 Byrne, D. (1971). *The Attraction Paradigm*. New York: Academic Press.

6 Hatfield, E. (1985). 'Passionate and companionate love'. In R.J. Sternberg & M.L. Barnes (eds.), *The Psychology of Love* (pp.191–217). Cambridge, MA: Yale University Press.

7 Traupmann, J., & Hatfield, E. (1981). 'Love and its effect on mental and physical health'. In R. Fogel, E. Hatfield, S. Kiesler, & E. Shanas (eds.). *Ageing: Stability and Change in the Family*. (pp.253–74). New York: Academic Press.

8 These questionnaires are based on: Hatfield, E., & Sprecher, S. (1986). 'Measuring passionate love in intimate relationships'. *Journal of Adolescence*, 6, 383–410. Sprecher, S. & Fehr, B. (2005). 'Compassionate love for close others and humanity'. *Journal of Social and Personal Relationships*, 22, 629–52.

9 Beauman, F. (2011). *Shapely Ankle Preferr'd: A History of the Lonely Hearts Ad 1695–2010*. London: Chatto & Windus.

10 Asendorpf, J.B., Penke, L., & Back, M.D. (2011). 'From dating to mating and relating: Predictors of initial and long-term outcomes of speed-dating in a community sample'. *European Journal of Personality*, 25, 16–30.

11 Schachter, S. and Singer, J.E. (1962). 'Cognitive, social and physiological determinants of emotional states', *Psychological Review*, 69, 379–99.

12 This questionnaire is based on The Body Perception Questionnaire by Stephen Porges.

13 Anderson, C.A., Bushman, B.J., & Groom, R.W. (1997). 'Hot years and serious and deadly assault: Empirical tests of the heat hypothesis'. *Journal of Personality and Social Psychology*, 73, 1213–23.

14 Baron, R.A., & Bell, P.A. (1976). 'Aggression and heat: The influence of ambient temperature negative affect, and a cooling drink on physical aggression'. *Journal of Personality and Social Psychology*, 33, 245–55.

15 White, G.L., Fishbein, S., & Rutstein, J. (1981). 'Passionate love and the misattribution of arousal'. *Journal of Personality and Social Psychology*, 41, 56–62.

16 For a review of this work, see: Berscheid, E. and Walster, E. (1978). *Interpersonal attraction*. Reading, Massachusetts: Addison-Wesley Publishing.

17 Dutton, D.G. and Aron, A.P. (1974). 'Some evidence for heightened sexual attraction under conditions of high anxiety'. *Journal of Personality and Social Psychology*, 30, 510–17.

18 Meston, C.M., & Frohlich, P.F. (2003) 'Love at first fright: Partner salience moderates roller coaster-induced excitation transfer'. *Archives of Sexual Behavior*, 32, 537–44.

19 Driscoll, R.H., Davis, K.E., & Lipetz, M.E. (1972). 'Parental interference and romantic love: The Romeo and Juliet effect'. *Journal of Personality and Social Psychology*, 24, 1–10.

20 Hatfield, E., & Berscheid, E. (1971). 'Adrenaline makes the heart grow fonder'. *Psychology Today*, 6, 46–62.

21 Brookes, M. (2004). *Extreme Measures: The Dark Visions and Bright Ideas of Francis Galton*. London: Bloomsbury.

22 Galton, F. (1884). 'Measurement of character', *Fortnightly Review* 36, 179–82.

23 For a review of this work, see: Givens, D. (2005). *Love Signals*. New York: St Martin's Press.

24 Gergen, K., Gergen, M., & Barton, W.H. (1973). 'Deviance in the dark'. *Psychology Today*, 11, 129–30.

25 Wegner, D.M., Lane, J.D., & Dimitri, S. (1994). 'The allure of secret relationships'. *Journal of Personality and Social Psychology*, 66, 287–300.

26 Fraley, B., & Aron, A. (2004). 'The effect of a shared humorous experience on closeness in initial encounters'. *Personal Relationships*, 11, 61–78.

27 For a review of this work, see: Laird, J.D. (2007). *Feelings: The Perception of Self*. New York: Oxford University Press.

28 Epstein, R. (2006). 'Giving psychology away: A personal journey'. *Perspectives on Psychological Science*, 1(4), 389–400.

29 Epstein, R. (2010). 'How science can help you fall in love'. *Scientific American Mind*, January/February, 26–33.

30 Epstein, R. (2002). 'Editor as guinea pig: Putting love to a real test [Editorial]'. *Psychology Today*, May/June, 5.

31 Much of the information in the section is from: Epstein, R. 'Answers to 50 questions from the media: Regarding Dr. Epstein's "Learning-to-Love" Experiment'. PDF available at http://drrobertepstein.com/downloads/Q&A-Learning_to_Love-4-05-c_2005_Dr._Robert_Epstein.pdf

32 See: http://www.signonsandiego.com/news/2009/apr/10/1n10psych232525-love-put-test-psych-course/

33 Epstein, R. (2010). 'How science can help you fall in love'. *Scientific American Mind*, January/February, 26–33.

34 Strong, G., Fincham, F. , & Aron, A. (2009). 'When nothing bad happens but you're still unhappy: Boredom in romantic relationships'. In *Mind*, 8. Tsapelas, I., Aron, A., & Orbuch, T. (2009). 'Marital boredom now, predicts less satisfaction nine years later'. *Psychological Science*, 20, 543–5.

35 Reissmann, C., Aron, A., & Bergen, M. (1993). 'Shared activities and marital satisfaction: Causal direction and self-expansion versus boredom'. *Journal of Social and Personal Relationships*, 10, 243–54.

3. MENTAL HEALTH

1 Hohmann, G.W. (1966). 'Some effects of spinal cord lesions on experienced emotional feelings'. *Psychophysiology*, 3, 143–56.

2 For a more complete discussion of these findings, and the various attempts to replicate them, see: Laird, J.D. (2007). *Feelings: The Perception of Self*. New York: Oxford University Press.

3 Davis, J.I., Senghas, A., Brandt, F., & Ochsner, K.N. (2010). 'The effects of BOTOX injections on emotional experience'. *Emotion*, 10(3), 433–40.

4 Cited in: Chaves, J. and Barber, T.X. (1973). 'Needles and knives: behind the mystery of acupuncture and Chinese meridians'. *Human Behavior*, 2, 19–24.

5 Lanzetta, J., Cartwright-Smith, J., & Kleck, R. (1976). 'Effects of nonverbal dissimulation on emotional experience and autonomic arousal'. *Journal of Personality and Social Psychology*, 3, 354–70.

6 Bohns, V.K, and Wiltermuth, S., S. (in press). 'It hurts when I do this (or you do that): Posture and pain tolerance'. *Journal of Experimental Social Psychology*.

7 U.S. Federal Bureau of Investigation. (2010). *Uniform crime reports*. Washington, DC: U.S. Government Printing Office.

8 Cited in: Seligman, Martin E.P. (1993). *What You Can Change and What You Can't: The Complete Guide to Successful Self-Improvement*. New York: Knopf.

9 Much of the information in this section is taken from: Alvarado, C. (2009). 'Nineteenth-century hysteria and hypnosis: A historical note on Blanche Wittmann'. *Australian Journal of Clinical and Experimental Hypnosis*, 37, 21–36.

10 Simon, R.I. (1967). 'Great paths cross: Freud and James at Clark University, 1909'. *American Journal of Psychiatry*, 124(6), 139–42.

11 Straus, M.A. (1974). 'Leveling, Civility, and Violence in the Family'. *Journal of Marriage and the Family*, 36, 13–30.

12 Ebbesen, E.B., Duncan, B., & Kone ni, V.J. 'Effects of content of verbal aggression on future verbal aggression: A field experiment'. *Journal of Experimental Social Psychology*, 1975, 11, 192–204.

13 Goldstein, J.H., & Arms, R.L. (1971). 'Effects of observing athletic contests on hostility'. *Sociometry*, 34, 83–90.

14 http://www.telegraph.co.uk/news/uknews/scotland/8376041/Revealed-full-scale-of-Old-Firm-football-madness.html

15 Whitaker, J.L., Bushman, B.J. (2011). 'Remain Calm. Be Kind. Effects of Relaxing Video Games on Aggressive and Prosocial Behavior'. *Social Psychological and Personality Science*, 3, 88–89.

16 Bremner, R.H., Koole, S.L., & Bushman, B.J. (2011). 'Pray for those who mistreat you: Effects of prayer on anger and aggression'. *Personality and Social Psychology Bulletin*, 37, 830–7.

17 Bushman, B.J. (2002). 'Does venting anger feed or extinguish the flame? Catharsis, rumination, distraction, anger, and aggressive responding'. *Personality and Social Psychology Bulletin*, 28, 724–31.

18 Much of the information in this section is taken from Hunt, M. (1993). *The Story of Psychology*. New York: Doubleday.

19 Watson, J.B. (1930). *Behaviorism*. Chicago: University of Chicago Press.

20 Gustafson, C.R., Kelly, D.J, Sweeney, M., & Garcia, J. (1976). 'Prey-lithium aversions: I. Coyotes and wolves'. *Behavioral Biology*, 17, 61–72.

21 Cited in: Seligman, Martin E.P. (1993). *What You Can Change and What You Can't: The Complete Guide to Successful Self-Improvement*. New York: Knopf.

22 See, for example: Clark, D.M. (1986). 'A cognitive approach to

panic'. *Behaviour Research and Therapy*, 24, 461–70. Clark, D.M., Salkovskis, P.M., Hackmann, A., Wells, A., Ludgate, J., and Gelder, M. (1999). 'Brief cognitive therapy for panic disorder: a randomized controlled trial'. *Journal of Consulting and Clinical Psychology*, 67, 583–9.

23 Clark, D.M., Salkovskis, P.M., Hackman, A., et al. (1994). 'A comparison of cognitive therapy, applied relaxation and imipramine in the treatment of panic disorder'. *British Journal of Psychiatry*, 164, 759–69.

24 Goldfried, M.R., Linehan, M.M., & Smith, J.L. (1978). 'Reduction of test anxiety through cognitive restructuring'. *Journal of Consulting and Clinical Psychology* 46, 32–9. Goldfried, M.R., & Sobocinski, D. (1975). 'Effect of irrational beliefs on emotional arousal'. *Journal of Consulting and Clinical Psychology*, 43, 504–10. Langer, T., Janis, I., & Wolfer, J. (1975). 'Reduction of psychological stress in surgical patients'. *Journal of Experimental Social Psychology*, 11, 155–65.

25 Schnall, S., Haidt, J., Clore, G.L., Jordan, H. (2008). 'Disgust as embodied moral judgment'. *Personality and Social Psychology Bulletin*, 34(8), 1096–1109.

26 Zhong, C., & Liljenquist, K. (2006). 'Washing Away Your Sins: Threatened Morality and Physical Cleansing'. *Science*, 313, 1451–2.

27 I was only kidding about my grandfather's extreme generosity.

28 Ben-Noun, L. (2003). 'What Was the Mental Disease that Afflicted King Saul?'. *Clinical Case Studies*, 2, 270–82.

29 Huisman, M. (2007). 'King Saul, work-related stress and depression'. *Journal of Epidemiology and Community Health*, 61, 890.

30 Myers, D. (2001). *Exploring Psychology*. Worth Publishers: New York.

31 Cuijpers, P., van Straten, A., van Oppen, P., & Andersson, G. (2008). 'Are Psychological and Pharmacologic Interventions

Equally Effective in the Treatment of Adult Depressive Disorders? A Meta-Analysis of Comparative Studies'. *Journal of Clinical Psychiatry*, 69, 1675–85. Imel, Z.E., McKay, K.M., Malterer, M.B., & Wampold. B.E. (2008). 'A meta-analysis of psychotherapy and medication in unipolar depression and dysthymia'. *Journal of Affective Disorders*, 110, 197–206.

32 Schnall, S., & Laird, J.D. (2003). 'Keep smiling: Enduring effects of facial expressions and postures on emotional experience and memory'. *Cognition and Emotion*, 17, 787–97.

33 VanSwearingen, J.M., Cohn, J.F., and Bajaj-Luthra, A. (1999). 'Specific impairment of smiling increases the severity of depressive symptoms in patients with facial neuromuscular disorders'. *Aesthetic Plastic Surgery*, 23, 416–23.

34 Koch, S.C., Morlinghaus, K., & Fuchs, T. (2007). 'The joy dance. Effects of a single dance intervention on patients with depression'. *The Arts in Psychotherapy*, 34, 340–9.

35 Lewinsohn, P.M. (1974). 'A behavioral approach to depression'. In R.M. Friedman, & M.M. Katz (eds.), *The Psychology of Depression: Contemporary Theory and Research*. New York: Wiley. Lewinsohn, P.M., Antonuccio, D.O., Breckenridge, J.S., & Teri, L. (1984). *The 'Coping with Depression' Course*. Eugene, OR: Castalia.

36 For further information about Behavioural Activation, see: Veale, D. & Willson, R. (2007). *Manage Your Mood: Using Behavioural Activation Techniques to Overcome Depression*. London: Robinson publishing.

37 Dimidjian, S., Hollon, S.D., Dobson, K.S., Schmaling, K.B., Kohlenberg, R., Addis, M., Gallop, R., McGlinchey, J., Markley, D., Gollan, J.K., Atkins, D.C., Dunner, D.L., & Jacobson, N.S. (2006). 'Randomized trial of behavioral activation, cognitive therapy, and antidepressant medication in the acute treatment of adults with major depression'. *Journal of Consulting and Clinical Psychology* 74 (4), 658–70.

38 For a review of this work, see: Spates, C.R., Pagoto, S. & Kalata, A. (2006). 'A Qualitative and Quantitative Review of Behavioral Activation Treatment of Major Depressive Disorder'. *The Behavior Analyst Today*, 7(4), 508–18.

4. WILLPOWER

1 Kohn, A. (1993). *Punished By Rewards: The Trouble with Gold Stars, Incentive Plans, A's, Praise, and Other Bribes*. New York: Houghton Mifflin.

2 Curry, S.J., Wagner, E.H., & Grothaus, L.C. (1991). 'Evaluation of Intrinsic and Extrinsic Motivation Interventions with a Self-Help Smoking Cessation Program'. *Journal of Consulting and Clinical Psychology*, 59, 318–24.

3 Geller, E.S., Rudd, J.R., Kalsher, M.J., Streff, F.M., & Lehman, G.R. (1987). 'Employer-based programs to motivate safety belt use (a review of short-term and long-term effects)'. *Journal of Safety Research*, 18, 1–17.

4 See, for example: McQuillan, J. (1997). 'The Effects of Incentives on Reading'. *Reading Research and Instruction*, 36, 111–25.

5 Cited in: Kohn, A. (1993). *Punished By Rewards: The Trouble with Gold Stars, Incentive Plans, A's, Praise, and Other Bribes*. New York: Houghton Mifflin.

6 Amabile, T.M. (1985). 'Motivation and Creativity: Effects of Motivational Orientation on Creative Writers'. *Journal of Personality and Social Psychology*, 48, 393–9.

7 Deci, E.L. (1971). 'Effects of externally mediated rewards on intrinsic motivation'. *Journal of Personality and Social Psychology*, 18, 105–15.

8 Lepper, M.R., Greene, D., & Nisbett, R.E. (1973). 'Undermining children's intrinsic interest with extrinsic reward: A test of the "overjustification" hypothesis'. *Journal of Personality and Social Psychology*, 28, 129–37.

9 Janis, I.L., & Mann, L. (1965). 'Effectiveness of emotional role playing in modifying smoking habits and attitudes'. *Journal of Experimental Research in Personality*, 1, 84–90.

10 Mann, L. & Janis, I.L. (1968). 'A follow-up study on the long-term effects of emotional role-playing'. *Journal of Personality and Social Psychology*, 8, 339–42.

11 Pliner, P., Hart, H., Kohl, J., & Saari, D. (1974). 'Compliance without pressure: Some Further Data on the Foot-in-the-Door Technique'. *Journal of Experimental Social Psychology*, 10, 17–22.

12 Beaman, A.L., Cole, M.C., Preston, M., Klentz, B., & Mehrkens-Steblay, N. (1983) 'Fifteen years of foot-in-the-door research: a meta-analysis'. *Personality and Social Psychology Bulletin*, 9, 181–96.

13 Meineri, S. & Guéguen N. (2008). 'An Application of the Foot-in-the-Door Strategy in the Environmental Field'. *European Journal of Social Sciences*, 7, 71–4.

14 Guéguen, N., & Jacob, C. (2001). 'Fund-raising on the web: The effect of an electronic foot-in-the-door on donation'. *CyberPsychology & Behavior*, 4, 705–9.

15 Guéguen, N., Pascual, A., Marchand, M. & Lourel, M. (2008). 'Foot-in-the-Door Technique Using a Courtship Request: A Field Experiment'. *Psychological Reports*, 103, 529–35.

16 Cialdini, R.B., Cacioppo, J.T., Basset, R., & Miller, J.A. (1978). 'The low-ball procedure for producing compliance: Commitment then cost'. *Journal of Personality and Social Psychology*, 36, 463–76.

17 Zeigarnik, B.V. (1927). 'Über das Behalten von erledigten und unerledigten Handlungen (The Retention of Completed and Uncompleted Activities)', *Psychologische Forschung*, 9, 1–85.

18 Staub, E. (1989). *The Roots of Evil*. New York: Cambridge University Press.

19 Purcell, A.H. (1981). 'The world's trashiest people: Will they

clean up their act or throw away their future?'. *The Futurist*, 2, 51–9.

20 Burn, S.M. & Oskamp, S. (1986). 'Increasing Community Recycling with Persuasive Communication and Public Commitment', *Journal of Applied Social Psychology*, 16, 29–41.

21 Martin, S. (1993). *What You Can Change and What You Can't: The Complete Guide to Successful Self-Improvement*. New York: Knopf.

22 Mann, T., Tomiyama, A.J., Westling, E., Lew, A., Samuels, B., & Chatman, J. (2007). 'Medicare's search for effective obesity treatments: Diets are not the answer'. *American Psychologist*, 62, 220–33.

23 Förster, J. (2003). 'The influence of approach and avoidance motor actions on food intake'. *European Journal of Social Psychology*, 33, 339–50.

24 Webber, L.S., Catellier, D.J., Lytle, L.A., Murray, D.M., Pratt, C.A., Young, D.R., Elder, J.P., Lohman, T.G., Stevens, J., Jobe, J.B., & Pate. R.R. (2008). 'Promoting Physical Activity in Middle-School Girls: Trial of Activity for Adolescent Girls'. *American Journal of Preventative Medicine*, 34, 173–84.

25 Schachter, S. (1968). 'Obesity and eating: internal and external cues differentially affect the eating behavior of obese and normal subjects'. *Science*, 161, 751–6.

26 Nisbett, R. (1968). 'Determinants of food intake in obesity'. *Science*, 159, 1254–5.

27 Goldman, R., Jaffa, M., & Schachter, S. (1968). 'Yom Kippur, Air France, dormitory food, and eating behavior of obese and normal persons'. *Journal of Personality and Social Psychology*, 10, 117–23.

28 Wansink, B. (2004). 'Environmental Factors that Increase the Food Intake and Consumption Volume of Unknowing Consumers'. *Annual Review of Nutrition*, 24, 455–79.

29 Herman, C.P., Olmsted, M.P., & Polivy, J. (1983). 'Obesity,

externality, and susceptibility to social influence: An integrated analysis'. *Journal of Personality and Social Psychology*, 45, 926–34.

30 Sentyrz, S.M., & Bushman, B.J. (1998). 'Mirror, mirror on the wall, who's the thinnest one of all? Effects of self-awareness on consumption of fatty, reduced-fat, and fat-free products'. *Journal of Applied Psychology*, 83, 944–9.

31 Neal, D., Wood, W., Wu, M., and Kurlander, D. (2011). 'The Pull of the Past: When Do Habits Persist Despite Conflict With Motives?'. *Personality and Social Psychology Bulletin*, 37, 1428–37.

32 Riskind, J. (1984). 'They stoop to conquer: Guiding and self-regulatory functions of physical posture after success and failure'. *Journal of Personality and Social Psychology*, 47, 479–93.

33 Hyung-il, A., Teeters, A., Wang, A., Breazeal, C. & Picard, R. (2007). 'Stoop to Conquer: Posture and affect interact to influence computer users' persistence'. The 2nd International Conference on Affective Computing and Intelligent Interaction (ACII 2007), 12–14 September, Lisbon, Portugal.

34 Fletcher, B. (C). & Stead, B. (2000). *(Inner) FITness and the FIT Corporation (Smart Strategies)*, London: International Thomson Press.

35 Hung, Iris W. and Aparna A. Labroo (2011), 'From Firm Muscles to Firm Willpower: Understanding the Role of Embodied Cognition in Self-Regulation'. *Journal of Consumer Research*, 37, 1046–1058.

36 Friedman, R., Elliot, A.J. (2008). 'The effect of arm crossing on persistence and performance'. *European Journal of Social Psychology*, 38, 449–61.

37 Fletcher, B.(C)., Page, N. & Pine, K.J. (2007). 'A new behavioural intervention for tackling obesity: Do something different'. *European Journal of Nutraceuticals and Functional*

Foods, 18, 8–10. Fletcher, B.(C)., Hanson, J., Pine, K.J. & Page, N. (2011). 'FIT – Do something different: A new psychological intervention tool for facilitating weight loss'. *Swiss Journal of Psychology*, 70, 25–34. Fletcher, B.(C), & Page, N. (2008). 'FIT Science for weight loss – a controlled study of the benefits of enhancing behavioural flexibility'. *European Journal of Nutroceuticals & Functional Foods*, 19, 20–3.

38 See, for example: Fletcher, B(C), Penman, D., & Pine, K.J. (2006). *The No Diet Diet: Do Something Different*. London: Orion. Fletcher, B(C), & Pine, K.J. (2012). *Flex: Do Something Different*. Hatfield: University of Hertfordshire Press.

5. PERSUASION

1 Korea: 'Twenty-Three Americas'. *Time* magazine, 5 October 1953.

2 Aronson, E. (2004). *The Social Animal* (Ninth Edition). New York: Worth Publishers. p.150.

3 Kassarjian, H.H., and J.B. Cohen. (1965). 'Cognitive dissonance and consumer behavior', *California Management Review*, 8, 55–64.

4 Jones, E.E., & Kohler, R. (1958). 'The effects of plausibility on the learning of controversial statements'. *Journal of Abnormal and Social Psychology*, 57, 315–20.

5 Bickman, L. (1972). 'Environmental attitudes and actions', *Journal of Social Psychology*, 87, 323–4.

6 Batson, C.D., Thompson, E.R., & Chen, H. (2002). 'Moral hypocrisy: Addressing some alternatives'. *Journal of Personality and Social Psychology*, 83, 330–9. Batson, C.D., Thompson, E.R., Seuferling, G., Whitney, H., & Strongman, J. (1999). 'Moral hypocrisy: Appearing moral to oneself without being so'. *Journal of Personality and Social Psychology*, 77, 525–37.

7 For a review of this work, see: Maio, G.R., & Haddock, G. (2010). *The Psychology of Attitudes and Attitude Change.* London: Sage.

8 Peterson. A.V. Jr, Kealey, K.A., Mann, S.L., Marek, P.M., & Sarason, I.G. (2000). 'Hutchinson Smoking Prevention Project: long-term randomized trial in school-based tobacco use prevention – results on smoking'. *Journal of the National Cancer Institute*, 92, 1979–91.

9 Wakefield, M., Terry-McElrath, Y., Emery, S., Saffer, H., Chaloupka, F., Szczypka, G., Flay, B., O'Malley, P., & Johnston, L. (2006). 'Effect of televised, tobacco company-funded smoking prevention advertising on youth smoking-related beliefs, intentions and behavior'. *American Journal of Public Health*, 96, 2154–60.

10 Monitor 2010: Fresh fruit and vegetable production, trade, supply & consumption monitor in the EU-27 (covering 2004–2009). Report produced by Freshfel Europe. Story reported at: http://www.dailymail.co.uk/health/article-1264937/Millions-spent-5-day-mantra-eating-LESS-vegetables.html.

11 Hornik, R., Jacobsohn, L., Orwin, R., Piesse, A., & Kalton. G. (2008). 'Effects of the National Youth Anti-Drug Media Campaign on Youths'. *American Journal of Public Health*, 98, 2229–36.

12 Clark, K.B. & Clark, M.K. (1940). 'Skin color as a factor in racial identification of Negro preschool children'. *The Journal of Social Psychology*, 11, 159–69. Clark, K.B. & Clark, M.K. (1950). 'Emotional factors in racial identification and preference in Negro children'. *Journal of Negro Education*, 19, 341–50.

13 For an account of this work, see: Kleinke, C.L. (1978). *Self-perception: The psychology of Personal Awareness.* San Francisco: Freeman.

14 Halberstam, D. (1976). *The Best and the Brightest.* New York: Random House.

NOTES

15 Elms, A.C. (1966). 'Influence of fantasy ability on attitude change through role playing'. *Journal of Personality and Social Psychology*, 4, 36–43.

16 Janis, I.L. & King, B.T. (1954). 'The influence of role-playing on opinion change'. *Journal of Abnormal Social Psychology*, 49, 211–18.

17 Laird, J. D. (2007). *Feelings: The Perception of Self*. New York: Oxford University Press.

18 Schein, E. H. (1956). 'The Chinese Indoctrination Program for Prisoners of War'. *Psychiatry*, 19, 149–72.

19 Myers, D. G. (2010). *Social Psychology* (10th ed.). New York: McGraw-Hill.

20 Chandler, J. & Schwarz, N. (2009). 'How extending your middle finger affects your perception of others: Learned movements influence concept accessibility'. *Journal of Experimental Social Psychology*, 45, 123–8.

21 Wells, G.L., & Petty, R.E. (1980). 'The effects of overt head movements on persuasion: Compatibility and incompatibility of responses'. *Basic and Applied Social Psychology*, 1, 219–230. Tom, G., Pettersen, P., Lau, T., Burton, T., & Cook, J. (1991). 'The role of overt head movement in the formation of affect'. *Basic and Applied Social Psychology*, 12, 281–9.

22 For more information about this exercise, see: Peters, W. (1971). *A Class Divided: Then and Now*. New Haven: Yale University Press.

23 Bloom, S.G., 'Blue-Eyes, Brown-Eyes: The Experiment that Shocked the Nation and Turned a Town Against its Most Famous Daughter'. Retrieved from: http://www.uiowa.edu/~poroi/seminars/2004-5/bloom/poroi_paper.pdf

24 For Jones's first-hand account of the experiment, see: http://libcom.org/history/the-third-wave-1967-account-ron-jones

25 Chaiken, S., & Baldwin, M.W. (1981). 'Affective-cognitive consistency and the effect of salient behavioral information on

the self-perception of attitudes'. *Journal of Personality and Social Psychology*, 41, 1–12.

26 Brehm, J. (1956). 'Post-decision changes in desirability of alternatives'. *Journal of Abnormal and Social Psychology*, 52, 384–9.

27 Knox, R.E. & Inkster, J.A. (1968). 'Postdecision dissonance at post time'. *Journal of Personality and Social Psychology*, 8, 319–23.

28 Zhong, C.B. & Leonardelli, G.J. (2008). 'Cold and Lonely: Does Social Exclusion Literally Feel Cold?'. *Psychological Science*, 19, 838–42.

29 Williams, L.E., & Bargh, J.A. (2008). 'Experiencing physical warmth promotes interpersonal warmth'. *Science*, 322, 606–7.

30 Brehm, J.W. (1960). 'Attitudinal consequences of commitment to unpleasant behavior'. *Journal of Abnormal and Social Psychology*, 60, 370–83.

31 Glass, D.C. (1964). 'Changes in liking as a means of reducing cognitive discrepancies between self-esteem and aggression'. *Journal of Personality*, 32, 531–49.

32 Hatfield, E., Cacioppo, J.T., & Rapson, R.L. (1994). *Emotional Contagion*. New York: Cambridge University Press.

33 See, for example: Friedman, H.S. & Riggio, R. (1981). 'The effect of individual differences in nonverbal expressiveness on transmission of emotion'. *Journal of Nonverbal Behavior*, 6, 96–104.

34 Andréasson, P., & Dimberg, U. (2008). 'Emotional Empathy and Facial Feedback'. *Journal of Nonverbal Behavior*, 32, 215–24. Dimberg, U., Andréasson, P., & Thunberg, M. (2011). 'Emotional empathy and facial reactions to facial expressions'. *Journal of Psychophysiology*. 25, 26–31.

35 This questionnaire is based on scales described in: Friedman, H.S., Prince, L.M., Riggio, R.E., & DiMatteo, M.R. (1980). 'Understanding and assessing nonverbal expressiveness: The

Affective Communication Test'. *Journal of Personality and Social Psychology*, 39, 333–51. Mehrabian, A., & Epstein, N. (1972). 'A measure of emotional empathy'. *Journal of Personality*, 40, 525–43.

36 Sherif, M., Harvey, O.J., White, B.J., Hood, W.R., & Sherif, C.W. (1961). *The Robbers Grave Experiment: Intergroup Cooperation and Conflict*. Norman, OK: University of Oklahoma.

37 Wiltermuth, S.S. & Heath, C. (2009). 'Synchrony and cooperation'. *Psychological Science*, 20, 1–5.

6. CREATING A NEW YOU

1 For an excellent overview of this work, see: Matthews, G. & Deary, I.J. (1998). *Personality Traits*. Cambridge: Cambridge University Press.

2 For a description of this study, see: Ross, L., & Nisbett, R.E. (1991). *The Person and the Situation: Perspectives of Social Psychology*. New York: McGraw-Hill.

3 Hartshorne, H., & May, M.A. (1928). *Studies in the Nature of Character* (Vol.2). New York: Macmillan.

4 Comer, R., & Laird, J.D. (1975). 'Choosing to suffer as a consequence of expecting to suffer: Why do people do it?'. *Journal of Personality and Social Psychology*, 32, 92–101.

5 Foxman, J. & Radtke, R.C. (1970). 'Negative expectancy and the choice of an aversive task'. *Journal of Personality and Social Psychology*, 15, 253–7.

6 Kellerman, J., & Laird, J.D. (1982). 'The effect of appearance on self-perception'. *Journal of Personality*, 50, 296–315.

7 Carney, D., Cuddy, A.J.C., & Yap, A. (2010). 'Power posing: Brief nonverbal displays affect neuroendocrine levels and risk tolerance'. *Psychological Science*, 21, 1363–8.

8 Schubert, T.W. (2004). 'The power in your hand: Gender differences in bodily feedback from making a fist'. *Personality and Social Psychology Bulletin*, 30, 757–69.

9 Briñol, P. & Petty, R.E (2003). 'Overt head movements and persuasion: A self-validation analysis'. *Journal of Personality and Social Psychology*, 84, 1123–39.

10 Griffin, J. H. (1961/2010). *Black Like Me*. San Antonio: WingsPress. For an account of Griffin's life, see Bonazzi, R. (1997). Man in the Mirror: John Howard Griffin and the Story of "Black Like Me" New York: Orbis Books.

11 Guéguen, N. (2009). 'Man's Uniform and Receptivity of Women to Courtship Request: Three Field Experiments with a Firefighter's Uniform'. *European Journal of Social Sciences*, 12, 235–240.

12 Townsend, J.M. and Levy, G.D. (1990). 'Effects of potential partners' physical attractiveness and socioeconomic status on sexuality and partner selection'. *Archives of Sexual Behavior*, 19: 149–64.

13 Green, W.P., & Giles, H. (1973). 'Reactions to a stranger as a function of dress style: The Tie'. *Perceptual and Motor Skills*, 37, 676.

14 Frank, M.G., & Gilovich, T. (1988). 'The dark side of self and social perception: Black uniforms and aggression in professional sports'. *Journal of Personality and Social Psychology*, 54, 74–8.

15 Johnson, R.D. & Downing, L.L. (1979). 'Deindividuation and valence of cues: Effects of prosocial and antisocial behavior'. *Journal of Personality & Social Psychology*, 37, 1532–8.

16 Tenzel, J.H. & Cizanckas, V. (1973). 'The uniform experiment'. *Journal of Police Science and Administration*, 1, 424. Tenzel, J.H., Storms, L. & Sweetwood, H. (1976). 'Symbols and behavior: an experiment in altering the police role'. *Journal of Police Science and Administration*, 1, 21–7.

17 Leung, A.K.-y., Kim, S., Polman, E., Ong, L., Qiu, L., Goncola,

J., & Sanchez-Burks, J. (in press). 'Embodied metaphors and creative "acts"'. *Psychological Science*.

18 For further information about this work, see: http://www.prisonexp.org/links.htm. Zimbardo, P.G., Maslach, C., & Haney, C. (2000). 'Reflections on the Stanford Prison Experiment: Genesis, transformations, consequences'. In T. Blass (ed.). *Obedience to Authority: Current Perspectives on the Milgram Paradigm* (pp.193–237). Mahwah, N. J.: Erlbaum.

19 Roberts, B.W. (1997). 'Plaster or plasticity: Are adult work experiences associated with personality change in women?'. *Journal of Personality*, 65, 205–31.

20 Kohn, M.L. , & Schooler, C. (1978). 'The reciprocal effects of the substantive complexity of work and intellectual flexibility: A longitudinal assessment'. *American Journal of Sociology*, 84, 24–52.

21 For more information about these approaches, see: Winter, D.A. (1987). 'Personal construct psychotherapy as a radical alternative to social skills training'. In R.A. Neimeyer and G.J. Neimeyer (eds.), *Personal Construct Therapy Casebook*. New York: Springer, pp.107–23. Beail, N., & Parker, C. (1991). 'Group fixed role therapy: A clinical application'. *International Journal of Personal Construct Psychology*, 4, 85–96. Lira, F.T., Way, W.R., McCullough, J.O., & Etkin, W. (1975). 'Relative effects of modeling and role playing in the treatment of avoidance behaviors'. *Journal of Consulting and Clinical Psychology*, 43, 608–18.

22 Clore, G.L., & Jeffrey, K.M. (1972). 'Emotional role playing, attitude change, and attraction toward a disabled person'. *Journal of Personality and Social Psychology*, 23, 105–11.

23 The exercises described here are designed to provide a general insight into the sorts of techniques that are used by psychologists. If you believe that you have a serious problem in your life, consult a professional.

24 This list is based on work described in: Peterson, Christopher & Seligman, M.E.P. (2004). *Character Strengths and Virtues: A Handbook and Classification.* Washington, D.C.: APA Press and Oxford University Press.

25 If you have decided to make this change, then please feel free to get in touch with me: http://richardwiseman.wordpress.com

26 Yee, N., Bailenson, J.N., & Ducheneaut, N. (2009). 'The Proteus Effect: Implications of Transformed Digital Self-Representation on Online and Offline Behavior'. *Communication Research*, 36, 285–312.

27 Fox, J.A., & Bailenson, J.N. (2009). 'Virtual self-modeling: The effects of vicarious reinforcement and identification on exercise behaviors'. *Media Psychology*, 12, 1–25.

28 Hershfield, H.E., Goldstein, D.G., Sharpe, W.F., Fox, J., Yeykelis, L., Carstensen, L.L., & Bailenson, J.N. (2011). 'Increasing saving behavior through age-progressed renderings of the future self'. *Journal of Marketing Research*, 48, S23–S37.

29 Rodin. J., & Langer, J.E. (1997). 'Long-term effects of a control-relevant Intervention with the Institutionalized Aged'. *Journal of Personality and Social Psychology*, 35(12), 897–902.

30 Langer, E.J., Rodin, J., Beck, P., Weinman, C., & Spitzer, L. (1979). 'Environmental determinants of memory improvement in late adulthood'. *Journal of Personality and Social Psychology*, 37, 2003–13.

31 Langer, E.J., Beck, P., Janoff-Bulman, R., & Timko, C. (1984). 'The relationship between cognitive deprivation and longevity in senile and non-senile elderly populations'. *Academic Psychology Bulletin*, 6, 211–26.

32 For further information about this project, see: Langer, E. (2009). *Counter Clockwise: Mindful Health and the Power of Possibility.* New York: Ballantine Books. Langer, E. (1989). *Mindfulness.* Reading, MA: Addison-Wesley. Hsu, L.M., Chung, J., Langer, E.J. (2010). 'The Influence of Age-Related Cues on

Health and Longevity'. *Perspectives on Psychological Science*, 5, 632–48.

33 Langer, E., Djikic, M., Pirson, M., Madenci, A. & Donohue, R. (2010), 'Believing is Seeing – using mindlessness (mindfully) to improve visual acuity'. *Psychological Science*, 21, 661–6.

34 Hsu, L.M., Chung, J., Langer, E.J. (2010). 'The Influence of Age-Related Cues on Health and Longevity'. *Perspectives on Psychological Science*, 5, 632–48.

35 Verghese, J., Lipton, R.B., Katz, M.J., Hall, C.B., Kuslansky, G., Derby, C.A., Ambrose, A.F., Sliwinski, M., & Buschke, H. (2003). 'Leisure activities and the risk of dementia in the elderly'. *New England Journal of Medicine*, 348: 2508–16.

36 Hsu, L.M., Chung, J., Langer, E.J. (2010). 'The Influence of Age-Related Cues on Health and Longevity'. *Perspectives on Psychological Science*, 5, 632–48.

CONCLUSION

1 For an accessible account of this debate, see: Waterfield, R. (2002). *Hidden Depths: The Story of Hypnosis*. London: Pan Macmillan.

2 Delgado, J.M.R. (1969). *Physical Control of the Mind: Towards a Psychocivilized Society*. New York: Harper and Row.

extracts reading groups
competitions books new
books discounts extracts extracts events
competitions reading groups discounts reading groups
books new extracts events
reading groups events books discounts
new events books reading groups
books extracts
new titles reading groups
interviews
books events extracts extracts books
discounts events new books
new books events interviews books extracts
events new events new interviews new extracts
discounts extracts discounts books

www.panmacmillan.com

extracts events reading groups
competitions books extracts new books